The
Answer
For Life

Donna Fiorini

The Answer For Life
by Donna Fiorini

ISBN: 978-1-935018-45-2

For permission to republish or reprint any portion of this book, please contact Donna Fiorini at:

df@rochester.rr.com

New Testament Christian Church

349 North Avenue

Rochester, New York 14626

585-723-1400

www.donnafiorini.com

Interior Design: Leo Ward
Editors: Lynda Ventura, Mary Pratt, Kate Fox and Janis Olson
Graphic Designer: Jenelle Penders VanZutphen

PUBLISHED BY:
Five Stones Publishing
A DIVISION OF:
The International Localization Network
randy2905@gmail.com
ILNcenter.com

Beloved, I wish above all things that thou mayest prosper and be in health, even as thy soul prospereth. III John 2

To my pastor, Jim Crowley, for recognizing giftings and talents within the body, for ordaining me and giving me a platform on which to minister and teach, for encouraging me to walk in my destiny and the call of God on my life and for not letting me give up every time discouragement paid me a visit.

To my spiritual parents, Kenneth and Gloria Copeland, who still have a profound effect on my life. You may never know on this side of eternity what you have done for me.

To my handsome husband, Mark, my best friend and the love of my life, for seeing the call of God on my life and giving me your faithful support, love and encouragement.

To my close friend, Pat Zarpentine, who, as a woman in ministry, mentored me and helped me to step up to the plate.

To my parents, sisters, family and friends for believing in me and supporting my vision and the call of God on my life.

To my daughter Jenelle and her family you are such a blessing to me and I adore you all.

My desire in writing this book is to expose the root to many of the problems we encounter in our lives and show you how to find *The Answer* for living an abundantly blessed life.

The problem resides in our soul, which is made up of our mind, will and emotions. Our soul shapes our ability to think, forms what we believe and how we feel. Through it we filter the events of life, creating our perceptions, which activates our behaviors.

We make decisions based on our feelings, which are not always telling us the truth, affecting the lives of the people around us. Then we bring these patterns into our relationships, raise our children with them and they are carried on to future generations.

In this self help book I openly share my quest for 'answers' to my own internal struggles and my journey to overcome life's issues. I will show you step by step; why we have the problems we do, how to dismantle toxic thoughts and emotions that have negatively impacted the direction our life has taken, and show you how to find peace and live the blessed life.

This book is a necessary read for every person. I believe that no matter what your background is or what mistakes you have made, you too can find *The Answer* and improve your quality of life as I have.

I would like to give a very special thanks to all the ministers from whom I have learned so much. Each and every one of you has had a part in leading me to *The Answer.*

Kenneth and Gloria Copeland
Creflo Dollar
Dutch Sheets
Don Colbert, M. D.
Joyce Meyer
Paula White
Dr. Caroline Leaf
Gregory Dickow
Liberty Savard
Dale M. Sides
Henry Malone
Larry Huch
Perry Stone
Mac and Lynn Hammond
John and Paula Sanford
Frank and Ida Mae Hammond
Peter and Doris Wagner
Luis and Pamela Perez
Singing Waters Ministry
Susan Goodnight
Fay Gilson

The Fall Of Man

What happened to the spirit and soul of man at the fall? I will take an x-ray of the inner workings of our soul, which is comprised of our mind, our will and our emotions. We will expose the damage that unmet needs, unhealed hurts and unresolved issues have had on our lives and how they still affect us today.

Chapter One

In the beginning The Bible says, *"And God said, Let us make man in our image, after our likeness"* - Genesis 1:26. God created man to be a triune being like Him. We are a spirit. Our spirit has a soul, and we live in a body. We'll talk about our soul and body a little later.

At creation Adam's spirit possessed God's life (Zoë - life as God has it, all of the spiritual forces and characteristics that make up Father God), The Father's DNA was breathed into Adam's spirit. So at creation the human spirit possessed the Father's life, His logic, reason and intelligence. The spirit of man was to be the dominant force of his triune being. The only information Adam received was from the Father. Adam viewed everything through the eye of his spirit.

At the fall in Genesis 3:5-10 the Word tells us that after eating of the tree of the knowledge of good and evil, *"their eyes were opened, and they knew that they were naked."* Adam's spirit was severed from the Father's. The two were no longer one. Man was "born again" from life to death. Man lost his God-given spiritual vision and the eyes of his soul / flesh were now open, he knew evil and experienced fear.

Adam no longer received his logic, reason or intelligence from the Father. Man's spirit was no longer the dominant force of his being. The ability to have control of self (the soul) that was in the spirit of man was now severed.

Adam's soul (mind, will and emotions) was the dominant force of his being instead of his spirit and man was receiving his logic, reason and intelligence from Satan, who was now his lord and the major source of his influence - John 8:44.

Before the fall, there was only the law of life and everything was righteous and right in the world. When Adam disobeyed God, Luke 4:5-6 tells us: *"all the kingdoms of the world were delivered unto Satan establishing the law of sin and death."* Everything became unrighteous and wrong in the earth.

With the separation of man's spirit from God's, the law of life in this earth was severed and perverted, *"...establishing the law of sin and death."* - Romans 8:2. All of the blessings God had designed for man to live in were perverted in the hands of Satan and became a curse.

- Life was turned to death.

- Love was turned to selfishness and hate.

- Faith was turned to fear.

- Health was turned to sickness and disease.

- Prosperity was turned to poverty and lack.

- Security was turned to insecurity.

Man's character was now the same as his new father, lord and master and man was receiving perverted logic, reason and intelligence from him. John 8:44 tells us, *"You are of your father the devil and the lusts of your father ye will do:..."*

The soul, now independent of the spirit and the Father's influence, was unleashing self-will. It had evil appetites. It was totally self-centered.

In fact you can see the beginning of the soul's development in a child as that child begins to display selfishness and rebellion. Did you ever notice that you don't have to teach a child to behave badly? They naturally tell you no, they aren't thrilled about sharing and they cry when they don't get their own way.

We, as children, are born with this tendency, as it is our sin nature. Man is now ruled by deception, selfishness, pride, and rebellion. The sin of Lucifer was passed on through the sin of Adam to infect all of mankind.

JESUS SAID, *". . .YE MUST BE BORN AGAIN."* - JOHN 3:3

Peter elaborates on what that means when he says, *"...being born again (that's the Greek word - anagennao. It means to regenerate, or have new genetics) not of corruptible seed, but of incorruptible, by the word of God, which liveth and abideth for ever."* - I Peter 1:23

When we were created in the womb of our mother under the law of sin and death, the entire DNA that would determine our genetic future was present. For example, the color of our hair and eyes; our height, were all programmed within our DNA.

Generational blessings as well as curses were programmed as well. For instance, if there was a weakness in the immune system that would cause a person to develop sickness of any kind, it was present at conception. This is how genetic disease runs in our family lines.

When Adam sinned, he was born again from spiritual life to spiritual death - Genesis 3:7. His spiritual eyes were shut and his natural eyes were opened and he knew he was naked. The Father has made a way through Jesus for us to be born again from spiritual death back to spiritual life.

When we were born again of incorruptible seed by the word of God, something happened inside our spirit. As a result of our new birth, present within us again is the DNA of God. Once our spirit man has been regenerated by our Heavenly Father's DNA we can *"... see the kingdom of God"* - John 3:3. Jesus told us, *"...the kingdom of God is at hand:"* - Mark 1:15. The kingdom is here in the earth now for us to live the blessed life, but without a regenerated spirit you can not see it or live in it.

The Greek word for seed is *spora* - that is where we get the word sperm from. We understand in the natural world that within every seed there is a blueprint to produce after its own kind. Human seed reproduces humans, animals reproduce other animals. Tomato seeds produce tomatoes. You can't get a tomato seed to produce corn, it just can't happen.

Something supernatural happens within us at the new birth. We begin to be regenerated by our Father God's genetics and change from the inside out by the incorruptible seed of the word of God. That means the Father's nature; His fruits, His giftings, His abilities and all that entails

15

are resident within our born again spirit. Our spiritual eyes are open to see and perceive the kingdom of God and now our new character can begin to be developed. Much like a caterpillar transforms into what the blueprint inside of it has already declared it to be. It breaks free from its cocoon and turns into a butterfly.

II Corinthians 5:17 says, *"Therefore if any man be in Christ, he is a new creature: old things are passed away; behold, all things are become new."*

Now after my conversion I stopped smoking, drinking and doing drugs, yes those things passed away. But I still struggled with things like anger, rage, fears, insecurities, and a bad attitude. I was born again and I could sense the change in my spirit but I was not demonstrating the character of God in my life yet. As I was struggling, many well-meaning Christians, in an attempt to minister to me, would say, "Donna, old things are passed away; behold, all things are become new." As if my soul issues should have naturally passed away already or as if just quoting that scripture would somehow make me feel better and I would suddenly be different.

This only caused me to cry out, "Lord, why then, am I still struggling with the old?" Struggling with my sin nature was my biggest problem as a Christian; it hindered my life, my prayers from being answered and my emotional well being. I know that I was not alone in this struggle.

In Romans 7:15 - 8:2, I combined the KJV and Amplified Bibles here to help you really understand this.

> Paul identifies his struggle. He says, *"I do not understand my own actions. I do not practice or accomplish what I wish, but I do the very thing that I loathe which my moral instinct condemns. However, it is no longer I who do the deed, but the sin principle which is at home in me and has possession of me."*

Yes, that is exactly how I felt. I was not thinking, feeling, or acting like I wanted to. A sin principle was hindering me from doing what was right. Paul goes on to say,

> *"I can will to do what is right but I cannot perform it. I have the intention and urge to do what is right, but no*

power to carry it out. But the evil deeds that I do not desire to do are what I am ever doing. If I act out what I do not desire to do, it is no longer I doing it but the sin principle, which dwells within me, fixed and operating in my soul."

This was certainly identifying my struggle; I too had the intention to do what was right but no ability to carry it out. There was a sin principle called the law of sin and death and it was fixed and operating in my soul. I could see the problem!

Paul goes on to say, *"I find it to be a law (a rule of action of my being) that when I want to do what is right and good, evil is ever present with me and I am subject to its insistent demands. I endorse and delight in the Law of God in my inmost self (spirit) with my new nature. But I discern in my bodily members, in the will of my soul, a different law at war against the law of my reasoning, making me a prisoner to the law of sin that dwells in my appetites and will of the flesh / soul."*

Paul identified exactly what I was dealing with. Wanting to do what is right and good, but evil, being ever present within me, is making me subject to its insistent demands. Like Paul I knew in my spirit man there was a new nature. Yet I could also feel a pressure at war within me making me a prisoner to the law of sin and death at work in my soul - mind, will and emotions. Paul concludes by saying, *"Oh wretched man that I am, who will deliver me? Oh thank God He did through Jesus Christ our Lord. For the Law of the Spirit of Life in Christ Jesus has made me free from the law of sin and death."*

You see, when we accepted Jesus as Lord and we were "born again," our spirit was regenerated and infused with life / Zoë. All of the spiritual forces and characteristics that make up the DNA of Father God was within us once again, bringing us back to the same condition Adam had before the fall.

I could feel the new life within my spirit but it certainly wasn't flowing out of me. The reason is that when we accepted Christ our spirit was saved instantly. However, our soul has not been renewed. Our soul is still conditioned to and contaminated or infected with a sin nature. This is the curse of the fall, called the law of sin and death. This is the reason we struggle, it is the root of all the problems in our lives.

The salvation and regeneration of our Spirit was immediate upon receiving Jesus. However the salvation of the soul is progressive. It is the process of restoring our mind, what and how we think, our will and our emotional well being to a place of wholeness.

This is the maturing process of manifesting the nature of the Father's Zoë life through our soul. This is what our Christian maturity is all about. In fact the whole book of 1st Peter is all about this journey!

WHIRLPOOL EFFECT

Have you ever been in a swimming pool and made a whirlpool? You know in the force of the flow of that water you can pick up your feet and the flow will just carry you. That is how I think of the force of the law of sin and death in the world. I liken it to what I call a whirlpool effect. You don't have to do a thing. You're born into it with a sin nature and the course of this world system will just carry you in its direction of sin and death with no effort on your part. Like the definition of the word whirlpool, the kingdom of darkness has produced a depression into which floating objects (you) may be drawn.

However, in a swimming pool you can put your feet down in the current and press against the pressure. You can walk against the force of the flow. It's hard, but it can be done. That is what it's like when you're walking in the law of the Spirit of Life in Christ Jesus. You're being led by your spirit and directing your soul. You're pressing against the current or flow of the world's system, the current or flow of the pressures within your soul - what and how you think and feel. If you build up enough momentum in the pool, pressing becomes easier and you can go in the other direction. Likewise if you build up enough momentum in your spirit, pressing against the pressures of your soul become easier.

This is why Paul could say, *"There is therefore now no condemnation to them which are in Christ Jesus, who walk not after the flesh, but after the Spirit. For the law of the Spirit of life (that's the Kingdom of God) in Christ Jesus (at work in our spirit) hath made me free (liberates and delivers me) from the law of sin and death."* (That's the kingdom of darkness at work in our soul) - Roman 8:1-2.

When you are continually walking in the spirit, the law of life you are creating becomes a force going in the opposite direction and it is making you free from the whirlpool flow of sin in your soul.

THE THREE PARTS OF MAN

IThessalonians 5:23 says, *"And the very God of peace sanctify you wholly; and I pray God your whole **spirit** and **soul** and **body** be preserved blameless unto the coming of our Lord Jesus Christ."*

We are a spirit. Our spirit has a soul, (mind, will and emotions) and we live in a body. When we receive Jesus and become born again only our spirit has been preserved blameless. That is why Paul's prayer for us is that our whole spirit, soul and body would be preserved blameless. God's part was to regenerate our spirit with His DNA. Our part is to use that DNA and bring restoration to our soul and body.

Spirit is the Greek word - *pneuma* - it is in our spirit where we are conscious of God. Our conscience is the voice of our spirit, and acts as a window between our soul and spirit. The Holy Spirit speaks to us in our spirit man which contains our conscience and our intuition; this is where we receive logic, reason, intelligence, understanding and revelation from the Holy Spirit's presence within us.

Body is conscious of the world around you. Our physical senses are the voices of our body. We communicate with the physical world through our five sense organs; sight, touch, hearing, smell and taste.

The mouth tells the real you. It reveals what is in our soul, *"...for out of the abundance of the heart, the mouth speaks."* - Matthew 12:34. If you listen to someone talk for any length of time you will know what is inside of them. Jesus said, *"...by their fruits ye shall know them."* - Matthew 7:20.

19

The body tries to boss us around with demands like, "Feed me, pamper me", etc. Our spirit is always willing to do what is right, but our body and soul work against it.

Soul is the Greek word - *psuche (psoo-khay)* This is your mind, will and emotions. The soul, which is now left unsurrendered and independent of the spirit because of Adam's disobedience, is limited in its abilities. The soul, no longer governed by God, has left us with a mind that needs renewing, a will that needs surrendering and emotions that need healing.

Reason is the voice of our soul. Communication with others is made possible by the use of our soul. Included in the mind portion of our soul is our conscious and subconscious memory. Within the soul is what and how we think, our image center and imagination; housing our ideas, beliefs, the filters of life's events that form our opinions, perceptions, attitudes and activates our behaviors. It is our ability to reason and have logic. It is our emotional make-up, housing all of our feelings like happiness, sadness, etc. Before the fall, the soul was surrendered to and dependent on knowledge from the Spirit of God. After the fall, the soul was influenced by the kingdom of darkness, leaving it unsurrendered and independent from the knowledge of God.

Our soul is the 'control tower' between the natural world our body relates to and the supernatural world our spirit relates to. When our soul is unsurrendered to God, it chooses which world we will most identify with. The entrance to our soul can come through our eye and ear gates. We call them gates because they give entrance to our soul; therefore we are to guard them. What we see and hear affects what we think and do. Our actions are the fruit of our lives and will reveal how well we have guarded the gates.

The unsurrendered soul is now limited in its abilities. When we are living life ruled by our constantly changing emotions, we are soulish or carnal Christians.

I don't talk much about controlling the flesh because what the Bible calls the flesh is the result of the soul and body working together. The flesh is a way of thinking. If we were to literally crucify the flesh we would physically die. In Galatians 5:24-25, Paul is referring to crucifying or bringing death to wrong thinking that leads to wrong actions so we can live from our spirit. I understand that the key to controlling the flesh is controlling the soul / what you think. If we will take care of the soul we won't have a problem with the flesh.

Just as a car only moves when maneuvered by its driver, the body only moves when acted upon by the soul. Just as a bad driver is capable of damaging the vehicle and causing danger to themselves or others; so too the soul, by virtue of what we think, is capable of leading the body into dangerous territory, endangering itself and possibly others.

UNDERSTANDING THE SOUL

One of the functions in the part of our soul called the mind is our conscious and subconscious memory. I do not fully understand all the principles of secular psychology. I am using the term "subconscious memory" simply to refer to the part of the soul that acts involuntarily of the conscious mind and stores all information.

The subconscious is aware of everything going on around us right now even if we are not consciously paying attention; things like birds chirping, the furnace going on, an airplane flying overhead. Our subconscious mind never forgets anything. It can be likened to a storage center for every experience we have ever had in our life. Every feeling and emotion we have ever had is stored there, much like the hard drive on your computer will record and save all your information. Our soul records and saves every feeling, event and memory in our lives. It is through this filter that we see life.

We were created to be able to retain knowledge without having to think about it consciously. In fact, that is where information is when it is on the tip of our tongue! It's in the subconscious someplace, and we are trying to bring it up to our conscious mind to remember it.

All of our habits are stored in the subconscious. We were designed to be able to do things without consciously thinking about them every time we do them. A great example of this is driving. Did you ever arrive at your destination and not remember the lights and turns that got you there? These things become a habit where we can do several things at once without even thinking about them.

What is stored here in the subconscious portion of our mind / memory is really our belief system. It determines what we really believe, forms our personality, our habits both good and bad and dictates our actions and reactions. What we believe is stored in the subconscious and becomes the 'filter' through which we see everything.

All of the information we have gathered from life's experiences come together to form our beliefs. If asked what we believe about things like: ourselves, other people, God, the Bible, love, marriage, child rearing, religion, races, relationships, government, society, schooling and everything else that pertains to life, our beliefs would cause us to have an automatic reaction when asked or provoked.

So whatever is in the basic belief system in our subconscious memory, we will act out. Everything we believe and everything that ever happened to us is kept in our subconscious memory.

In Dr. Caroline Leaf's book *Who Switched Off My Brain* - she teaches that in the cortex of our brain are around 100 trillion nerve cells. Each nerve cell is capable of growing up to 70,000 branches called dendrites - (from the Greek word Dendron meaning "tree"- Google brain dendrite). As information comes into us, we create memory that literally forms a branch / dendrite on a nerve cell in our brain that looks like a tree. Thoughts have a chemical response attached to them which are our emotions.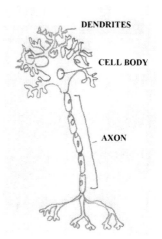

Therefore you cannot separate a thought from an emotion. As a result of the fall thoughts are either faith based or fear based. Dr. Leaf describes fear based emotions such as, "hate, worry, anxiety, anger, hostility, rage, ill-will, resentment, frustration, impatience, irritation, etc; saying these produce toxic attitudes which produce toxic responses in the body."

When thoughts are negative or fear based, a thorn will develop on the dendrite branch.

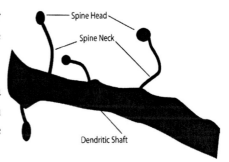

This image is an illustration of a microscopic image of a dendrite. In neuroanatomical terms thorns are described as spines.

As a thought is developed it activates the hypothalamus, which is the chemical factory of our endocrine system and responder to our thought life, to release the chemical emotion related to the thought. If the thought was negative or fear based and produced a thorn, then the chemicals we would secrete would be toxic, producing toxic responses in the body.

We filter everything through these trees / dendrites that have recorded the events of our life. We have heard of the old expression, looking at life through rose colored glasses. That means you have an attitude of seeing everything in a pleasant light. That has not been my experience in life; in fact it was quite the opposite. My filter was more like looking through glass block. Everything I viewed in life was twisted, perverted, always in a negative light with fear attached to it. I can now understand that my perception of the information and the circumstances of my life were primarily negative. Fear based seeds sown in my mind and the fruit my trees produced were thorny; creating the filters by which I viewed life.

For years I dreaded Christmas. As soon as the fall season would come around I began feeling dread knowing winter and Christmas were coming. It wasn't until putting my class together that I realized I had a filter on that season, which was put in place after my parents divorced when I was sixteen. The holidays weren't the same and my negative thoughts produced negative emotions and even depression associated with that time of year.

Those emotions remained with me for twenty-five years. The last fifteen of those years I had become a Christian with that filter still firmly in place. It was only the material presented here in *The Answer* that gave me my freedom. Now every year when fall turns into winter those old familiar 'feelings' will try to put pressure on me, but now I know how to resist and overcome them and you will too as you keep reading!

A friend said to me one day that she hated the smell of flowers because they reminded her of her father's funeral. I had another friend who said that the smell of cleaning products produced a happy feeling with him as it reminded him of his mom cleaning on a summer day. These are perfect examples of a smell triggering a memory and emotion.

Many times my husband would be flipping through the channels and stop and watch the television show *Cops*. After a few minutes of seeing domestic violence and dysfunctional behavior I would notice myself becoming enraged. It would trigger emotions of anger, bitterness, fury, criticisms, and judgments. I found myself being disgusted with the people I was watching. My stomach would be in knots and my peace would be gone. Inevitably I would have to leave the room and it would take me some time to find peace again.

This was happening to me because I experienced that same dysfunctional lifestyle before I came to know Christ and it was triggering those old feelings. Memories were being pulled up from my sub-conscious mind to my conscious mind along with all the feelings attached to them. Remember all of the information we have gathered from life's experiences form the trees of our mind holding our beliefs and releasing our emotions.

Let's talk about the will. The will is actually like the enforcer of the soul. There is actually a place in our DNA coding in our nerve cells that is our free will. As information is processed, there is an electrical, chemical and magnetic flow of that information through the brain. It is with the corpos callosum part of the brain that we start to think and analyze the information in our free will. Depending on what you believe and feel, the will gives the orders to accept or reject information, thereby determining which course of action we will take.

A word, a smell or even a frightening situation can trigger a memory from our past, pulling up an emotion, before we even have time to think about it. Our will is triggered causing us to act out or respond to what we are experiencing.

24

DECEPTION IN OUR PERCEPTION

You see, what we believe to be true in the subconscious portion of our mind is what controls us, whether our beliefs are based on truth or not. **Information doesn't have to be true to control us. We just have to believe it's true.** It then becomes what we will feel and act out.

All of our opinions, reactions and what we will say and do are triggered by our beliefs and acted out through our will. We can believe a lie, having what I like to call "deception in our perception," and those wrong thoughts will control us.

I was married when I was twenty-one and had my daughter from that marriage. Her father and I were both very young and immature at the time. I was still emotionally sixteen because that is the age when a trauma occurred in my life due to my parents' divorce. Many times when a trauma occurs your emotional maturity is stunted at that age, as mine was. I was looking to my first husband to meet my needs, be the replacement for my father who had moved away and provide, for me, the home and family that I had lost. That was a lot of expectation to put on a young man who, himself, came with his own baggage.

I left that marriage and dated another man who was no good for me either. As a result of the disappointments I had in my life; from the men in my family, to the men I was in relationships with, I developed a "belief system" that all men were pigs.

When I was twenty-six and my daughter Jenelle was five years old we found Jesus and I married my wonderful husband Mark. He was a blessing from God to me. Mark's mom is a Christian and she mentored me in my Christian faith.

There were times when she would hear me explaining things to Jenelle and often I would say to her that men would always hurt you, because they all are pigs. So one day she took me aside and said to me that I shouldn't tell Jenelle that, she said it wasn't true and that it would color her view of men. I listened to my mother-in-law's advice and I never said that to Jenelle again, but on the inside I still believed it.

This belief that all men were pigs was a "deception in my perception." It was based on my life's experiences. It wasn't true. It didn't have to be true, I believed it and therefore it controlled me. It controlled the way I viewed men, the way I treated them, the way I felt about them and so on.

It was a filter on my soul like glass block that caused me to see men in a twisted and perverted light. I heard Joyce Meyer say that, "hurting people hurt people." That helped me a lot. I needed to see that just as I have unintentionally hurt people out of my own personal pain, other people have unintentionally hurt me out of their pain.

What I want to say to you is, not everything you believe is true. Don't believe everything you think. We all think that what we believe is the truth. I often ask my students when I teach this class, "How many of you think everything you believe is true?" They raise their hands. Then I ask, "How many of you think you're believing any lies?" No one raises their hands. Isn't that funny?

Yet most of us believe many lies. We believe lies about God, about ourselves, what we can and can't do. We believe lies about the people and situations of our lives. You see we don't know we're deceived - because we're deceived.

At this point we need to stop and pray this out loud,

> "Lord, I ask you to reveal to me every place I believe a lie, about any person including myself. Show me all deception in my perception and when you do I will be quick to repent and line my thinking up to yours. In Jesus' name Amen."

AN X-RAY OF MY SOUL

What would we see if we could x-ray our soul? Just as tree experts can tell the history of a tree by its rings, they can look at a slice of tree and see which years the tree may have experienced drought, insects or fire. An x-ray of our soul would show the trees in the cortex of our mind, our experiences in life, the good times and the bad.

We all have images that have made impressions deep into our being, especially concerning our longing for love and value, which have become fixed beliefs / dendrite branches on the nerve cell trees in our mind. As soon as a familiar situation triggers a memory and emotions arise, our reactions will respond.

Much like when we walk through a house of mirrors, our body can look all distorted. We can look taller and thinner or shorter and fatter. Our self-image responds in much the same way.

When I teach this class I share with my students the x-ray of my soul. The Greek word for soul is *psuche (psoo-khay)* and it can sound like the word suitcase. So I bring a suitcase to class and I unpack all the junk in my trunk so to speak. We all come with baggage and we seem to think we are the only ones struggling with that particular junk in our trunk.

People tend to look at me as a teacher and think I didn't have to overcome some of the things that they have to. So I unzip my suitcase and begin pulling out signs to show them some of the 'stuff' I have overcome. They look like signs as I hold them up to my students, but to me they were labels, belief systems, coats that I wore. They were a blueprint of the thorny trees of my mind. They are my description of who I was even many years into my Christianity.

So I begin pulling out signs, the first being abandonment. Abandonment came into my life when I was sixteen years old and my parents divorced. Although my father didn't literally abandon me, the death of my family unit created the feeling of abandonment and it became a fracture on my soul that I didn't know was there until I was putting this class together.

I was insecure at the core of who I was. As a young Christian I opened my home for someone else to lead a Bible study, I had no desire to be a leader. My friend Josie used to say, "Donna you're a leader." I never thought of myself as a leader and was shocked anyone would ever say those words to me. She used to encourage me to lead. If you asked me to do anything in church my first answer was always no because I was afraid, I could see no value in me and had no self worth or confidence.

I also struggled with depression. I didn't have highs and lows I was just gray, no joy, no peace. I had a lot of fears. Fear was handed down generationally. My parents had a lot of fears and my thoughts and actions were primarily fear based. As a result of abusive relationships, I had some feelings of rejection, a lot of anger and a very short fuse. Whenever I saw bad behavior in anyone I wanted to make it stop. These issues led me to want to be in control. I thought if I could control people's behaviors they couldn't hurt me. I was bitter and had negative opinions and judgments. I was not shy about sharing my opinions and you heard my attitude of bitterness and anger come out when I shared them.

As a result of all this junk I felt extremely worthless. Feeling worthless is painful. You don't have any value in yourself. You feel like God doesn't value you. It colored and filtered the way I viewed God, the way I prayed to Him, my inability to receive from Him. That led to condemnation, I condemned myself for everything. Every time I stepped out to do something for the Lord the voice of condemnation would come immediately and stay for days. Life's experiences had left my mind full of thorns years into my Christianity.

The last sign I pull out is one that says wholeness. Over the years, as my class developed, the Lord was exposing all these places within me. Little by little I was recognizing areas where I had deception in my perception. I was repenting, changing my mind and choosing to think righteous thoughts. In so doing I was pruning the trees of my mind, cutting off all the thorns and growing a new healthy branch in its place. In the process I was renewing my mind and changing my internal blueprint. As a result, the Lord has healed me in all these places through the material in this book. As you continue through each chapter I share my journey of healing!

We all have junk in our trunk; we all come with a lot of baggage, as for me I had never found anything to reverse the damage in my soul quite like *The Answer* does. I know I am not alone here; it isn't a pleasant picture when you decide to x-ray your soul. But this is where we start; by identifying the soul, then x-raying the soul. We must understand that what we think about ourselves or a situation is a result of our life's experience and the filters on our soul. We look out at life through those filters and the deception in our perception. What we see doesn't have to be true, what I believed about myself wasn't truth. But because I believed it, it controlled me.

We have all held onto our beliefs, disappointments, hurts, anger, past memories, wrong attitudes, bitter-root judgments, wounds and offenses.

The soul doesn't want us to forget these things, but rather likes us to remember them, as well as to remind others of them.

The enemy takes these facts of our life (they are not truth, because truth is what God's word says) and interprets them for us, using his deception and distortions. By doing so he builds into us what he wants us to believe.

He will take circumstances and try to interpret these for us in order to continue developing the deception in our belief systems. What we believe about ourselves, others and God will be seen through this colored filter, giving us deception in our perception. Then we act it out, whether it is right or wrong.

For nine years after Mark and I got married I tried to have another baby. Every month I experienced depression. Every time I heard of a friend getting pregnant I went into deeper depression. When I would see a teenager in the store who was pregnant I would think, "God don't you love me? You'll let a kid get pregnant and not me?" I reasoned with God, I told him, "I am a Christian now, I'll raise my child to know You." I viewed my situation as God not loving me enough to bless me with more children.

You see, this belief system was not truth; my ability to conceive had nothing to do with how much God loved me. But I believed it to be true and therefore it controlled my thoughts, my emotions and twisted my view of God. To me He was a respecter of persons, and I was always crying out for His love and approval.

In Liberty Savard's book, *The Unsurrendered Soul,* I like how she identifies the damage within us. She says the damage comes from three main areas - needs that have never been met, hurts that have never been healed and issues that have never been resolved.

Many people have needs that have never been met. They have a need for love, value, approval, acceptance, significance, security and dignity. They have experienced hurts that still ache years after they were inflicted. All these together create many of the issues in life that haven't been resolved. We cannot change anything that has happened to us, but we can change how these things affect us now - by changing the power they have over us!

THE SALVATION OF OUR SOUL

Just as our spirit received new life and genetics with the DNA of the Father and was born again from death to spiritual life, so too our soul requires an experience of salvation. It requires an ongoing decision on our part to say, "Lord, not my will but Thy Will be done."

Peter instructs us by saying, *"...that you must receive the end (goal or conclusion) of your faith, which is the salvation (this word literally means - restoration, healing, deliverance, wholeness) of your soul / psuche."* - I Peter 1:9

Have you noticed that the Lord will not force Himself upon our thoughts or our will to work in our soul? It is up to us to daily examine our thoughts, behaviors, actions and reactions and ask the Lord to expose the root of why we act and think the way we do.

Peter goes on to say, *"Seeing ye have purified (to make clean, sanctify) your souls in obeying the truth through the Spirit unto unfeigned (sincere, without hypocrisy) love of the brethren, see that ye love one another with a pure heart fervently: Being born again, not of corruptible seed, but of incorruptible, by the word of God, which liveth and abideth for ever."* - I Peter 1:22-23

Peter said, *"ye have purified,"* this is our responsibility. God does not do this for us. Now if we are honest, we will admit that we struggle at times with a host of things like walking in love, fears, insecurities, anger, jealousy, lust, the inability to discipline our life and control our mind, worry, past hurts resulting in bondages, roots of rejection, a negative self-image, eating disorders and sexual, emotional or verbal abuse. The church is full of people just like us.

Remember, when we received Jesus, our spirit man was born again. We know that *"old things have passed away and all things have become new"* (2 Cor. 5:17) in our spirit. However, we may still have a soul that has not been purified and is somewhat distorted because the junk in our trunk has defiled our subconscious mind / soul.

This is why the apostle John prayed for us saying, *"Beloved, I wish above all things that thou mayest prosper and be in health, even as (in direct proportion, with the same measure) thy soul / psuche prospereth."* - III John 2

With the understanding of how our brain processes information, I have gotten a deeper revelation of what Peter and John are saying. Our goal after we have received Jesus is to have our souls / mind / brain healed, delivered and restored to wholeness - I Peter 1:9. We do this by obeying the truth of the Word of God and walking in love. It prunes the thorns of wrong thinking and makes our soul / mind clean - I Peter 1:22-23. As we do, we will begin to prosper and be in health, even as, or in direct proportion to, the prosperity of our soul / mind / brain - III John 2.

Peter and John both understood that how we prosper in our life, family, relationally, in our health and finances is in direct proportion to how well we have surrendered our soul to the process of restoration. The prosperity of our soul / mind is the key to living a whole and prosperous life.

Healing can come from the "inside out." So what affects or influences your mind - affects your body. There is a mind-body connection.

> In the book *Deadly Emotions* by Dr. Don Colbert, he says what we feel emotionally often becomes how we feel physically. There are devastating consequences of "disease" in the human heart. Dis-ease is emotional and spiritual discomfort. It is disharmony of the soul.
>
> It is often related to plaguing doubts, painful memories, hurtful stress, not forgiving and unforgiven sins. Dis-ease produces disease in the body. Not all disease is caused by dis-ease of the soul and spirit, but a good percentage of it is.
>
> The mind and body are linked. How you feel emotionally can determine how you feel physically. Certain emotions release hormones that, in turn, can trigger the development of a host of diseases.
>
> Specifically, research has linked emotions such as depression to an increased risk of developing cancer and heart disease. Emotions such as anxiety and fear have shown a direct tie to heart palpitations, mitral valve prolapse, irritable bowel syndrome and tension headaches, as well as other diseases.

If we don't treat the core stress, the symptoms may become chronic. New, deeper symptoms can also arise: sleeplessness; weight loss or gain; muscle aches, especially back and leg pain; general lethargy or feelings of exhaustion; sluggish thinking; and lack of ambition.

The difference in whether the event is stressful or not lies in our perception. It lies in what the individual believes to be the importance of the event. When it comes to stress, believing is key.

The brain doesn't distinguish whether a memory is short term or long term. Once the idea of a memory is released into biochemical code, the body responds to the chemicals.

Stress is the body and mind's response to any pressure that disrupts the normal balance. It occurs when our perceptions of events don't meet our expectations, and we don't manage our reactions to the disappointment.

This is why it is so important for us to understand and deal with the spirit / soul connection before it turns into the soul / body connection (psychosomatic) and affects our health.

Dr. Caroline Leaf says that, "What you think affects your whole body. 87% of mental and physical illness that we experience comes from our thought life. Your brain speaks to your body and your body speaks to your brain. There is a constant conversation going on in our mind body connection. There is a whole symphony of electro magnetic chemicals moving through our body."

Fear based thoughts trigger more than 1400 known physical and chemical responses in your body, and activate more than thirty different hormones and neurotransmitters. They are activated in such a way that it has an incredible physical effect on your body. For instance, harboring anger and bitterness have the ability to shut down your immune system for up to six hours. When your thoughts are primarily negative or fear based the stress chemicals being secreted are now in higher quantity, which alters their formula, making them toxic. Left unchecked, the perpetual release of the stress hormones adrenaline and cortisol can sear the body in a way that is similar to acid searing metal. They do damage to our cell receptors, organs and immune system. Even hours later these hormone levels can remain high and continue to do their damaging work converting our thought life into disease.

Begin to think about what situations have the ability to cause you stress. Daily examine your thoughts, behaviors, actions and reactions and ask the Lord to expose the root of why you act and think the way you do. As He reveals the roots be sure to write them down and journal what He is showing you. Then begin the process of changing the way you think and perceive events. For example, you may have thoughts of dread knowing you have to go to work on Monday, but you have the ability to change your perception. For example, you can choose to think I am so blessed to have a job to go to in this economy. I am grateful for a paycheck and benefits. Who can I bless in my environment today? You can take any negative thought and turn it into a positive thought by changing your perception. The Holy Spirit is with you to help you do this, reveal all truth and empower you to live a life of victory.

I encourage you to stop making excuses today for not dealing with your soul issues so that you won't experience health problems tomorrow.

SPIRIT MAN VS. SOUL MAN

In I Corinthians 2:14 it says, *"But the natural man receiveth not the things of the Spirit of God: for they are foolishness (Greek word – moria, where we get the words moron or moronic from) unto him: neither can he know them, because they are spiritually discerned."*

The natural man or soul man does not accept the things of the Spirit of God. He cannot understand them. They must be spiritually discerned.

33

If we start talking to a soulish person about spiritual things, their soul / *psuche* or what I refer to as their "suitcase" just comes unzipped and all their stuff starts to come undone!

They just can't relate to it. The things of the spirit are foolishness (moronic) to them, ridiculous and absurd.

As a Christian, our spirit should embrace the things of the Spirit and of faith. For instance, when the Bible says, "By his stripes we were healed," our spirit says, "That's right, I'm healed!" But our soul says, "I'm not sure I believe that. I'll believe it when I see it and I feel it."

Many Christians are soulish Christians and that is why they struggle to understand spiritual things and never seem to gain any victory in life.

Too often we attempt to know God with our natural mind and it doesn't work. If we want to commune with God, Scripture tells us we must worship Him in spirit and in truth.

There was a girl in our church some years ago; I will call her Sally, who had been saved from a life on the streets and drug abuse. When she found Jesus, she was so grateful for her new life and was so much in love with Jesus, that during worship she would dance almost like a ballerina, around the front of the church and up and down the aisles. It didn't seem to bother Sally what other people thought about her, all she cared about was expressing her love and grateful heart to her Savior in worship.

Well a new person came into the church and was in one of my classes. After class she asked me about Sally and the way she danced during worship. She said she thought it was pretty fleshy and wanted to know what I thought about it. I told her I thought her judgment of Sally was actually what was fleshy and explained to her exactly what Sally was saved from and how grateful Sally was for all the transformation in her life. After my explanation she could better see how her thoughts were deceiving her.

Have you ever been in worship in a church service and felt like you were just singing songs? You're thinking about what you have to do after church, your mind is wandering. You start watching the people around you and then you're bothered by their expressions of worship? You end up being a spectator instead of a participator. If that's you, you are being soulish or a carnal Christian. When you are in worship the best thing you can do is close your eye gates. What you see will distract you from your place of worship. If your eyes are closed you won't see how others are worshiping and you won't judge them!

The transformation of the soul is progressive. After we are born again, our spirit, now filled with life, begins to try to express itself. The spirit has to work through the mind and emotions to get to the will and be expressed out of the soul through the body. That's no problem until what is being released out of the spirit contradicts what is programmed into the soul.

> **Your spirit says**, "Be quiet; your opinion doesn't matter here."
> **Your soul says**, "I have a right to my opinion, and they need to hear what I think."
> **Your spirit says**, "Walk in love, go the extra mile, be a blessing!"
> **Your soul says**, "No way, they don't deserve it."
> **Your spirit says**, "Obey the Lord with your tithes and offerings."
> **Your soul says**, "I can't afford to."
> **Your spirit says**, "I can do all things through Christ who strengthens me."
> **Your soul says**, "I can't, I am afraid."
> **Your spirit says**, "I believe."
> **Your soul says**, "I'll believe it when I see it."

When your spirit and soul disagree, there is a war within your members until one of them submits.

Here is how to read the following chart left to right:

Your spirit is born again when you receive Jesus. Your soul is in the process of being transformed and your body has to be controlled.

Next line – your spirit is saved. Your soul is in the process of being saved. Your body will be saved.

Next line – In your spirit, that is who you are in Christ. In your soul that determines what you do and how you act. Your body will basically obey the soul.

I think you get it!

Spirit	Soul	Body
Born again	Transformed	Controlled
Saved	Being saved	Will be saved
Who you are in Christ	Determines what you do and how you act	Basically will obey the soul
II Cor. 5:17 (become new)	James 1:21 (the engrafted word that saves *psuche*)	Romans 6-8 (Paul's struggle to yield himself)
I Peter 1:23 (born again)	II Cor. 3:18 (changed image into the image of Christ)	I Cor. 9:27 (we are to keep body in subjection)
	Romans 12:1,2 (renewal of your soul)	
	I Peter 1:9 (Our goal is the salvation of our soul)	

HE RESTORETH MY SOUL

Jesus said, *"I am come that they might have **life** (Zoë), and that they might have it more abundantly. I am the good shepherd: the good shepherd giveth his **life** (psuche) for the sheep."* - John 10:10b, 11

Now this is very interesting, there are three Greek words for the word "life." The first is *Zoë*, which is the God kind of spiritual life. The second is *bios*, which is our biological life; and the third is *psuche*, which is our soul (mind, will and emotional) life.

When Jesus said He came to lay down His life for the sheep, He didn't use the word *bios* for His biological life, even though He did lay down His physical life.

He didn't say that He came to lay down His Zoë (spiritual life). He said, *"I came to lay down psuche (His soul life) for you."*

Jesus said that He only did what He saw the Father do - John 5:19. He depended totally upon His spirit man to hear from the Holy Spirit. He then directed His soul and lived it out through His body.

36

Jesus, the second Adam, was reversing what the first Adam did when he severed the connection from the Father in the Garden of Eden. At the fall, Adam became independent and unsurrendered to the will of God.

Jesus reversed this act by not allowing His soul to lead him. He yielded to His spirit by only doing what the Father told Him to. Jesus came as our representative. He did something for us that we could have never done for ourselves.

He brought an exalted, independent and unsurrendered soul / *psuche* to the cross, reversing the effects of sin from the first Adam. Since the fall, man has lived from the outside in, meaning that outside pressures affect the way we think, feel, talk and act. Jesus lived from the inside out. Meaning that from His spirit He walked in authority directing His soul no matter what outside pressures there were, He always walked in grace and love.

Jesus said, *"Father, if thou be willing, remove this cup from me: nevertheless not my will, but thine, be done. And there appeared an angel unto him from heaven, strengthening him. And being in an agony he prayed more earnestly: and his sweat was as it were great drops of blood falling down to the ground."* - Luke 22:42-44

Four thousand years earlier in another garden, the Garden of Eden, Adam basically said, *Father, not your will, but my will be done* by partaking of the forbidden fruit. Jesus the second Adam, in the Garden of Gethsemane, was literally reversing this act of sin and the death it brought to our souls.

Jesus said, *"If any man will come after me, let him deny (abstain) himself, and take up his cross, and follow me. For whosoever will save his life / psuche shall lose (perish, destroy) it: and whosoever will lose his life / psuche for my sake shall find it."* - Matthew 16:24-25

Jesus was telling us the answer to a successful life. *Psuche*, our soulish life, must live at the cross daily to bring death to the contamination of the sin principle that infected our soul. I am not talking about death to the functions of our mind, will and emotions. God gave us these functions to display the workings of our spirit man. We want our thoughts influenced by the logic and the knowledge of God, instead of the tree of the knowledge of good and evil. We want balanced, healthy emotions. We want our spirit and soul working in perfect harmony, acting out the will of God on earth as it is in heaven.

Our goal as believers is not to have the soul functioning independently of the spirit any longer, but rather controlled by the spirit.

Think about how your mind, will and emotions, if controlled by your spirit, would act differently. In fact, I believe a phrase has been coined about it called - W.W. J.D. What would Jesus do? You would walk in love with all the people around you. You would put their needs, interests and desires above your own. All your relationships would improve. Your stress levels would go down. The blessings are endless. This is our spiritual maturity we're talking about.

Jesus must have lordship over every throne in our soul. Our soul can shut down the flow of the spirit because it acts like the 'release valve' that determines what will flow out of our spirit. This principle is the reason that one minute we can be in the spirit and the next minute our soul can be rising up and taking the lead. This very thing happens to all of us on a daily basis.

For example, maybe you're arguing with your spouse and kids in the car on the way to church. When you arrive, you put on your church face to everyone. Oh good morning, praise the Lord! You begin singing, "He is Lord, He is Lord." Then you're back home and you're yelling at the kids and aggravated at your spouse. Your *psuche* or shall I say your suitcase has come unzipped and all your baggage is spilling out.

It is not enough for us to be born again, filled with the Holy Spirit, and then continue to live constantly under the dictates of our soul. We have a responsibility in the restoration of our soul. There was a judgment written on the cross of Calvary. It is our responsibility to execute that judgment; it doesn't come to us automatically. We have only executed the forgiveness side of what Jesus died to purchase for us, and we have neglected healing, deliverance, wholeness and the restoration of our soul.

Too many believers have only grown to the place of receiving Jesus and the forgiveness of their sins. And that is important; in fact it's what it takes to have eternal life. But there is more to what Jesus died to purchase for us. He wants us to benefit from all of His Covenant Blessings.

Ask the Lord for discernment to recognize and identify the areas of struggle in your life and whether these occur because of demonic attack or living from your soul. To war effectively, we must be able to distinguish what is of the enemy, the soul or the Lord. For many years I blamed every struggle I had on the enemy. When I began to understand the soul, I realized that my sin nature was still ruling my life and I was a carnal, soulish Christian. That was the reason for most of my problems. Identifying the soul and examining its issues has improved every area of my life.

God desires wholeness in us; but to reach wholeness, we must cooperate with Him. Healing for the damage in our soul is progressive. As He begins to deal with us in a particular area, we can choose to stuff it, medicate it, or allow it.

It is similar to an infection. If you leave it alone or just cover it with a band-aid, the infection will just get worse.

Toxic emotions are volcanic in nature. When you suppress them, much like an infection they will erupt and cause damage. They are a chemical response to a toxic, negative or fearful thought. If not dealt with, they will continue to secrete toxic chemicals. Over time, as they flow through your body, they begin searing your organs and cells like battery acid breaking down your immune system and making you sick.

The Lord desires to expose these things so that He can get to the root and heal us. He doesn't want to deal with symptoms. He doesn't want us to just feel better. He wants to make us whole and complete.

A PROPHETIC PICTURE

I want you to see the prophetic picture in creation and what the fall of man produced. When God created, *"... He formed man of the dust of the ground..."* - Genesis 2:7. Then He *"...planted a garden... the tree of life and the tree of knowledge of good and evil."* - Genesis 2:8,9

Man was to *"...dress (work) and keep (guard, protect, attend to) the garden."* - Genesis 2:15. Just as we are to dress (work) and keep (guard, protect and attend to) our earth bodies. And the Lord God commanded the man, saying, *"Of every tree of the garden thou mayest freely eat: But of the tree of the knowledge of good and evil, thou shalt not eat of it: for in the day that thou eatest thereof thou shalt surely die."* - Genesis 2:16,17

Adam ate of the tree of the knowledge of good and evil. At that moment man was born again from spiritual life to spiritual death. He had knowledge of evil, experienced fear, died spiritually and death entered into the earth - Genesis 3:5-10.

Adam's rebellion gave Satan man's authority over the earth. As a result, *"...cursed is the ground for thy sake; in sorrow shalt thou eat of it all the days of thy life; Thorns also and thistles shall it bring forth to thee."* - Genesis 3:17-18

Seeds are planted in the ground and bring forth fruit. Seeds are also planted as a thought in the ground of our minds and bring forth fruit as well. The curse brought forth thorns in the ground of the earth and established the law of sin and death. The curse established a sin nature in the ground of our earth bodies and brought forth thorns on the trees of our mind. Death, darkness, evil and fear had invaded earth's envelope. Our thought life was now ground for the enemy to manifest his kingdom through us. Proverbs 23:7 tells us, *"As a man thinketh in his heart so is he."* We can see that what we think affects not only our bodies and physical health but the decisions we make and the direction our life will go. It all starts with the seed of a thought.

You can see the prophetic picture. The information seed comes in through our eyes as a light wave and our ears as a sound wave. It is planted in our brain. A nerve cell in the cortex of our brain will grow like a tree, roots, a stem, branches and fruit. The branches are called dendrites and if the thought was negative or fear based it will produce the fruit of a thorn and have a different chemical structure from that of a faith based, positive thought. The thorns in our mind disrupt our chemical balance bringing dis-ease to our bodies that eventually will bring forth death.

While purchasing our redemption, Jesus, the second Adam, bore a crown of thorns around the cortex of his mind and was hung on a tree. He could have worn thorns around his neck, wrist, ankle or even his waist. He could have been hung on a stake, but the way he was crucified was very specific to the reversal of the curse. The crown of thorns that was placed on Jesus' head had three-and-a-half-inch razor sharp spikes. It represented the thorns that hindered prosperity in the ground of the earth, as well as the prosperity in the ground of our minds. When they pressed that crown of thorns into His brow, blood came out. That blood reversed the curse of mental and natural poverty for us. There is power in pleading the blood of Jesus in prayer over our lives and as we do we are enforcing our covenant provisions for a prosperous life.

Just as every tree in the yard has its own unique blueprint and shape, the trees in our mind have created a unique blueprint for our life as well. Jesus said, *"You shall know them by their fruits. Do men gather grapes of thorns, or figs of thistles? Even so every good tree bringeth forth good fruit; but a corrupt tree bringeth forth evil fruit. A good tree cannot bring forth evil fruit, neither can a corrupt tree bring forth good fruit... Wherefore by their fruits ye shall know them."* - Matthew 7:16-20 We too are known by the fruit of our lives. It is the evidence of what has been sown in our minds.

For this reason the Apostle Paul told us to *"...be transformed by the renewing of our mind."* Coming out of agreement with wrong thoughts removes the thorns. Agreeing with what the Word of God says will renew our mind and change the nerve pathway of our internal blueprint - Romans 12:2.

Think of this - spirit / pneuma is the element in man that gives him the ability to think of God. It is man's vertical window while the soul / *psuche* is man's horizontal window.

It's a picture of the cross.

Father, I am so grateful that you sent Jesus to redeem us. Not only did He make a way for me to spend eternity with You, but He made the way for my sin-infected soul to be restored. Lord Jesus, I receive You as my Savior. I ask You to come into my heart, forgive my sins, and cleanse me from all unrighteousness.

I am so grateful for my new life. I know that I am created in Your image. I have Your likeness, Your character, Your nature, Your DNA within my born again spirit. Holy Spirit I ask you to baptize me in Your power and presence so I can live this Christian life from my spirit and daily overcome the issues in my soul.

Holy Spirit, I give You permission to daily reveal my soul nature to me. Help me to abstain from soulish living. I give You permission to put Your finger on areas of my soul and character that need changing and heal me from the inside out. I ask you to bring me to a place of spiritual maturity and development. Today I begin my born again journey in my Christian faith. I love You, Lord.

I am providing for you a list of "I am" scriptures telling you who you are in Christ. Use this to renew your mind and see yourself as God sees you!

Copy the list and put it where you can see it daily.

I Am List

1. I am able. (Phil. 4:13)

2. I am abounding in grace. (II Cor. 9:8)

3. I am above and not beneath. (Deut. 28:13)

4. I am accepted. (Eph. 1:6)

5. I am an ambassador for Christ. (II Cor. 5:20)

6. I am anointed. (I John 2:20)

7. I am anxious for nothing. (Phil. 4:6)

8. I am the apple of His eye. (Zech. 2:8)

9. I have authority over the devil. (Luke 9:1)

10. I am beautiful. (Psalm 149:4)

11. I am becoming a mature person. (Eph. 4:13)

12. I am becoming conformed to Christ. (Rom. 8:29)

13. I am a believer. (Rom. 10:9)

14. I belong to God. (John 17:9)

15. I am blessed. (Eph. 1:3)

16. I am blood bought. (I Cor. 6:19,20)

17. I am bold. (Prov. 28:1)

18. I am a branch of the True Vine. (John 15:5)

19. I am called. (I Peter 5:10)

20. I am cared for. (I Peter 5:7)

21. I am a child of God. (John 1:12)

22. I am cherished. (Eph. 5:29)

23. I am chosen. (I Peter 2:9)

24. I am a co-heir with Christ. (Rom. 8:17)

25. I am comforted. (Jer. 31:13)

26. I am confident. (I John 4:17)

27. I am confident of answers to prayer. (I John 5:14,15)

28. I am confident He will never leave me. (Heb. 13:5,6)

29. I am a conqueror. (Rom. 8:37)

30. I am courageous. (I Chron. 28:20)

31. I am created in His image. (Gen. 1:27)

32. I am crucified with Him. (Gal. 2:20)

33. I am dead to sin. (Rom. 6:11)

34. I am a delight. (Psalm 147:11)

35. I am delivered. (Psalm 107:6)

36. I am determined. (Phil. 4:13)

37. I am disciplined. (Heb. 12:5-11)

38. I am empowered to obey. (Phil. 2:13)

39. I am enlightened. (Eph. 1:18)

40. I am faithful. (Rev. 17:14)

41. I am far from oppression. (Isaiah 54:14)

42. I am favored. (Job 10:12)

43. I am filled with the fruit of the Spirit. (Gal. 5:22,23)

44. I am filled with the knowledge of His will. (Col. 1:9)

45. I am filled with joy. (John 17:13)

46. I am a finished product in progress. (Phil. 1:6)

47. I am fighting the good fight of faith. (I Tim. 6:12)

48. I am forgiven. (Eph. 1:7)

49. I am free. (John 8:36)

50. I am gifted. (Rom. 12:6)

51. I am God's child. (John 1:12)

52. I am granted grace in Christ Jesus. (Rom. 5:17,20)

53. I am guarded by God's peace. (Phil. 4:7)

54. I am the head, not the tail. (Deut. 28:13)

55. I am healthy. (Deut. 7:15)

56. I am holy. (Eph. 1:4)

57. I am humble. (Phil. 2:24)

58. I am the image of God. (Gen. 1:27)

59. I am an imitator of God. (Eph. 5:1)

60. I am indwelt by His Spirit. (Rom. 8:11)

61. I am inseparable from His love. (Rom. 8:35)

62. I am joyful. (Phil. 4:4)

63. I lack no wisdom. (James 1:5)

64. I am a light in a dark place. (Acts 13:47)

65. I am loved. (John 3:16)

66. I am loyal. (Psalm 86:2)

67. I am mighty in God. (Luke 10:19)

68. I have the mind of Christ. (I Cor. 2:16)

69. I am a minister of reconciliation. (II Cor. 5:18,19)

70. I am a mountain mover. (Mark 11:22,23)

71. I am prosperous. (Psalm 1:3)

72. I am protected. (Psalm 91:14)

73. I am provided for. (Matt. 6:33)

74. I am reconciled to God. (Rom. 5:10)

75. I am redeemed. (Gal. 3:13)

76. I am His representative. (Matt. 5:16)

77. I am rich. (I Cor. 8:9)

78. I am righteous. (Eph. 4:22)

79. I am rooted and built up in Him. (Col. 2:7)

80. I am safe. (Psalm 4:8)

81. I am satisfied. (Jer. 31:14)

82. I am secure. (Deut. 33:12)

83. I am sheltered. (Psalm 91:1)

84. I am stable. (Is. 6)

85. I am standing in His grace. (Rom. 5:2)

86. I am standing firm in Christ. (II Cor. 1:21)

87. I am strong in the Lord. (I Cor. 1:8)

88. I am transformed. (II Cor. 3:18)

89. I am triumphant. (II Cor. 2:14)

90. I am unafraid. (Is. 44:2; 51:12)

91. I have understanding. (II Tim. 2:7)

92. I am valuable. (Luke 12:24)

93. I am living in victory. (I Cor. 15:57)

94. I am a warrior. (II Cor. 10:4)

95. I am in a wealthy place. (Psalm 66:12)

96. I am being made whole. (Mark 5:34)

97. I am wise. (Prov. 2:6)

98. I am His worshiper (Psalm 95:6)

99. I am worthy. (Rev. 3:4)

100. I am yielded to God. (Rom. 6:13)

Strongholds
The Battle For Our Minds

We take a closer look at our thought life and the battlefield of the mind. You will discover that we all have a measure of deception in our perception coming from the filters of life's experiences. Learn how to be transformed from the inside out by the renewing of your mind.

Chapter Two

What is a stronghold? A stronghold is an entrenched and practiced way of thinking within the mind part of our soul, that has a strong hold on what we believe and shapes our thinking.

A stronghold can be constructive, positive and healthy. A pattern of thinking in which God and righteousness can rule. Or a stronghold can be destructive, negative and unhealthy; a pattern of thinking where the enemy and unrighteousness can rule.

In brain images, a stronghold looks like a tree network of tightly inter-twined branches. If the belief system is negative and unhealthy, it will look dark and heavy from the thorns and different chemical structure.

For instance, I used to have negative destructive thinking where healing was concerned. Back pain runs in my family. So my entrenched belief system was that when back pain came to my body, I just accepted it as part of who I was.

Now that I understand all that Jesus' death purchased for me, I have developed a positive, constructive belief system where healing is concerned. When any manifestation of the curse tries to put pressure on my body, my mind's first response is, "You have no legal right to me, by Jesus stripes I am healed." Then I put myself in a posture of resistance, by having positive thoughts entrenched in my belief system, based on the Word and will of God.

Therefore, strongholds would be the logic, reasoning, arguments, rationalizations, justifications and denials that we use to defend our positions and beliefs, whether they are right or wrong, positive or negative. Since these thoughts are so ingrained and a part of who we are, they cause us to have automatic reactions in our behavior that can be either good or bad.

We all have a belief system that rules our thinking. That belief system has a strong hold on what we believe, good or bad. We know that the kingdom of darkness has influenced the thought process and belief systems of man, establishing entrenched patterns of thinking that have become destructive strongholds within us.

THE SOUL

We have learned that the soul is made up of the mind, including our conscious and subconscious memory, our will and emotions. It is what and how we think. It is our image center and imagination. It houses our ideas and beliefs; the filters of life's events that form our opinions, perceptions, attitudes and it activates our behaviors. It is our ability to reason and have logic. It is our emotional make-up, housing all of our feelings like happiness, sadness, etc.

So then you can see how easily an "entrenched pattern of deception" can cloud our beliefs, forming our perceptions about anything, thereby affecting our feelings and behavior.

Have you ever been in a group of people and the topic of conversation turns to either religion or politics? Suddenly you will hear all kinds of negative strongholds (entrenched belief systems) being expressed. Conversations can become heated as their attitudes and judgments begin negatively affecting the way people feel and behave.

THE TWO KINGDOMS

As a result of the fall, there are two kingdoms on the earth. There is the Kingdom of God and the kingdom of darkness. In the Kingdom of God, Jesus is Lord and everything works according to the law of the spirit of life. If you obey the Lord and operate the law of life, the blessings of God will overtake you!

Deuteronomy 28:1,2 says, *"And it shall come to pass, if thou shalt hearken diligently unto the voice of the LORD thy God, to observe and to do all his commandments which I command thee this day, that the LORD thy God will set thee on high above all nations of the earth. And all these blessings shall come on thee, and overtake thee…"*

In the kingdom of darkness, Satan is lord and everything works according to the law of sin and death. Ephesians 2:2 tells us, *"…wherein in time past ye walked according to the course of this world, according to the prince of the power of the air, the spirit that now worketh in the children of disobedience."*

According to my whirlpool example, the course of this world; where sin, sickness and curses flow, has carried our lives in the direction of the kingdom of darkness naturally. But Jesus came preaching, *"The Kingdom of God is at hand."* He also said that, *"…the kingdom of heaven suffereth violence, and the violent take it by force"* - Matthew 11:12.

Jesus brought us the Kingdom of God and it is suffering violence here on the earth. The Greek translation means a forceful pressure is coming against it, just like the flow of that whirlpool. However, we as believers have the ability to overcome the kingdom of darkness in our lives by being violent and forceful ourselves; pressing against that whirlpool pressure by going in another direction. We press against that pressure with violent faith resisting the kingdom of darkness by speaking God's word and creating the Kingdom of God in every area of our life!

This is what Paul is describing in Romans 8:2 when he says, *"For the law of the Spirit of life in Christ Jesus (at work in our spirit) hath made me free (liberates and delivers) from the law of sin and death (at work in our soul)."* So when the Kingdom of God in our spirit is influencing our soul, and our soul is surrendered and submitted to our spirit; we have given Jesus Lordship. We are operating the law of Life and pressing against that whirlpool pressure, so that the blessings of God can overtake us!

However, when we are living from an unsurrendered soul, we are aligning ourselves to the course of this world, according to the prince of the power of the air. The law of sin and death in the kingdom of darkness operates in our lives, with the flow of that pressure. God has always left the choice up to us as to which kingdom and lord we will serve.

In Deuteronomy 30:19 it says, *"I call heaven and earth to record this day against you, that I have set before you life and death, blessing and cursing: therefore choose life that both thou and thy seed may live."* You see His will is that we would choose life!

THE BATTLEFIELD

Our mind is the battlefield. The enemy's primary plan of attack against us is through the ground of our soul / thought life. If we agree with his unhealthy, destructive thoughts, it will generate thorns on our dendrites that will secrete a toxic chemical emotion and negatively influence our behavior.

Proverbs 23:7 says, *"...for as a man thinks in his heart so is he:"* As we open the gate of our soul / mind, to either godly positive thoughts or the enemy's negative thoughts, it will not only affect our health but create our future.

Here is how that works: images from your eye and ear gates come together and form what you believe, creating a brain tree / pattern or practiced way of thinking, which determines what you will say and do.

These thoughts have made an impression on us. They come from our upbringing, life experiences, television, movies, society, etc. Once in place, those trees have created our own unique blueprint for life. So, you are not controlled by the actual truth of a matter, but by what you believe to be true.

The Placebo Effect - is a remarkable phenomenon in which a *placebo,* a fake treatment, an inactive substance, like sugar, distilled water, or saline solution, can sometimes improve a patient's condition simply because the person has the expectation that it will be helpful. Expectation plays a potent role in the placebo effect. The more someone believes he or she will benefit from a treatment, the more likely it is a benefit will happen. So the patient improves because of his or her belief and expectation, not because it was real medicine. The placebo studies prove the power of our mind to affect our bodies where our health is concerned.

This is a spiritual law we are identifying *"...for as a man thinketh in his heart so is he:"* - Proverbs 23:7. So obviously what we think about we bring about. Since our thoughts direct our actions on a daily basis, we all must examine our belief systems for areas of deception in our perception. What we believe to be true is what controls us, whether our beliefs are based on truth or not. That is why the placebo effect works on the people who believe it. **Information doesn't have to be true to control us. We just have to believe it's true.** It then becomes what we will feel and act out.

As was discussed before, we all struggle with needs that have never been met, hurts that still ache and issues that are left unresolved. Every one of us has developed some sort of coping mechanisms to deal with our thoughts and feelings, learning how to bury the need and to medicate the pain.

The result of these coping mechanisms is that we have developed entrenched patterns of thinking that are based on our perception of these life events.

What we are left with is a distorted view as seen through the filters / thorny dendrites on our soul / mind. These have become our unhealthy strongholds.

We all have been raised by people, who were also raised by people, who had their own *psuche* / suitcase full of baggage. The most loving parents can still have areas of darkness in their souls. Those impressions and imperfections in our family lines have created a blueprint in our thought process marking the souls of generations.

This book is entirely about identifying the patterns on our soul, putting an end to the blame game, and taking responsibility for where we are now, and then making the necessary changes to surrender our soul to the process of restoration.

The enemy knows exactly how we were raised and what our familiar patterns of thinking are. He uses his vast knowledge of every scar as an arsenal against us by making just the right suggestions to our mind.

When we come into agreement with the enemy by agreeing with a thought that is a deception or perversion of truth and contrary to the Word of God, it gives him power to bring destruction in that place of agreement.

Those places of agreement that are stored in our belief center become a stronghold in our thinking. They create tunnel vision from the filters / thorns on our soul / belief system. We end up viewing situations through these filters which prevent us from seeing anything outside of our limited perspective. This especially hinders us from seeing the Father's perspective.

As a negative or fearful thought is developed, it activates the hypothalamus - which is the heart of our endocrine system - and responds to our thought life to release the chemical emotion related to the thought. In so doing, it will translate your thought life into a physical state. This cycle is what puts your body into a stress reaction that can eventually make you sick. If your thought life is chaotic and messed up, you will feel and act that way too.

I bumped into a stronghold I didn't realize I had in a rather embarrassing way. I am on staff at my church and we went away for a staff retreat one weekend. As Pastor was going over the calendar for the year, he mentioned that a church in our inner city had requested that Pastor's wife come and minister. As she looked at her calendar she realized that she would be out of town that weekend. When Pastor asked me if I would go in her place, I froze. I was immediately stricken with fear and intimidation. The chemical related to that thought was secreting those emotions. My thoughts were being translated into a physical state. I hesitated, then began stumbling over my words while everyone was staring at me. They told me I got pale and looked sick. I told them to go on and come back to me in a minute.

As I was sitting there, I found myself mentally going through the processes that are included in this book. In a matter of seconds I began taking an x-ray of my soul. I asked myself why I was feeling this way. I knew it was because of my upbringing. My parents moved me out of that part of the city when I was very young. Growing up I heard about the dangers of the city; I heard their stereotypes of people. The things I heard were seeds planted in my thoughts that had a strong hold on me. I realized I had a negative belief system that wasn't true. I immediately changed my thinking to thoughts like, I had nothing to fear about that part of the city or the people there. I came out of agreement with the negative fearful thoughts and beliefs and committed my way to the Lord. In so doing I removed the thorns off my dendrites and came into agreement with a godly thought so I would produce good fruit. Jesus said, *"A good tree cannot bring forth evil fruit, neither can a corrupt tree bring forth good fruit...Wherefore by their fruits ye shall know them"* - Matthew 7:18-20.

Now I have to tell you as I am writing this, it seems so much easier than what I was actually going through at the time. You have to understand what it was like as I was going through this process. I was experiencing what felt like a wall in my chest and every fiber of my being was resisting this process. That is because as I touched those thorns / my belief system, I was pricked, so to speak. They began to secrete their toxic chemicals and my hypothalamus was also releasing the chemicals related to the thought, making me 'feel' like I had a wall in my chest and did not want to do this. My soul began rationalizing and justifying; I was thinking these people don't know me, they don't know that Pastor asked me to go, they'll never know how I am feeling. I don't know them, this doesn't matter.

I had a belief system and a thorny / filter in place that needed to be removed. Remember, a filter is like the saying, "looking at the world through rose-colored glasses." In my case I was looking through a thorn bush. So what I believed was not the truth. Everything I saw had been colored and distorted by my filters.

This is when we end up using justifications for our behavior. For example: you don't know how I grew up... my parents were... I was raised to believe...We argue, reason and rationalize our right to believe and behave the way we do.

As I was going through this process, I realized that I took some very deep breaths and everyone on staff had noticed my body language, so I was embarrassed as well. A couple of minutes later I spoke up and said, "I'll go!" Pastor said, "What?" I said, "I'll go." I had realized what was happening to me and I came out of the agreement with the negative, fearful thoughts, thereby breaking off the thorn. Then I replaced those thoughts with the truth that I had nothing to fear. My friends on staff commented on how they never saw someone go through the process of change that quickly. Well I knew what had to be done and I did it. I didn't feel like I wanted to do it, in fact it would have been much easier to just say no. But I had to do this for my own sake. And now with the knowledge of how our brain works, I realized I had to do it to stay healthy as well.

THOUGHT PATTERNS

Here are some of the most noticeable examples of destructive stronghold thought patterns. Remember negative or fear based thoughts create thorns on your dendrite trees, forming your own unique brain blueprint and internal image, affecting your decisions, health and reality.

1. Thinking that you need a man / woman to make you happy or complete you

I remember being a teenager and believing this. All my friends had boyfriends and I didn't, so I didn't feel happy or complete until I had one too. It didn't matter what kind of character that boy had, as long as he was interested in me I felt complete. I have watched women of all ages go from man to man all in an attempt to feel whole.

2. Giving yourself sexually to receive love or attention

This goes right along with needing someone to complete you. Or perhaps your love tank wasn't filled as a child. You may find that the only way you feel love is to give yourself sexually. When you do, the love you feel is very short lived. You have to ask yourself, is this really love or are you being used?

3. Any fear-based belief

Any time you are making a decision based on fear, you should examine what you really believe and ask yourself, does it line up with the Word of God. Fear is the foundational force of the kingdom of darkness; just as love is the foundational force of the Kingdom of God. Fear is having more faith in the enemy's ability to harm you than in God's ability to protect you.

4. Self-rejection

When we have self-rejection issues we tend to abuse ourselves, or let others abuse us because we have no self worth. We don't see ourselves the way God sees us. Behaviors can run from being needy and clingy to cold and distant. Many times our behavior may make others feel uncomfortable around us which only leads to more feelings of rejection.

5. Addictions

If you are addicted to anything, for example, a drug, food, activity, a person; if you believe you 'need' that thing, then it is a destructive stronghold. I believe the chemicals being secreted from this thought create your craving. Freedom is not found in suppressing the thought or its craving, it is found in removing the thorn by changing your mind!

6. Eating disorders

Someone with an eating disorder doesn't see themselves the way God sees them. They can look in a mirror and see a fat person, when in reality they are all skin and bones.

7. Prejudices

Whenever you pre-judge someone, you have an entrenched pattern of thinking colored by your belief system.

8. Religious belief systems

Every religion is based on a set of beliefs that are comfortable for the believer. I believe this is where we get denominational differences. We are divided according to what we believe. Instead, we should have the mind of Christ with our beliefs lined up with Him and His Word.

9. Fantasies

Any unrestrained, unreal thought process that doesn't line up to the will and Word of God is dangerous. What you think and believe will shape your image center. It is the creative part of you and you have to examine if you are using your image center to imagine the promises and blessings of God, or something of the kingdom of darkness.

10. A medical doctor's report

If you have been told you have something the Bible lists as a manifestation of the curse (in Deuteronomy 28:14-68) and you come into agreement with that, you are setting yourself up for more of it. It is okay to have a doctor diagnose a problem. However, if you agree with the doctor's report, if you use your image center to see yourself as having that disease, if you repeat to everyone what the doctor has said about you, then you are binding yourself to that diagnosis. Dr. Caroline Leaf says that, "Saying things like 'my' arthritis, or 'my' heart problem takes ownership of it and makes it part of you." If you are experiencing a manifestation of the curse then you can say: "I am dealing with symptoms of whatever you're resisting", just be cautious not to 'my' it. As soon as you 'my' it and take ownership you change the neuro-chemical structure of the way in which your body functions. That means your belief is creating a tree network / chemical structure in your body and will only enforce your 'having' what you're trying to resist. Your responsibility from the diagnosis forward is to know exactly what you're fighting and to get in agreement with what the Word says about you so you can begin the process of resisting. Jesus died to purchase your healing, begin to see yourself being made whole.

11. Suicidal thoughts

If you have ever thought or said, "I wish I were dead," you have agreed with the enemy and released a spirit of death into your life. Now let's say some time has gone by and you changed your mind or you even forgot about that thought or the words that you spoke. What you need to know is that the enemy has not forgotten and the assignment of death released against you is still in operation.

If you take a good look, you will notice that death has been at work in many other areas of your life. It could be your health, your finances, or your relationships. So it is at this time we must pray to break that agreement.

Say this prayer out loud: "Father, I come before you and confess, as sin, the thoughts, internal agreements and words spoken about wishing I was dead. I come out of agreement with that thought and I break the power in words of death I have spoken. I bind every spirit of death at work in any area of my life; I cancel your assignment against me and loose you out of my life in Jesus' name. I choose life; I choose to live in the power of the Blessing that Jesus died to purchase for me."

In all of these examples of stronghold thought patterns, our agreement with the enemy has given place to obsessive thoughts that consume so much of our emotional and mental energy. Like weeds spreading through our minds, they cripple our life and set us on a road to destruction. They become how we are wired, so to speak. Those networks of dendrites can look like a nest of wires that have programmed our hard-drive. The neuro-chemical structure of our image center has been defiled by destructive thoughts / thorn trees and a blueprint for our life has been created, translating our thought life into a physical state and putting our body into a stress reaction that makes us sick.

The behavior we have been experiencing is driven from within the damaged soul, for instance; a need for love, acceptance and companionship, fear of being alone, and a need for security. People could feel hopeless, confused, have wrong desires, etc. that keep them in the death cycle under the kingdom of darkness. They try to medicate these driving forces within their nature with offerings of sex, alcohol, food or drugs.

These offerings are substitutes and merely a temporary fix. They quiet the need and stuff the pain until the fix wears off. We often find ourselves crying out to God to change our spouse, kids, job, and situation or to send us someone who will meet our needs.

It is not God's will to change our environment so that our issues will be satisfied. It is God's will to get to the root of our issues so He can heal them. God cannot dismantle our entrenched patterns of thinking for us because He will not violate our free will.

The Lord has shown us through His Word that it is our responsibility to tear down these toxic strongholds and vain imaginings. At this point we all must recognize where we have believed lies, having deception in our perception in areas of our life. Now it is vitally important to change our thinking.

The Apostle Paul encouraged us to retrain our thought patterns when he said we are to rejoice in the Lord always. He said don't take thoughts of worry or care about things, but through prayer with thanksgiving make your request to God. And the peace of God, which passes all understanding, shall keep your hearts and minds through Christ Jesus. - Philippians 4:4, 5-7

So take your cares and turn them over to the Lord and leave them there. He knows how to take care of you. Then, with thanksgiving, start rejoicing and being thankful for *The Answer*! We can always thank the Lord for something. It is imperative that we have a heart that looks for the best and not the worst in life. Paul goes on to say, *"Finally, brethren, whatsoever things are true, whatsoever things are honest, whatsoever things are just, whatsoever things are pure, whatsoever things are lovely, whatsoever things are of good report; if there be any virtue, and if there be any praise, think on these things."* - Philippians 4:8

The word think here means to take an inventory, number and meditate. In other words we should be taking inventory of and counting our blessings along the way. Writing them down will help us to focus on the good in our life and not the bad; change our perspective and think better thoughts. We have turned our cares over to the Lord and our provision is on its way. Perception is everything. It is how we interpret the events of life that make the difference for us. The difference in whether an event is stressful or not lies in our perception. It lies in what we believe to be the importance of the event. When it comes to worry, fear and being in stress, what we believe is what got us stressed and it will be the key to getting us out of that emotional state.

For example, my mom had a tragic childhood and many losses in her life. After my father left she put herself through school to do hair and became a successful barber and hairdresser.

Many years later she found herself going through another divorce. This time she was having to move into an apartment and live alone for the first time in her life.

This event was triggering all the other losses in her life and was like pulling scabs off of many old wounds. She was experiencing a lot of fear, insecurity and depression. As a result of those toxic thoughts, they put her body into a state of great stress.

It was vital for her to change her thinking and her perception of the events in her life in order to survive and stay healthy. She began thinking thoughts like; I can do this, there is nothing to fear, the Lord is with me, I am not alone. The Lord saw this coming and has gone before me and made my provision, there is a benefit to living alone. I don't have to cook dinner every night anymore, I can come and go as I please, etc.

Then the Lord led her to become a volunteer at Monroe Community Hospital. That is a hospital in our area where people go to live who can't take care of themselves. She began feeding people who couldn't feed themselves. She took them for walks, pushing their wheel chairs outside so they could have fresh air. She played cards with them, hugged them and loved on them.

People who didn't receive any attention from their families were her patients and they absolutely loved her and looked for her every day. She was their light in a dark place.

Being a volunteer and meeting the needs of others totally changed the perception she had of her life. Instead of looking at all the losses in her life, she was instead able to count all of her blessings. At another difficult time in her life, things had turned into a great blessing, for her as well as for the people she mentored.

I am so proud of my mom and the amazing gift she has to give and show love. I am in awe of the ministry she has of being the hands and arms of Jesus to all the people she cares for and loves.

With my mom as an example, you can see that is vitally important to guard our thoughts as they are the first step in the creative process of our life. With our thoughts we begin to create an image of who we are and a blueprint for the direction our life and health will go. It will either be a life in the Kingdom of God or a life in the kingdom of darkness. A life where either blessings or curses can flow. My mother turned her life to good, and so can you.

PULLING DOWN STRONGHOLDS

II Corinthians 10:4-5 says, *"For the weapons of our warfare are not carnal (physical weapons) but mighty through God to the pulling down (overthrow and destruction) of strongholds (entrenched patterns of thinking); casting down (violently destroying) imaginations (mental creations, blueprints) and every high thing (elevated barrier) that exalteth (rises) itself against the knowledge of God and bringing into captivity (leading away) every thought to the obedience of Christ;..."*

We must understand that we have given the enemy legal ground in our soul where these strongholds exist. These are the cords of the yoke by which the enemy attempts to lead us.

For example, not many of us can look in the mirror and love what we see. For the most part we are extremely critical of what we see. It is very common for most of us to have low self-esteem and pick ourselves apart.

Just as we have to x-ray our soul in order to examine what we believe about ourselves, we must x-ray and examine what we believe about others as well. These belief systems that we have about ourselves and others are patterns of thinking rising against the truth of how God sees us.

I suggest writing down what you think about yourself, both good and bad. Then make a list of the people in your life. Write what you think about them. That will make it obvious to you exactly where your belief systems are and how they need to change.

How does the Father see us? How does He see others? If our thinking doesn't line up with that truth, then we have just identified some deception in our perception, a stronghold rising above the truth of God. We may have to forgive ourselves or someone else for words or deeds sown into us, or repent for judgments we may have placed on ourselves or someone else.

Now we are ready to repent for believing a lie and coming into agreement with the enemy. Then we can break the power of that agreement and choose to agree with what the Word of God says about us.

Once we know the mind of Christ on the matter, we can clearly see the deception in our perception and repent for the wrong agreement. Now take that list you made of yourself and others and write the truth next to your toxic belief systems. Now you can see why it is so important to remain teachable and ask the Lord to reveal to you where you are being deceived. We are all deceived somewhere.

When talking about this battlefield of the mind and how the enemy operates, please understand that the enemy cannot force us to do anything. His only power is to make suggestions to us.

His suggestions come in many forms, such as the way we were raised, our life's experiences, things we see on television, in movies, music, media and advertising portraying a way or style of life. They come in the form of other people's words, opinions and behaviors.

The enemy will try to wear us down by influencing other people's actions to affect us. Remember that this is all a part of how the kingdom of darkness flows naturally in the whirlpool of earth today.

The very first question I always ask people when I see them struggling or in an emotional upheaval is, "What are you thinking?" Tell me what you are thinking and what you believe about this particular situation or person.

As soon as they tell me, I am able to identify the deception in their perception. I can easily show them where they are coming into agreement with the enemy and believing a lie.

Thoughts come so fast that we subconsciously agree with them without even realizing it at first. It may be that these thoughts are a result of a life time of wrong thinking and mental agreement. The brain doesn't distinguish whether a memory is short term or long term. Once the idea of a memory is released into biochemical code, the body responds to the chemicals. The way we will know this has happened is that our feelings will start to be negatively affected.

We may begin to feel negative emotions like: fear, sadness, loneliness, anger, or anxiety. Your feelings will help you identify the wrong thought. It is the thought that is secreting the chemical, that is the feeling you are experiencing. So identifying your feelings will help you to identify the wrong thought that you took. After taking the thought and experiencing the feeling, the next thing you know, you will want to speak or act out that subconscious or conscious agreement.

Know this, that every thought the enemy suggests and we agree with, gives him power to destroy us in that area of life.

STOP COMING INTO AGREEMENT WITH THE ENEMY.
YOU ARE RELEASING POWER FOR YOUR OWN DESTRUCTION!

I remember a time when I could sense the Lord calling me to a higher place in Him. Mark wasn't where I was spiritually and I believed if I followed what the Lord was calling me to, that it would bring a great separation between my husband and me. I found myself withdrawing from fellowship with my Christian friends and sinking into a deep sadness. This lasted for many months. Chuck Pierce was coming to a church in our area and I went with some people to hear him. I don't remember a word he said, but at one point in the service I heard these words, *"Stop coming into agreement with the enemy, you are releasing power for your own destruction."*

Those words shot through me so hard I grabbed a pen and wrote them down. Then I saw it. I had agreed with the enemy that if I followed what the Lord was calling me to do it would bring a separation in my relationship with Mark. It was a lie, but I believed it, and because I believed the lie thorns had grown, translating my body into a state of depression. I broke that agreement and was free immediately. The truth of the matter has been that as I have followed the call of God on my life, it has caused my husband to grow even closer to the Lord and our marriage to grow even stronger.

As believers we haven't realized the destructive power of agreeing with the lies of the enemy. As I counsel people, I find their greatest freedom comes by helping them identify the deception in their perception. Once they can see the lies they believe and verbally break that agreement, removing the thorns, then I have them say the truth of what God says about them so as to create a new nerve pathway and internal blueprint for their lives. When they do this they are free.

Again I return to Dr. Caroline Leaf. From her books and videos, I came to understand that, "They have actually proven in the laboratory, with science, that you can build a new memory or thought over an old one once you have removed the thorns. Faith based chemicals are stronger than the fear based chemicals, so they remove the thorns and heal us. It is

STRONGHOLDS - THE BATTLE FOR OUR MINDS

a biochemical fact that this actually happens! She says it takes four days to change the chemical structure of your brain. Within twenty-one days of right thinking you will create a new nerve pathway."

We know naturally that if we do something for twenty-one days it will create a habit. It could be exercising or eating differently, etc. The reason it creates a habit is that we have grown a new nerve pathway of thinking. Now we understand that we have the power to change the structure of a thorn tree and grow our brains at will. Just by thinking correctly and using our brain properly we can begin to heal!

Remember, our mind is the control tower of our entire being. If the enemy can get us to agree with his suggestions, then we will speak his words and do his actions. Then his will, his kingdom of darkness can be accomplished in the earth.

THE WAY YOU THINK CREATES YOUR REALITY
WHAT YOU THINK ABOUT YOU BRING ABOUT

- Your thoughts determine your emotions.

- Your emotions determine your actions.

- Your actions determine your behavior and habits.

- Your behaviors and habits determine your character.

- Your character determines your destiny.

- And it all starts with a thought.

The enemy has no authority over us to make us do anything because Christ *"...disarmed principalities and powers and authorities...and made a public spectacle of them, triumphing over them by the Cross."* - Colossians 2:15

Yet the enemy knows that many believers do not know or practice the Word; and because of this, they are not familiar with his deceptive ways. We will always have to manage our thought life.

See, we may have received Jesus as our Savior, but may not have allowed Him to really become the Lord of our soul life, Lord over our words and behaviors. Most of us have not learned to discern between the functions of our soul and spirit.

With this in mind, we must determine to view people and the issues of life by rightly dividing what we are thinking. Our posture must always be, "Father, how do you see this? Show me the truth of what is really happening here, not the fact of what I just experienced or how I perceive a situation to be."

We can't be so quick to jump to a conclusion filtered through deception. Situations can appear to be absolutely true based on the facts of our experience and yet can be absolutely false based on God's Word and from His point of view.

Our goal then is to dismantle every entrenched pattern and practiced way of thinking which removes the thorns and rebuild a belief system that lines up with God's Word and His perspective creating a new nerve pathway - so that we walk, talk and act just like Jesus in every situation in life. This is what having the mind of Christ would look like!

When I learned this about strongholds and made a list of the people in my own life, I realized I had a belief system about one particular person who was a consistent source of emotional pain and anger for me. Now as a Christian I had consciously chosen to forgive him repeatedly, that was not a problem for me.

My problem was that I had an entrenched belief system about him that colored my view of him in a negative way. I had a thorny / filter on my soul where he was concerned and I couldn't see him any other way.

I knew I had to see him through the Father's eyes and not my own. It was at this moment that I felt my heart hardened, that old familiar brick wall in my chest. Thoughts of seeing him differently caused toxic chemical emotions to secrete making me 'feel' like I did not want to do this. It was the feeling of every thought, hurt, emotional pain and judgment I have ever believed about him. It was right there in my chest, a pressure within me resisting this process.

I was driving at the time and I remember literally gripping the steering wheel and crying out loud as I said, "Lord, I repent, I change my mind, I choose to let go of the way I see him and I choose to see him through your eyes." It was at that moment I could see a child who was hurt and had buried all of his pain. I heard what Joyce Meyer says, "Hurting people hurt people." For the first time I could see that his behaviors were the result of him acting out his pain and they were negatively affecting my life.

What I was doing was coming out of agreement with every lie I had ever believed about him and choosing to see him the way God sees him. God loves him, He can see why this person behaved the way he did. He could see the damage in his soul. He could see what I couldn't, until then.

I cried all the way home for my freedom. The next morning I was towel drying after a shower and skin was just rolling off my body. I was so grossed out I jumped back in the shower and began scrubbing, while saying, "Lord, what's happening?" He spoke immediately to me. He said, "Donna, what broke on the inside is shedding on the outside!" Now I can see that changing my mind removed the thorns. The chemicals that had been coursing through my body had returned to a normal healthy balance and I was shedding the toxic damage.

It wasn't too long after that an opportunity arose for me to get upset, angry and hurt by this person again. But this time it was different because I could see him differently. My perception had changed, that old belief system had been broken, a new nerve pathway of righteous thinking had been established. I wasn't about to come back into agreement with those toxic destructive thoughts again, I was free! Today I can say that I actually feel love for him, we get along great and I am forever grateful for this understanding!

James 4:7 tells us to, *"Submit yourselves therefore to God. Resist the devil, and he will flee from you."*

When we find ourselves in a test or trial, our immediate response should be, "Am I submitted to the will of God for my life?" If not, then align yourself spirit, soul and then body. Now you are prepared to resist the devil. That means resist acting like him!

Resist by saying "no" to him. No, I am not going to stay mad. No, I am not going to pout or take revenge. No, I am not going to medicate with food or any other substance. No, I am not going to sink into depression by meditating on the problem. I am submitted to God! It is after the submission and resisting that the enemy will flee from you.

Here is a practical way to stop a destructive thought process. Do this test and you will see how it works. Begin counting silently in your mind. Wait a few seconds and then say your name out loud. You will notice that your counting stopped when you said your name. You even know what number you were on when your silent counting stopped. Why is that? The lesson here is that when you are in the heat of the battle fighting to keep your thoughts pure, you don't overcome thoughts by just thinking a different thought. You overcome thoughts with words.

So when you find your mind being negatively tormented about anything, you must begin saying, out loud, what God's Word says about the situation. Start quoting a scripture that pertains to your situation. You can begin thanking God for your desired outcome, or declaring a positive outcome. If you are in a conflict with a person and all you can think about is how much that person upsets you, then get a piece of paper and every day write out and verbally declare all the good qualities about that person. Write down what you appreciate about them. Focus your attention in a positive, constructive way by verbally thanking God for the good and before you know it you won't be meditating on the bad! When we speak, what we hear is a sound wave that gets converted into electricity and goes through the same process of building the trees of our mind. So saying something positive will construct a healthy brain dendrite and rewire you for success.

BE TRANSFORMED FROM THE INSIDE OUT!

Romans 12:2 tells us exactly how to do this. It says, *"And be not conformed to this world: but be ye transformed by the renewing of your mind, that ye may prove what is that good, and acceptable, and perfect, will of God."*

I am going to amplify this scripture so you can see it better.

Be not - Conformed (*suschematizo*) We get the word schematic from this Greek word, and it means together with; to be fashioned together with the world.

- It is saying, don't let outside pressures or the circumstances of life dictate who we are going to be, what our schematic or brain blueprint is and what our life is going to look like.

But be -Transformed (*metamorphoo*) We get the word metamorphose from this Greek word, we are being instructed to be transformed from the inside out! From your spirit through your soul.

- This is the process of change from one form to another, just like a caterpillar transforms into a butterfly.

By the renewing or restoration of our mind / soul.

- This is the goal for mankind - 1 Peter 1:9.

That you may - Prove

- God knows that there is an ability within our born-again human spirit, where the DNA of God is, to act righteously; and He wants us to develop and demonstrate that righteousness. We must surrender our soul to the will of God and let this transformation process take place.

What is that good, and acceptable, and perfect will of God

- We have learned that the DNA of the Father is within our spirit. We have His character, His nature and the fruits of the Holy Spirit within us and it is acceptable when we let them flow from our spirit and be demonstrated out through our soul.

Perfect - means to be complete or totally mature.
- Much like a caterpillar transforms into what the blueprint inside of it has already declared it to be. It opens its cocoon and turns into a butterfly. In the same way, we will be proving or demonstrating the perfect will of God as we develop in our own spiritual maturity.

So let's re-read Romans 12:2 with the definitions you have learned so we can see exactly how to be transformed. This is how it reads:

Be not conformed by being fashioned together with the world. Don't let outside pressure dictate who you are going to be. But be transformed from the inside out; allow the transformation process to bring change, a metamorphosis, from one state of being to another, by the renewing or restoration of your soul / mind. Prove that there is ability resident in your spirit to act good, acceptable and righteously by demonstrating that through your soul. This behavior makes you perfect, complete and totally mature, which is the will of God for you!

WHAT DOES PROVING THE WILL OF GOD LOOK LIKE?

It is so important that you understand the real way the Lord proves us. Let's start by saying that He doesn't tempt or test us with sickness or anything damaging. As we have seen these are the manifestations of the curse that come naturally through the open door of sin and giving place to the enemy.

Ecclesiastes 10:8 says to us, *"He that diggeth a pit shall fall into it; and whoso breaketh an hedge (enclosure, fence, wall), a serpent shall bite (strike, sting, oppress) him."* The hedge was put in place by God. It is activated through our obedience and deactivated through our disobedience. Our disobedience causes us to "give-place" to the enemy, then he can secure his position in our lives, homes and families for generations.

This is something I believe the body of Christ does not understand. When we participate in the kingdom of darkness, when we take wrong thoughts and act on them, thorns will develop on the trees of our mind, then we have dug our own pit, we took the bait, we have broken the hedge of protection around us and we position ourselves for the serpent to bite us. We find ourselves living under the kingdom of darkness and the dis-ease that comes with it.

When the Lord proves us, it requires an action of obedience on our part that will prove or demonstrate to us what is in our soul. The Lord already knows what's in us. Whatever circumstance we find ourselves in, one thing is for sure; our behavior will expose where we have thorns and the level of our spiritual maturity.

This happened to me repeatedly only I had no clue that it was exposing my level of maturity. When I came in contact with people that had the ability to "push my buttons" (I think those buttons might be the thorns on our dendrites) I would react in an unrighteous way. I would think, talk and behave badly. Of course I would feel badly and repent for my behavior when I was done, but that did nothing to change my character. It was my unsurrendered soul infected with a sin nature that was my problem. What changed my character and brought me to a place of maturity was understanding my soul and the material outlined here in *The Answer*.

As Christians we must be able to discern the difference between the Lord proving us and the various temptations and trials of life. Jesus said, "*...In the world (cycle of the kingdom of darkness) ye shall have tribulation: but be of good cheer; I have overcome the world.*" - John 16:33

James 1:13-15 brings more clarity to this when he says, "*Let no man say when he is tempted, I am tempted of God: for God cannot be tempted with evil, neither tempteth he any man. But every man is tempted, when he is drawn away of his own lust, and enticed. Then when lust hath conceived, it bringeth forth sin: and sin, when it is finished, bringeth forth death.*"

James, the Lord's brother says, don't say the temptation is coming from God - don't even say it! What he's saying is that when we sow to our own lusts and enticements we've conceived sin. Then we reap the consequences of wrong thoughts leading to evil temptations, testing and trials bringing forth death (stealing, killing and destruction).

It never occurred to me that what I was experiencing was the reaping process of what I had sown. It wasn't the Lord trying me at all. When life happens we should ask the Lord, is this the result of a seed sown, am I being affected by the reaping process, is it a result of soulish behavior, or deception in my perception? After making the proper adjustments, when we find ourselves in these trials we are to repent for wrong thinking thereby removing the thorns, release our faith, do spiritual warfare and enforce the Kingdom of God on earth as it is in Heaven. This response will cause us to mature as well as gain the victory.

When it is the Lord giving us an opportunity to "prove" ourselves, it is something He already knows we have the ability to pass. He wants us to mature enough to begin to let righteousness flow out of our spirit, through our soul, by way of our thoughts, words and actions of life.

This is exactly how we treat our children. We tell them, for example, to go clean their room because we know they are well able. We tell them that if they don't, they will lose their television or phone for the week.

Sometimes they may fail the test, but we keep on giving it to them. Why? Because we know they have an ability within them to do the job and do it right. What are we doing? We are training them for maturity in every area of life.

We want to help them develop that ability, so we keep giving them the same opportunity over and over until we don't have to tell them anymore. At some point in time they just do it as part of their lifestyle because they know it is expected of them, and they do it right.

Then we give them something else to do that we know they are capable of. All the while we are proving and demonstrating to them that the ability to do what is right and do it correctly is within their spiritual DNA if they will just yield to it.

I remember the Lord doing this with me when it came to bringing my shopping cart back to the store. My soul wanted to leave it in the parking lot, especially when the weather was nasty. My spirit could hear the voice of the Lord prompting me to put the cart back. As I obeyed in this area, so did my maturity. Then greater opportunities arose to walk in love, hold my tongue, turn the other cheek and so on.

Now we may squirm a bit just like our kids do when the Lord requests something of us that isn't very comfortable, that we don't like, or that stretches us out of our comfort zone a bit, like walking in love, going the extra mile or holding our tongue.

We squirm under these situations because we are responding out of our soul, and God expects us to obey from our spirit. The wonderful thing about the Lord proving us is that we can just keep trying over and over until we mature.

THE LAW OF JUDGMENTS

The Bible is full of spiritual laws. We have been talking about the law of the Spirit of life in Christ Jesus and how it makes us free from the law of sin and death.

The law of sowing and reaping operates under both laws. Galatians 6:7, 8 says, *"Be not deceived; God is not mocked: for whatsoever a man soweth, that shall he also reap. For he that soweth to his flesh / soul (wrong thoughts) shall of the flesh reap corruption (because negative thoughts will eventually corrupt our physical being); but he that soweth to the Spirit shall of the Spirit reap life everlasting."*

There are natural laws that the world understands, such as the law expressed in chemistry that every equation or formula must balance. Then there is the law expressed in physics that says for every action, there must be an equal and opposite reaction.

Romans 2:1 is clear when it says, *"Therefore you are without excuse, everyman of you who passes judgment, for in that you judge another, you condemn yourself. For you who judge practice the same things."*

Matthew 7:1-2 instructs us further, saying *"Judge not, that you be not judged. For with the judgment you pronounce you will be judged, and the measure you give will be the measure you get."* When we agree with a judgment thought against another person, that thought is negative and fear based, meaning it will produce a thorn on our tree and therefore we will be judged by reaping the same measure.

I don't think we have reverenced this law or grasped the effect that when we pass a judgment we condemn ourselves to practice the same things, and with the same measure we measure out, we must receive. It's a law.

Here is another law we probably have not recognized: *"Honor thy father and thy mother, as the LORD thy God hath commanded thee; that thy days may be prolonged, and that it may go well with thee, in the land which the LORD thy God giveth thee."* - Deuteronomy 5:16

These are all one basic law described differently in each field. When our judgments are dishonoring to our parents (regardless of how badly they hurt us), by thinking incorrectly we have activated the reaping process of those toxic thoughts, secreting toxic chemicals and translating them into dis-ease in our bodies, which says that our days will not be prolonged on the earth and life will not go well with us. Now I can see why.

When we sow these judgment seeds, the law states that we sleep and rise night and day and the seed springs and grows up, first the blade, then the ear, then the full corn in the ear - Mark 4:27-28. It is usually not until we've reaped the full corn in the ear, so to speak, that we begin wondering, how did this happen? Why is my marriage in trouble, why are my children behaving like this? Remember, somewhere we violated a law. I suggest examining the harvest field of your mind and see what kind of fruit is on your trees. Search for any judgments you may have made against your parents or any other people and change your thinking.

Perhaps life isn't going too well for you. You may be experiencing health problems and don't know how or why this is happening. The longer these judgments remain undetected, neglected and unrepented of, the larger the harvest grows in the trees of your mind, sending toxic chemicals coursing through your body and searing your organs and cells like battery acid until you're really sick.

Bitter-root judgments are the most common, most basic sins in all our relationships. In fact, we get married with our *psuche* / suitcase loaded with this type of baggage.

In Hebrews 12:15, Paul says, *"...See to it that no root of bitterness springing up trouble you, and thereby many be defiled."*

John Bevere said, "Bitterness is a root. If roots are nursed, watered, protected, fed and given attention to they increase in depth and strength and become hard to pull up." They defile our character.

If our thorny dendrites are nursed, watered, protected, etc. they certainly will defile our character as well as our health.

The fact that derogatory, negative thoughts or a sharp, cynical attitude are springing up means there is a root producing this thorny fruit.

These roots not only trouble us, but when we express them, they actually defile the people around us. Our responsibility is to see to it that these hidden, beneath the surface, problematic roots get destroyed.

I had judgments against my parents, my grandparents, and people in my life that hurt me; teachers, the school system, the government, the church, God, etc. Every time I opened my mouth about any of these things I defiled the people around me with my opinions. I colored the way they saw the people and events in my life causing them to partake in my judgments.

We now understand that spiritual laws operate whether we know of or are ignorant of them, believe or disbelieve them. It is impossible to hold a judgment or do a deed without setting in motion forces which must return to us.

For this reason the Apostle Paul in Romans 12:2 told us, "…be not conformed to this world: but be ye transformed by the renewing of your mind…" We can do this from the inside of our thought life out, by coming out of agreement with every wrong negative and fear based thought. We forgive and release every judgment we have made against ourselves and others for every expectation we may have had in us or them to have behaved differently.

This requires the act of repentance. That word means - to think differently, reconsider and change your mind about what you have believed. Without repentance thorns cannot be removed and healing cannot take place - Matthew 6:15; Mark 11:26; Matthew 5:23, 24. Then bring your thinking into agreement with the Father and see things from His perspective. This will help you to develop the 'mind of Christ'.

We will, however, have to catch ourselves at maintaining this posture. While we still might feel hundreds of pockets of 'guerrilla resistance' here and there in our soul nature, we need to remind ourselves of these truths and refuse to be moved by what we feel.

Some of the thoughts on bitter-root judgments were gleaned from the book *The Transformation of the Inner Man* by John and Paula Sandford, Bridge-Logos, 1982.

1. Make a list of the people in your life and write down what you think about them. This will help you to identify every destructive stronghold and judgment. You may also have judgments against establishments (like your job, school, government, etc.) that you will need to examine as well.

2. Allow Jesus to be Lord over your thoughts, your will and all your emotions. Choose to see people through His eyes.

3. Identify every area of deception in your perception and take back your power of agreement from the enemy. Disown those beliefs as being a part of who you are. Change your negative perceptions to positive ones. Choose to see things from the 'Father's eyes.'

4. Forgive everyone who may have helped to shape those belief systems within you.

5. Break the power of the bitter-root judgments you have made over others and break the force of the reaping process in your own life and family.

6. Replace all negative, destructive thoughts with the truth of what God and His Word say about you and your situation. Knowing that: *"The law of the LORD is perfect, converting (restoring) the soul;..."* - Psalm 19:7. The Lord is showing us in this scripture that when we do this it literally changes the dendrite structure of our brain, restoring our soul!

The key to your success is in daily managing your thought life by asking yourself, "What am I thinking? Why do I 'feel' this way? What thought did I take that is producing this 'feeling?'

HOMEWORK OF SELF EVALUATION:

Go to the people in your life that you trust to be honest with you, give them permission to speak honestly with you.

- Ask them what they see in you.

- Are you teachable?

- Are you approachable or easily offended?

- Do they have to walk on eggshells around you?

- Are you controlling or manipulative?

- Do you twist events in your mind?

- Are you a worrier or fearful?

- Are you afraid of me?

- Do I make you uncomfortable in any way?

Write down what they say and then repent where you are wrong. Use what you have written to x-ray your soul and work on yourself, begin to see yourself the way God sees you. See your character changing, see yourself maturing spiritually and manifesting the fruits of the Holy Spirit. See the blueprint of your life changing on the inside, see your brain bringing your body back into perfect chemical balance.

Ask the Lord to magnify yourself to you. I remember when the Lord did this with me. For the first time I could hear myself. I could hear how I spoke with my daughter, my husband, the people in my life. I could hear the tone in my voice; I could hear my negative, critical, judgmental words. I was so grieved, but it changed me more than any test or trial ever did.

PRAYER TO BREAK UNGODLY STRONGHOLDS

AND BITTER-ROOT JUDGMENTS

Father, I repent for all the deception in my perception and for coming into agreement with the enemy and releasing power for my own destruction. I realize I have unrighteously judged my parents, myself, You, other people and establishments.

I repent for judging the facts, as I perceived them through my limited knowledge. I repent of the sin of anger and pride by changing my mind about these wrong belief systems, attitudes, criticisms, judgments and bitterness that I have had, the wrong things that I have felt emotionally, clung to, and verbalized about others, defiling the people around me by sharing my judgments with them and speaking evil of others.

I choose to break the power of those wrong agreements and wrong words that I have spoken. I release all destructive patterns of thinking about these situations, including wrong beliefs about others and the significance I have placed on what they have done, what is fair and how my feelings have been hurt.

I ask You for forgiveness, Lord, and receive by faith the cleansing from all the unrighteousness of all my judgments so it can go well with me and I can live long on the earth. I choose to bind my mind, will and emotions to the will of God so that the gates of hell will not prevail against me.

I break the power of the harvest, the return of these seeds that I have sown as a result of my disobedience in judging. I stand on Galatians 3:13 which says that Christ has redeemed me from the curse of the law. Jesus bore a crown of thorns for me and shed blood for my redemption. Therefore I plead the blood of Jesus over my mind and declare I have the mind of Christ concerning every situation. I consciously prune the trees of my mind and receive the healing of my soul so I can prosper and be in health.

I ask you, Father, to reverse the effects of my sins; and open my ears so I can hear the way I talk to and about other people. Make me sensitive to the areas where you are trying to mature me. As I begin to sow positive, constructive thoughts, I choose to bless these people and establishments by praying for them and asking Your blessing upon them in Jesus' name. Amen.

Soul Ties

A Soul Tie is a term used to describe when our soul (mind, will and emotions) are tied or connected to someone or some thing. People are unaware of the destructive power that unhealthy emotional attachments have on their lives. We will take a close look at the soul's ability to be tied to people, places, memories and things. Find examples of how these soul ties may feel and how they affect our thinking. Once identified; we will break their power, setting us free.

Chapter Three

A soul tie is a term used to describe when our soul / mind, will and emotions are tied or connected to someone or something. Soul ties are more commonly known as a mental or emotional attachment.

Strongholds and soul ties are inter-related and function much in the same way. Wherever you have a belief system about someone or something, you will notice that you have an emotional response there as well. Dr. Caroline Leaf says, "You are made up of two systems: one chemical (the endocrine system) and the other electrical (the nervous system). Essentially this means that the currency of your body is electromagnetic energy and chemicals. A thought and the emotion attached to it take shape in your body and mind as electro-chemical responses occurring in the depths of the brain." So the dendrite tree is housing your belief system / stronghold as well as your emotional response / soul tie.

Soul ties can be healthy or unhealthy, just as a stronghold can be constructive or destructive. A healthy tie is when there are no negative emotional attachments and you maintain perfect peace in your life and relationships.

An unhealthy tie is when a person, place or memory of an event has the power to trigger negative thoughts and emotions. The object of this chapter is to identify the unhealthy ties that have caused so much trouble in our lives and held us in bondage.

Our Heavenly Father has designed the bonding of emotional soul ties between husbands and wives, parents and their children, siblings and friends to be bonded in love. These are the types of ties that will produce the fruit of health and wholeness in our lives.

He also has established protective boundaries that make up these healthy ties between people. However, as a result of the fall of man and a sin nature infecting the souls of mankind, too often these boundaries get violated.

When these boundaries are violated, a destructive stronghold / belief system develops and the soul / emotional tie becomes unhealthy. The soul may become wounded, fragmented and damaged, creating unhealthy and even dysfunctional relationships.

For example, extreme violation of boundaries could be: verbal, physical, emotional or sexual abuse, control or trauma. Less extreme violations that often go undetected are things like: withholding love and affection, not communicating, selfish behavior, a refusal to resolve issues.

The first mention of a soul tie is in Genesis 2:24 where it says, *"For this cause a man shall leave his father and his mother, and shall cleave to his wife; and they shall become one flesh."* The word *"cleave"* means adhere to, abide fast or be joined it is a description of a soul tie.

God has purposed that a man and woman be joined in marriage and the two shall become one flesh. *"...What therefore God hath joined together, let not man put asunder."* - Matthew 19:6

This soul tie is one of the most powerful soul ties we experience in life. This is why we feel so much pain in divorce. It violently tears mental, physical and emotional ties.

This tearing fragments our soul. When you are married you have a neuro-chemical bonding (glue) that takes place with your partner. You imprint on each others brains. So when separation occurs there is a physical pain because the bond is still there and it takes time to dissolve.

When two people come together in marriage, they each bring their own baggage in to the relationship. They each have needs in their wounded souls that no other human being can ever meet. There are some obvious needs that will be met in marriage, but the soul tie created between two wounded souls will cause them to look to each other to get their needs met. They end up developing an expectation from their partner for such things as security, healing, assurance, fulfillment and guidance before looking to God to meet those needs.

When we are looking to our partner to meet our needs and make us feel whole, instead of to God, we are setting ourselves up for disappointment. What happens is we then have two wounded people depending on each other to meet the emotional needs in each of their damaged, wounded souls.

One very basic need we all bring to a relationship is a need to feel loved. For example, everyone has their own love language with which they either show or receive love. For instance, words of affirmation, quality of time, receiving of gifts, acts of service and physical touch are all part of that language. (Suggested reading, *The Five Love Languages* by Gary Chapman)

You may show love by acts of service, such as paying the bills and providing for the needs of the family. Your mate, on the other hand, may receive and feel love through quality of time and physical touch. This would leave your loved one longing, feeling their needs haven't been met because they have an expectation and are looking to you to speak their love language.

These things, left unresolved in relationships, will eventually feed that wound even deeper, with pain and hurt. Bitterness and resentment then develop because your expectations and needs have not been met.

These unhealthy relationships produce thorny fruit. The evidence of that fruit is often destructive, oppressive and brings all concerned into bondage. Our soul / thoughts and feelings may experience pain, confusion, fear, intimidation and depression. Bitterness and resentment then develop. We are now tied to that person with an unhealthy emotional / soul tie.

In marriage for example, if you are drawn emotionally to another person in order to fulfill needs that are not being met by your spouse, you are walking in very dangerous territory.

You may say, "I could never talk to my wife about these things like I can talk to you." Or "You understand me so much better than my husband does."

When we are seeking and finding comfort, approval, understanding and acceptance outside of the marriage, an unhealthy soul tie will be formed on an emotional level with another person. It is then easily taken to the next level, which is a physical consummation of that tie.

TIES BETWEEN PARENTS AND CHILDREN

The bearing of children is another one of the most powerful soul ties we experience in life. It is probably as close as we can get to the experience of the Father's perfect, unconditional love toward us. It should be the most healthy soul tie formed, resulting in security, love and the soundness of a child's personality and stability in life. Unfortunately for many this has not been their experience.

To help you x-ray your soul for unhealthy ties, I want to give you some examples of what unhealthy emotional and mental attachments can look like between a parent and child, at any age. These soul ties may happen when the parents do not bond in a healthy way with their child at birth. Or, for many reasons, the relationship may grow to become dysfunctional and fragmented. Remember, we have all been raised by imperfect people who were also raised by imperfect people. So in many cases, the parent is a damaged soul and is not capable of having a healthy relationship. This, in turn, damages the soul in their child and the cycle continues for generations.

THE FRUIT MIGHT LOOK LIKE THIS

If a parent has caused you pain by wounding your soul, then every time you speak with that parent you may feel anger, want to cry or even want to avoid them completely. I remember after my parents divorce my dad's job moved him out of state. He tried to parent me long distance. Every time he called wanting to know how I was, I remember all I could do was cry. At the time I didn't know why I cried when I talked with him, one of my sisters had the same emotional response. I watched another young girl whose parents were divorced. After returning from a weekend with her dad she would cry and be depressed for days. Remember that divorce violently tears mental, physical and emotional ties.

This tearing fragments the soul of the child as well as the adult's.

Being very critical and judgmental toward a parent and constantly rehearsing their shortcomings in your own mind and sharing them with the people you meet is an indication of not only an unhealthy tie but an offense as well.

Using things like manipulation, unreasonable control, guilt, fear, anger, rejection, hurtful words and dishonest dealings, to get your way with a child or parent, in order to control their behavior, meet your needs or please you in some way, forms an unhealthy tie and an offense.

It is not allowing the child to individuate and become a mature independent adult. You may feel a constant source of anger toward them as they are trying to break away from you. Even "empty nest" is a restructuring of a soul tie.

Another sign could be having one's priorities out of order, such as putting one's parents' preferences or feelings before those of the spouse. In this example a matter of priority makes this soul tie unhealthy. So a soul tie doesn't always have to feel bad.

Resistance to guidance concerning child rearing is a sign. If you are yielding to a child's manipulation, because you feel guilty for divorce or you feel sorry for them, this makes discipline very difficult. You are training the child to think this is the way to get their needs met. This is doing more of a disservice to the child and perpetuating an unhealthy tie.

A parent who sexually, emotionally or verbally abuses their child, not only creates an unhealthy tie, but also damages their soul.

Not being able to leave your child with others because of your fears and insecurities passes those fears and insecurities on to the child and prevents them from being emotionally healthy.

There is a tie between a mother and an aborted child. You must forgive yourself and release that child to the Lord. A woman in her seventies came to the office for ministry. She said that she had an abortion in her twenties. She said years later she had a miscarriage and then she was never able to conceive again. The fact that she never had any children had been a source of depression for her for all these years. I told her that what she believed was not true, she had two children and they are both in heaven and can't wait to meet her! I told her that her life on this earth was just a blink of the eye compared to the eternity she would spend in heaven with her two children. At that moment she began to say, "Oh my God!" repeatedly as she was staring off as in a daze. I said, "What?" She couldn't answer me. Several minutes went by before she was able to tell me what happened to her. When she finally spoke she said she saw darkness leave her. She was watching it move across the room and go out the window. All her depression and sorrow about this situation left. What happened to this woman was that she had "deception in her perception." It was a lie she had believed for over fifty years about never having children. The stronghold that was tied to that loss was broken in her soul and she was healed. The demonic oppression that went with that belief system had to leave as well. The oppression had no more lie to support it. Her soul became tied to the time when she would meet her two children and have them with her forever. John 8:32 says, *"And ye shall know the truth, and the truth shall make you free."* If you have had an abortion, your soul may be tied to shame or guilt. It is important to grieve your loss, forgive yourself, and release the tie you have had.

In these examples of unhealthy soul ties, you can also see the mental belief systems in operation from the destructive strongholds. Remember a healthy tie is when there are no negative emotional attachments and you maintain perfect peace in your life and relationships. An unhealthy tie has the power to trigger negative thoughts and emotions.

TIES IN RELATIONSHIPS

The Bible actually has a lot to say about soul ties. I Samuel 18:1 tells us that, *"...the soul of Jonathan was knit to the soul of David, and Jonathan loved him as his own soul."* Jonathan loved David so much that he was willing to lay down his rights to the throne of Israel. Healthy and godly soul ties are always based on godly love.

Soul ties are like cords of many strands, like a rope that can tie people together. These cords act as a pipeline through which influence passes in both directions. All of these ties can be either positive or negative. To help you x-ray your soul for unhealthy ties I want to give you some examples of what an unhealthy emotional and mental attachment can look like with other people in your life.

I Corinthians 15:33 from the Amplified Bible says, *"Do not be so deceived and misled! Evil companionships (associations) corrupt and deprave good manners, morals and character."* It is important to choose right friends. Wrong relationships have the power to ensnare us, and we find ourselves being corrupted by their influence.

Proverbs 22:5, 24-25 say that, *"Thorns and snares are in the way of the froward (distorted, crooked). He that keeps (guards) his soul shall be far from them. Make no friendship with an angry man lest you learn his ways and set a snare for your soul."* Interestingly the Bible tells us thorns come from being influenced by distorted people. Their wrong thinking can negatively influence us causing thorns in our thinking and setting a snare for our soul.

II Peter tells us that Lot was vexed by living in Sodom and Gomorrah. The things he saw and heard *vexed his righteous soul* from day to day.

So you can see that unhealthy relationships produce destructive, oppressive, thorny fruit and bring all concerned into bondage. Our soul (thought life and feelings) will experience many negative emotions like pain, confusion, fear and maybe even intimidation when you have an unhealthy soul tie. We have deception in our perception and are believing a lie if we think that we 'need' that relationship to feel self-worth, dignity or value. Only our relationship with the Lord can meet those needs within us.

Our children develop these types of ties in school when they hook up with the wrong group of kids. It is important to monitor their time on the phone and computer as well as social times, as their young souls may be getting vexed.

Friends that we have an unhealthy soul tie with can entice us and lead us away from strong, godly commitments and values. Like Lot, their spiritual garbage will easily come to us, and our spiritual righteousness will be squashed.

There is so much power and influence in these types of soul ties that we need to carefully guard and examine all of our relationships. Our soul (mind, will, and emotions) can be systematically brought into bondage in an unhealthy relationship.

An unhealthy soul tie may be formed with any person toward whom we may have feelings of fear or unresolved anger; whether it's because of hurts, frustrations, disappointments, unmet needs or unresolved issues. Any time we get out of the protective boundaries the Father has established for relationships, we create an environment in which the enemy can work.

EXAMPLES OF PEOPLE WE MAY BE TIED WITH
EVALUATE ALL YOUR RELATIONSHIPS!

People who have violated, injured or assaulted us or our loved ones through sexual, verbal, emotional or psychological manipulation and control. If you or a loved one has been injured or hurt by someone else it is easy to have a negative emotion toward them.

Teachers or others who have belittled us or taught us things that were not true. If what someone else has said or imparted into you has hindered your life in a negative way you will have an unhealthy tie with them.

People we are tied to as a result of wrong decisions and choices we made. Many times remembering things we did and the people we did them with, leaves us with a negative emotion toward them or even ourselves. You may be tied to yourself in an unhealthy way by having a negative self image. This will require you examining yourself and changing your mental agreements to agree with what God says about you.

Music and movie stars or anyone else whom we have idolized or worshiped. Images of these people lead us to have mental agreements to want to be like them. We bind our soul to them and hinder our God given destiny. I strongly suggest monitoring who is impressing your children. What posters are in their rooms, what books do they like to read, what movies are they drawn to, what games are they playing. Guard their soul as you would guard your own.

People with whom we have sinned with, bought or used drugs with, your memories / soul is still tied to them. Have you ever been out and seen someone and turned the other way to avoid talking to them? Your soul may be tied to shame in association with them.

Societies, organizations, jobs or churches with which we have been associated. If you have a negative emotion about these places then there is an unhealthy tie. I see Christians go from church to church for many different reasons; they didn't like what the Pastor said and got offended or sister so and so didn't say hello, etc. These are being led by their soul, they are offended and are carrying a tie in an unhealthy way. God wants us planted where He places us and He wants our roots to go deep. I encourage you not to have expectations in other people, you will be left disappointed. We tend to think that everyone in church should be spiritual and know what we need from them. Remember we are all at different places in our level of maturity and many Christians are still soulish Christians and will fail us.

INNER VOWS

The binding of ourselves with an oath is another area where our souls get tied. People we have been in secret societies with (such as Freemasonry or sororities). Vows and oaths are taken in such societies. Numbers chapter 30 is entirely about vows and oaths. I strongly suggest you read it. Words are a powerful force, Numbers tells us of our responsibility and the authority we have over our lives and our children's lives concerning vows. It says that when we swear an oath or vow we bind our soul with a bond. When we hear our children say things like, "I will never," or "no one will ever tell me what to do," it is our responsibility to break those vows so their souls will not be bound. You will have to do some self examination to see if you have any of these places in your life or household.

I remember one time while teaching this class a woman jumped up and said, "I see it!" She said when she was young she had a relationship with a man outside of marriage. They vowed that they would love each other forever even if they weren't together. Years went by and she married

89

another man. Over all those years she was haunted with thoughts of this man from her past. She would dream about him and thoughts of him would come up all the time. She took it before the Lord for years asking Him to take away the troubling thoughts, memories, and feelings about this other man. She finally understood the power of a vow. They vowed a vow to each other and that vow had power to bind her soul for many years. A neuro-chemical bond took place with her partner and he was imprinted on her brain. After finding truth that night and breaking the vow, she was made free!

HOW UNHEALTHY SOUL TIES MAY FEEL

When we are emotionally bound to a person in an unhealthy relationship, we may "feel" that we need this other person to make us happy, bring us security, meet a need or fulfill our life in some way. Regardless of how unhealthy or self-destructive the relationship may be, it keeps us in bondage.

When our thought life is being consumed with someone else, we can be angry, upset or disappointed with them. Or, we may experience constant thoughts of how to please them or get their approval. We may find ourselves constantly thinking, imagining or fantasizing a way to be with this person or get this person to notice us.

Thoughts of seeing a person can bring out negative emotion such as fear, anxiety, dislike or frustration. Perhaps someone else's behavior is able to control us or have any kind of negative effect on us. It could be any person in our life that makes us feel this way. We may be afraid of disappointing them and losing their love, or we may fear their rejection.

If our attitude, perception, or opinion about someone has become colored we can't see them clearly the way God sees them. We must remember when God looks at us He sees our whole life and knows what shaped us and why we act the way we do. He loves us in spite of us.

It could be as simple as putting our friends above our spouse, or having an obsessive preoccupation with someone. We might be looking to someone else to fix a need or pain inside of us. Even in our marriage, our spouse

90

is not there to fix, medicate or stroke the pains inside us. We need to be set free.

There are times we all may struggle with an inability to really forgive and release someone. Examine if you have patterns of blame, anger and accusation. When this is happening, your mind may be tormented with thoughts playing over and over in your head like a tape. If going to sleep is like pushing the pause button but as soon as you open your eyes you are back on play, you can know that your soul is tied.

Soul ties may also exist between us and any "thing" that consumes our thought life, emotions, desires or behavior in a compulsive way. For example, you can be tied to your job, sports, games, gambling, animals, watching television, eating, drugs, smoking, drinking, etc. in an unhealthy way. Remember that *"A false balance is an abomination to the Lord;..."* - Proverbs 11:1.

All of these examples we just went through of how unhealthy soul ties may feel, reveal the stronghold / soul tie connection in operation. These are indications that our thoughts have gone toxic and produced the fruit of thorns. Imagine what a web of thorny branches might look like in the network of your mind where these people have negatively imprinted on your life.

SOUL TIE TO A MEMORY

Let's look at a soul tie where a memory is concerned. I remember long after I was a Christian I could drive by different places around town and memories from my past would bother me. I had repented over and over again, but these places were still emotional triggers for me. I realized my soul was tied to the memories of those events and the thorn of shame was still attached in that place on my soul. I learned that repenting over and over was not fruitful as the Lord had forgiven me the first time I repented. I realized that I was not using my authority as a believer. Every time I would drive by an emotional trigger, I needed to forgive and release myself, then break the power that event had in my life and was still holding over my soul. Once I did this, then I could release my faith and see the sting of that thorn being removed.

Your soul can be tied to a season or time of year. For example one woman had a miscarriage in the spring. So every spring she would experience depression. The season became a trigger for her. Another woman lost a loved one in the fall. So every fall she would experience depression. Your soul can be tied to memorabilia, pictures, jewelry, etc. Any "thing" that can bring up a negative emotion or pain is an unhealthy soul tie.

Now the reverse is true as well, anyone of these things can cause you great joy. Well then that would be a healthy soul tie!

SOUL TIES HAVE THE ABILITY TO BECOME DEMONIC

Just as a godly, healthy tie is based on love, a demonic soul tie is based on lust or "pressure." There is an open door for evil spirits to enter when God's protective boundaries are violated. A soul tie to a memory, event or season left unchecked can give place to an oppressive spirit in that place of agreement.

We have been learning that the enemy cannot go beyond the rights that we give him. He can only work within the authority of what we allow him to do. He will hold us in bondage until we recognize this, take back our authority, and break the soul tie the very same way we had to come out of agreement with him in order to break a stronghold.

In a relationship, the initial wound to our soul is where it is fragmented. That place is usually the root and may be the entry point for a wounded spirit and other evil spirits to keep us in bondage. Their presence can perpetuate unhealthy, dysfunctional relationships in our future.

Demonic soul ties can exist between two people who engage in sin together through sexual relations, drug use, criminal acts, gang activity, witches' covens, physical abuse, verbal abuse or various forms of manipulation. They are a product of wrong agreements between these people. If the protective boundaries set by God, which govern all our relationships, are not honored, our relationships can become perverse and demons may enter.

OCCULT PRACTICES
DEUTERONOMY 7:25-26, 12:3, 18:10-12

The Occult is an expression of idolatry because you are looking for information outside of your relationship with the Lord. Scripture tells us that person has joined or tied himself to an idol in Numbers 25:3. *"And Israel joined himself unto Baal-peor: and the anger of the Lord was kindled against Israel."*

Even though seeking a fortuneteller or psychic is prevalent in today's society, we cannot deny that it still joins us to occult practice, thereby opening the door for demonic influence in our lives and for generations to come.

Involvement with occult practices such as the Ouija Board, astrology, divination (the foretelling of future events), palm reading or tarot cards creates a spiritual soul tie. One has spiritual intercourse or soul to soul fellowship with demons.

We must repent for our involvement and break the curse that follows in order to stop those demons from traveling down through the generations.

TIES FORMED THROUGH FORNICATION

I Corinthians 6:16 says, *"Do you not know that he who is joined to a harlot is one body (as a whole, spirit and soul) with her? For the two shall become one flesh."*

When we have an intimate relationship with another person outside of marriage, then demonic soul ties are created. Promiscuity scatters and fragments our soul.

There is an exchange of spiritual forces and familiar spirits. When we cross the line of godly sexuality (anything outside of marriage), we have opened the door for that connection to take place. Some people become so enslaved that they will put up with verbal and physical abuse, manipulation and control. They may feel they cannot lose that person and are willing to put up with anything to keep them.

Those who engage in sex outside of marriage become the one flesh which God purposed solely for a husband and wife. Even petting outside of marriage violates God's protective boundaries so that soul ties are created because passions and emotions have been aroused. The lust that accompanies it makes the tie unclean. This opens the door for demonic spirits.

Pornography ties our mind and emotions as well as our bodies with images, that leave the door open for perverted sexual spirits. Just as an STD can get passed to your partners, so can spiritually transmitted dis-eases be passed from partner to partner.

BIBLICAL EXAMPLES OF DEMONIC SOUL TIES

II Samuel 13 is the story of King David's children. Amnon, the son of David, loved his sister Tamar; he was so *vexed*, that he *fell sick* for his sister. So Amnon tricked her to come to him and then forced himself upon her. Amnon had a destructive stronghold and soul tie with Tamar that led to rape. After the rape his obsession turned to hatred for her. Absalom Tamar's brother hated his brother Amnon for doing such a thing to their sister. Absalom festered with thoughts of hatred for two years, developing a demonic soul tie toward Amnon to the point of plotting to have his brother murdered.

There is another example like this found in Genesis 34:2-3. *"Dinah the daughter of Leah and Jacob went out to see the land and Shechem the Hivite, prince of the country, saw her, he took her, and lay with her, and defiled her and his soul clave unto Dinah..."*

Judges 16:16 says that, Delilah pressed Samson daily with her words, *"... and urged him, so that his soul was vexed unto death."* He told her the secret of his strength. Samson's unhealthy soul tie with Delilah cost him his life.

In these examples of Amnon, Shechem and Samson you can see how their thoughts established a stronghold thought pattern that began the process of growing a neuro network of thorny dendrites. Their souls were tied in an unhealthy way. Each of them became obsessed. That demonic obsession led to rape, control, manipulation and even death.

94

Our eyes must be opened to the power of soul ties not only for our own well being, but for the well being of our children. Our children, in their ignorance, are creating unhealthy soul ties with each other and those ties are causing them to be snared in destructive relationships. Now that we know, we can be pro-active in our parenting and able to help our children get free with us.

SOUL TIES WITH THE DECEASED

Psalm 116:15 says, *"Precious in the sight of the Lord is the death of His saints."* We are on one side of eternity essentially experiencing a loved one going, going then finally gone. On the other side of eternity they have received notice that the deceased is on their way. So they are experiencing the person coming, coming then finally home. When the deceased arrives there is a great family reunion! I choose to look to the future, become heavenly minded and focus on eternity and not my loss.

I know that my loved one is not in my past, but my future. That person is very much alive, experiencing great joy and reconnection with family and friends. I will see my loved one again. It will help you to remember this as well knowing that Jesus took the sting out of death - 1 Corinthians 15:55-56.

When we experience loss, there is a season of grief and sorrow where our soul is adjusting to losing that person. We go through a period of adjustment where it is necessary to express the emotion and release the pain we are feeling. Remember you imprint on each others brains. So when separation occurs there is a physical pain because the bond is still there and it takes time to dissolve. Biblically, mourning normally lasted from seven to thirty days - Genesis 50:10; Numbers 20:29; Deuteronomy 34:8.

Prolonged mourning and the stress that extended grief brings will create an opportunity for spirits of sorrow, grief and loneliness to enter. Also, Scripture warns if one attempts to communicate with a deceased loved one, he can easily acquire a familiar spirit. (Suggested reading, *Confronting Familiar Spirits* by Frank Hammond)

95

A woman who had lost her husband ten years earlier came in for ministry. After his passing she experienced great loss, grief and depression and she eventually walked away from the Lord. When we ministered to her she was willing to come out of agreement with all the destructive thinking she had, she was willing to let the soul tie be broken in a healthy way and start a new future. We bound the spirit of grief and with great ease it left her. She was so totally set free that in a very short time her entire life has turned around. She is walking strong with the Lord and being blessed again.

Through this book, we can see that breaking unhealthy and even demonic ties is essential to set our present relationships on the path to wholeness. We begin developing unhealthy soul ties as children and carry them through our lives. So I encourage you to keep watch over the souls of your children.

Remember that a healthy tie is where there are no negative emotional triggers, you maintain perfect peace in your life and relationships. An unhealthy tie is when a person, place or memory of an event has the power to trigger negative thoughts and emotions.

HOMEWORK

If you didn't make your list of names from the first two chapters I highly suggest you make it now. We need to examine all of our past and present relationships. Think of each person. Determine if our tie to them was healthy or unhealthy. As you do this you may identify areas of strongholds you might have missed in the last chapter.

Determine if your relationships were based on need, lust, perversion, acts of sin, medicating a pain, bringing validation, establishing self-worth or any other negative thought driven emotion. This will help you to x-ray your soul for strongholds you may have overlooked. Make the proper mental adjustments, come out of agreement with deception in your perception and come into agreement with God's truth concerning your situations.

Many times we have to maintain a relationship with these people. They may be family members, co-workers or long-time friends. It is important to remember to have healthy God given boundaries and to walk in love towards one another.

Confession and repentance of your own involvement in the unhealthy soul tie is necessary before the tie can be broken. It is not unusual for healing and or deliverance to occur immediately after unhealthy soul ties have been broken. Then it is vital to replace your wrong thinking with what God's word says about you and your situations.

It is important to remember that unhealthy soul ties can be easily re-connected. This can be done in many ways:

- By revisiting unforgiveness.

- By entering into sin with that person again.

- By coming back into agreement with wrong thoughts we had of someone or something.

- By getting our value or self-worth from our relationship with that person again.

- By letting someone have power over us to wound us.

- By violating Gods protective boundaries in your relationships.

Psalm 23:3 tells us the Lord our Shepherd *"restores our soul"* and Psalm 19:7 says that, *"The law of the LORD (the word of God) is perfect, converting (restoring) the soul."* Applying the Word of God as well as His boundaries to our life will make us whole and restore our souls. It has worked for me and I know it will work for you.

STEPS TO FREEDOM

1. Stay out of agreement with the devil and stop releasing power for your own destruction.

2. Walk in a maintenance program of forgiveness and agape love toward others.

97

3. Repent for every place that you have violated God's ordinances. It is wise to get alone before the Lord and name each sexual partner and renounce your ties with them so as to close all possible doors.

4. Cut off all unhealthy soul ties as you evaluate your relationships.

5. Now you can begin to call back the restoration of your fragmented soul in prayer, applying the blood of Jesus over every scar for healing. When you have an unhealthy soul tie with someone, there is a neuro tree network woven into your brain that they hold. When you break that soul tie, you want to mentally see yourself releasing them out of you; then see every part of your soul coming back into wholeness.

   It is our responsibility to take back all the soul ground we have given over to the kingdom of darkness and loose off any demons attached to these ties in the name of the Lord Jesus Christ.

6. Break any ungodly vows you may have made with others by coming out of agreement with wrong thoughts, break the power of the words you spoke, and make a declaration over your life of what God and His Word say about you. Using your I AM list will help.

7. Now, by making godly decisions, we can begin to employ boundaries that make up healthy soul ties in our relationships.

8. Search your heart before praying. Are there ties with family members, friends (old as well as new), teachers, pastors, other denominations, co-workers, organizations, occultists, the dead, secret societies or fraternities? If so, make the necessary heart adjustments.

PRAYER TO BREAK SEXUAL SOUL TIES

Father, I confess that I may have allowed myself to hold anger, resentment and bitterness in my heart against others (name them). I acknowledge this as sin and I now repent and turn from this behavior. I ask You to forgive me and cleanse me.

As an act of my will, I now choose to forgive those who have hurt me. (Name out loud the people that need to be forgiven.) I release each and every one of these people into the freedom of my forgiveness.

Father, I humbly ask You to forgive me and cleanse me from the sin of fornication. I acknowledge it as sin and ask You to help me forsake it completely. I thank You for Your forgiveness and the cleansing of all unrighteousness.

I prune any and all unhealthy soul ties created by sexual acts between me and anyone else (say their names). By the power of the Holy Spirit, I separate and loose my soul from the soul of anyone with whom I have had ungodly sexual contact. I loose them out of my mind and emotions.

I also loose and release any parts of their (name persons) soul that I hold, and I release it back to them. I plead the blood of Jesus over all my gates (senses) for cleansing.

I cleanse my eye gates from defilement of things I shouldn't have seen. I cleanse my ear gates from every sound I should not have heard, from every defiling word or noise. I cleanse my nose gate from smells and odors that were unclean and defiling. I cleanse my mouth gate from any unclean things I should not have tasted. I cleanse my sexual gates from defiling touch and acts. I call back to myself a sense of purity and innocence.

I declare that the blood not only cleanses me, but closes the door of any possible access through which the enemy can trouble my family or me. By the authority of the name of the Lord Jesus Christ, I break the power of any and all vows, covenants, contracts, dedications or commissions made over me (or my children, if any).

In the name of Jesus Christ, my Lord, I now command any and all demons, which may have come into me by ungodly soul ties or any other sin, to loose me at once, never to return. I cancel your assignment against me in the name and by the blood of Jesus.

PRAYER TO BREAK NON-SEXUAL SOUL TIES

Jesus, I confess as sin and ask You to forgive me for every place my soul is tied to another person (name them) in an unhealthy way. I choose to break the soul tie that I have formed with them

99

(name persons). I ask You to make each of us whole. I release any parts of them (name person) that I hold in Jesus' name.

I repent of and renounce all participation that I have had in the occult. Jesus, You are my Lord and I will not look anywhere else for my guidance or answers. I stand on Galatians 3:13 that says, Christ has redeemed me from the curse of the law and I break the power of any curses that have come on my life or my family's lives as a result of occult involvement of any kind.

According to Your Word, You have given me authority over demons and every power of the enemy. In the name of Jesus, I command any and all demons to leave me now.

DEALING WITH ABORTION

If you have:

- Had an abortion

- Are the father of an aborted child

- Paid for an abortion

- Drove someone to an abortion clinic

- Counseled someone and agreed that abortion was the answer

- Played any part in the process

- Have family history of abortion

We labor under a curse for our participation in the shedding of innocent blood.

Psalm 106:37-39 says, *"They even sacrificed their sons and their daughters to demons, and shed innocent blood, even the blood of their sons and daughters, whom they sacrificed to the idols of Canaan; and the land was polluted with blood. Thus were they defiled with their own works."*

Isaiah 59:7- 8 says, *"Their feet run to evil, and they make haste to shed innocent blood: their thoughts are thoughts of iniquity; wasting and destruction are in their paths. The way of peace they know not; and there is no judgment in their goings: they have made them crooked paths: whosoever goeth therein shall not know peace."*

I found out there had been an abortion a few generations back in my family line. I never thought it affected me until I saw these scriptures. I realized a generational curse was established and through that my family line was polluted. I could see defilement, crooked paths and not knowing peace was all over my family history; aborted dreams, visions, marriages and family units. I stood in the gap and repented for the sin that opened that door in my blood line for myself and all future generations.

PRAYER TO BREAK THE CONSEQUENCES OF ABORTION

Father, I confess to You my abortion or my aiding in an abortion as sin. Your Word says, "Thou shalt not kill." I repent for breaking Your commandment. I ask You to forgive me and to cleanse me from all unrighteousness.

I choose to forgive myself and everyone concerned in decisions that led to abortion. I release myself and all others from every expectation to behave differently and to have made better choices. I release and remit these sins off of me. I ask the baby to forgive me, and I receive forgiveness for what I have done.

I have confessed, repented of, and renounced all sexual sins that I have committed that led to my connection with an abortion. I break every place my soul is tied to others where this is concerned. I loose all damaging memories off my soul and emotions. I apply the blood of Jesus to remove the pain from the memory of this sin in Jesus' name.

I stand in the gap on behalf of anyone in my family that may have opened the door to a spirit of death through abortion, and I repent on their behalf and ask You, Father, to forgive the sin and cleanse the unrighteousness from my family line.

I break all generational ties to this sin in my family and close all doors that allowed the spirits of murder, death, lying, self-hatred, guilt, shame and condemnation to operate in our blood line. I also cancel the effects of the curse from the shedding of innocent blood, including aborted marriages, failed projects, unfulfilled purposes and destinies in our lives. I command you to loose me and my family in Jesus' name.

I declare Galatians 3:13 over my family line that says, *"Christ hath redeemed us from the curse of the law, being made a curse for us: for it is written, Cursed is every one that hangeth on a tree:"* I break this curse off my family, off my children and grandchildren in Jesus' name.

Forgiveness Therapy

Did you know that we are forgiven with the same measure that we forgive others? We will x-ray your soul for areas of offense. You will learn what to do if you've been wronged and how to overcome those offenses. You will discover the steps to releasing others and letting go so that you can be free.

Chapter Four

In the last several chapters we have carefully identified many of the functions of our soul. We are going to see that taking up an offense and harboring unforgiveness is another open door, giving the enemy legal ground to not only torment us but to destroy our lives.

We have learned that the enemy's primary plan of attack is to make a suggestion to our thought life in our soul. When we come into agreement with that thought we begin to develop dendrites, then chemical emotions are secreted and we act on them.

This behavior on our part has built the strongholds and soul ties that we have been identifying, causing us to harbor bitter-root judgments as well as unforgiveness thorns.

In Psalm 55:12-14 when David was on the run from King Saul he said, *"For it was not an enemy that reproached me; then I could have borne it: neither was it he that hated me that did magnify himself against me; then I would have hid myself from him: But it was thou, a man mine equal, my guide, and mine acquaintance. We took sweet counsel together, and walked unto the house of God in company."*

This scripture is telling us that it is the people who are our companions and close friends, especially our family and loved ones, that have the greatest potential to hurt us.

As was discussed before, we all struggle with needs that have never been met, hurts that still ache and issues that are left unresolved in our lives. We all have been raised by people who were also raised by people who had their own *psuche* / suitcase full of baggage.

Yet we still have expectations of these very same people to meet our needs. We expect them to do what is right. We expect them to have behaved differently toward us. We expect them to know better. Many times the more expectation we have in them, the more we are disappointed and hurt when they let us down.

What we are left with is a distorted view of these people as seen through the filters of pain and disappointment on our soul. These filters cause us to harbor unforgiveness and bitter-root judgment thorns, thereby forming unhealthy soul ties.

We have unspoken expectations in the people closest to us to meet our needs. When these expectations are not met we are left disappointed, hurt or angry. We often find ourselves thinking, well they should have known I needed a hug, or they should have known I wanted them to spend time with me. I encourage my students to ask the people in their lives, "How can our relationship be better, what do you need from me, what do you like or dislike?" This helps to open lines of communication and improve relationships. I think the highest form of our love walk would be to look for ways, on purpose, to meet the needs of the people in our life; choose to be a blessing on purpose to the people around us.

In Luke 17:1 Jesus said, *"It is impossible (unthinkable or unallowable) that no offense (skandalon) should come but woe to the person through whom it comes."*

Jesus was saying, it is unthinkable that you could live without encountering a situation that could snare your soul (mind, will and emotions) in the trap of an offense. That means that we will always be presented with opportunities to become snared and offended.

The word offense comes from the Greek word *skandalon.* It was the trigger or stick on a trap set for animals. They would put some bait or a piece of raw meat on the stick. When the animal would take the bait, the trap would be sprung, and the animal would be caught.

When we become offended or are taken up in a scandal, we take the bait. For example when people aggravate us, treat us badly or let us down an opportunity is presented to us to either respond in love or take the bait. If we choose to take the bait we become snared and taken captive by the enemy.

If we have been ensnared by this trap, you can say that we have "taken the bait of Satan." We have yielded to the enemy's influence on our soul.

Once we are in this trap of an offense, our soul's reasonings and justifications begin to form negative thoughts and attitudes, developing strongholds. Our words become sharp and even cynical.

Remember that we are viewing these people and situations through filters which prevent us from seeing anything outside of our limited perspective. This hinders us from seeing God's perspective.

The deception in our perception causes us to believe we have been wronged. We will often form conclusions because our information is inaccurate as a result of the filters on our soul.

Even if the information is accurate we can misinterpret it because we are looking through filters of deception. Our soul will begin experiencing a host of negative emotions such as: hurt, anger, bitterness and resentment. These are all the strings / dendrites that make up an unhealthy soul tie. At this point we usually want to share what has upset us with someone who will be on our side and agree with us. We begin spreading and sowing the seeds of 'bad mouthing' the people who hurt us, which only defiles the people we are talking to, with our misguided opinions and judgments.

We know there is a root of bitterness producing fruit if negative thoughts or sharp cynical attitudes are being created. These roots not only trouble us, but by the force of reaping, they actually defile the people around us and destroy our relationships.

In Hebrews 12:15 Paul says, *"...See to it that no root of bitterness springing up trouble you, and thereby many be defiled;..."*

When we find ourselves in the trap of an offense, we should never call someone who is going to agree with us or be on our side. As we share with them what we are upset about, our story will be sowing seeds in their minds, while painting a picture in their image center. This, in turn, may cause them to pick up our offense and share in our destructive belief systems. When we do this we are causing someone else to sin.

We need to call someone who will jerk the slack out of us and cause us to see where we are in error. Call someone who will not take sides but show us a different perspective reminding us that hurting people hurt people. It is our human nature to see only from our perspective. What we really need is to see the truth of the whole picture from God's perspective. If we ask the Holy Spirit, He will reveal to us what the other person was thinking or show us why they reacted the way they did. Don't just lean on your own understanding of a situation; always seek to see both sides of the story.

Our responsibility is to see to it that these hidden, beneath the surface, defiling roots get destroyed. Let's remember what we learned about the laws of God concerning sowing and reaping judgments; they will operate whether we know of them or are ignorant, believe or disbelieve them. It is impossible to hold unforgiveness and a judgment without *setting in motion* forces which must return to us.

If we do not quickly deal with the fact that we became offended, the stronghold of bitterness that we just picked up and came into agreement with will cause a breakdown socially, mentally and physically. The thorns on our dendrites cause our hypothalamus to secrete toxic chemicals that will poison our life and cause an unhealthy soul tie that effects the lives of all those around us.

So ask yourself this question, have you been offended with someone? Who have you judged? Have you judged God, churches, establishments, family members, co-workers? In all of these places of judgments we have taken the bait, become offended and have fallen into the trap. We have a network of dendrites in our brain full of toxic thinking, secreting toxic emotions. Add this information to the homework list you have been making.

WHAT WE LEARNED ABOUT BITTERNESS

It is a stronghold, an entrenched pattern of thinking in our belief system. John Bevere said in his book *The Bait of Satan,* Charisma House, 2004, that, "Bitterness is a root. If roots are nursed, watered, protected, fed and given attention to they increase in depth and strength and become hard to pull up."

Once you have been angry and bitter with someone for any length of time it is hard to let go. Especially after you have nursed that belief system, watered it and told others about it. Now it has become a large tree in the soil of your mind and its roots are strong and go deep affecting your life and health. Many times people will then develop a victim mentality, this belief is a stronghold rooted in deception and will hold them in bondage until they choose to come out of agreement with it.

The soul doesn't want us to forget these things, but would rather that we remember them as well as remind others of them. Instead of the fruit of righteousness flowing freely from our spirit, we will see a harvest of anger, resentment, jealousy, hatred and strife flowing from our soul. Jesus calls these evil fruits - Matthew 7:19-20. I never thought of myself as evil, I thought of myself as hurt, wounded, a victim and abandoned but never evil. I never perpetrated evil against someone else on purpose. Anything I did was usually in an attempt to protect myself or to meet my own needs. Yet things that I said and did could have been viewed as offensive or evil by someone else.

Remember what was said about people who are deceived – they believe they are right even when they are wrong. We don't need any help seeing people or situations through our eyes. We need help seeing through the Father's eyes.

In Matthew 18:23-35 Jesus is telling the parable of the king and his two servants. The king forgave one servant a great debt. That servant went out and found one who owed him a small debt. He laid hands on him and took him by the throat and said, "pay me what you owe me." Then he threw him in prison till he should pay the debt. We'll pick up the story in verse 32. *"Then his lord, after that he had called him, said unto him, 'O thou wicked servant, I forgave thee all that debt, because thou desiredst me: Shouldest not thou also have had compassion on thy fellow servant, even as I had pity on thee? And his lord was wroth, and delivered him to the tormentors, till he should pay all that was due unto him. So likewise shall my heavenly Father do also unto you, if ye from your hearts (soul / will) forgive not every one his brother their trespasses."*

When we don't forgive we set in motion a spiritual law that delivers us into the hands of the tormentor.

In the prayer known as the *Our Father* (Yes, it is being singled out and is a printed document) Jesus says, *"And forgive us our debts, as we forgive our debtors."* You can see that it is a spiritual law that we are forgiven with 'the same measure we forgive' - Matthew 6:12. If you want to be forgiven completely you need to forgive completely.

In John 20:23 Jesus said, *"...whosesoever sins ye remit (forgive), they are remitted (forgiven) unto them; and whosesoever sins ye retain, they are retained (keep, lay hold)."*

Jesus is making it very clear in all these scriptures that if we make a decision not to forgive with the same measure God has forgiven us, we have retained the sin. When we retain the sin a thorn grows on our dendrites that will poison our life. We have kept someone on the hook of our expectation and opened the door to the enemy by our disobedience, giving demons a legal right to torment us.

So when an opportunity to get offended is presented it is either going to be a stepping stone to maturity or a tombstone to bondage, again the choice is always ours.

As a Christian I had a measure of understanding about forgiveness. I knew that forgiveness is an act of our will and has nothing to do with how we feel. I knew that we choose to forgive because it is the right thing to do. So I would always choose to forgive but I never understood what it meant to release someone.

Jesus said, *"...whosesoever sins ye retain (keep) they are retained"* - John 20:23. I was quick to forgive, however I was keeping their sin by maintaining my judgments and opinions of them. This imprinted a network of dendrites with thorns within me. So I certainly did retain them.

To release is to take that person off the hook of our expectation and release our judgments of them. They don't owe us anything, not even an apology. We forgive them completely and release them from any obligation. To forgive is an act of great strength and maturity. In Matthew 18 the wicked servant threw his fellow servant in prison and wanted repayment of the debt. He was an immature Christian, holding on to his wants, instead of forgiving.

Now this is where I missed the mark. I would forgive by faith and obedience as an act of my will. However, I would still have feelings and thoughts of anger and resentment. I carried bitter-root judgments in my heart toward others because I had an expectation in that person to know better or to have made a better choice. I arrogantly thought to myself, "I would never do what they did" or "how could they do that?" Those negative thoughts were toxic and therefore grew thorns and secreted toxic emotions keeping me in prison.

Now I know I am not alone here, we all think like this. Once I understood what it means to forgive and release it took me to another level and I became freer.

I had a girlfriend from high school who was still bound by alcohol and a bad lifestyle. I bent over backwards to help her all the time. I prayed constantly for her. One day I was having a garage sale and selling a lot of stuff and she wanted a big portion of it. My husband, Mark, told me not to sell to her and not to trust her for the money, but I didn't listen. When she didn't pay and didn't return my calls I became furious. My mind was in torment, I kept thinking of all I had done for her; how could she do this to me. Not to mention that Mark had told me not to do it.

One beautiful, hot summer day as I was driving, the Lord spoke and said go home, clean out your clothes closet, even some good stuff, bring it to her and bless her with it. Well my first reaction was, "What?" After all she had taken from me! It's too nice a day to clean out my clothes. Then I realized what He was trying to teach me; if I would bless my enemy and give what I thought she owed me, I wouldn't feel robbed. She wouldn't owe me anything and I would have forgiven and released her from the debt, securing my freedom.

So I obeyed, filled a bag and left it on her porch, as she wasn't home. In my heart I sowed all of it as a seed toward her salvation. I left a note and told her she didn't owe me for all the garage sale stuff and that I loved her. However, in my heart, I did expect a phone call at some point acknowledging the bag and what I had done for her. She never called or responded in any way and I had to get over that too. The enemy tried to use that to keep me bound but I continued to maintain my posture of forgiveness and release. I realize now that I kept my heart pure on purpose and didn't allow thorny dendrites to take root. It took a few years but she showed up at my door very late one night and asked for prayer. She later gave her life to the Lord and I was blessed to be able to mentor her spiritual growth.

I encourage you to make a conscious decision to forgive and release the people in your life. If we don't, we deliver ourselves into the hands of the tormentors. We are tormented because our retaining and laying hold of that sin produces thorns and secretes toxic emotions that poison our life. Now we can literally see why the wages of sin is death - Romans 6:23.

Many times it is not a conscious decision to be offended. We may not even realize that we have taken the bait and fallen into a trap of offense until the torment begins. Then we wonder, "Why am I feeling so bad?" We find ourselves rehearsing tormenting thoughts, feeling sad, anxious, angry or upset. Remember these emotions are a chemical reaction to a toxic thought. So they should be an alarm for us to check our thought life.

Areas of offense very often go undetected when we are upset with God or have trouble forgiving ourselves. So many times we don't receive an answer to prayer in the way or in the time frame that we want and we get upset with God. Then we begin to entertain the thoughts that He doesn't really love us. To add to our trouble, we gain all new patterns of wrong belief systems surrounding these offenses.

Once I was married to Mark, we spent nine years trying to have another child. The doctors said there was no medical reason why we were not conceiving. Over time, when I would see a pregnant teenager, the thought would come, "God, you let them conceive but not me." This belief system that I agreed with had a destructive thorny stronghold on my mind, secreting toxic emotions, putting me into states of depression every month. I believed that God was a respecter of persons; that He would bless others but not me.

That deception in my perception caused me to be offended with God having a wrong perception of Him. This led to years of mental and emotional torment and sadness surrounding this offense. I believed the Lord would do anything, just not for me. As time went by I could see that, for me, having children was a band-aid, a way for me to medicate a broken place within me. I had a belief system that being a mom would give me purpose and a destiny. I discovered what I wanted was to feel whole on the inside. Once I found wholeness all desire for more children went away.

Perhaps we've had a loved one become ill and we've prayed for their healing but they died anyway. Then we blame God. We become offended with Him. We had an expectation that wasn't met the way we thought it should have been. There are many factors involved in healing; many times spiritual laws have been set in motion and we find ourselves perishing for lack of knowledge - Hosea 4:6. Some of those factors and spiritual laws are being outlined in this book.

It is hard to forgive one's self. So many times it is easier to forgive someone else while we keep ourselves on the hook. By the time my daughter was two I was divorced, lost, and medicating my pain.

I found my husband Mark and came to the Lord by the time my daughter was six years old. Fifteen years later as I was teaching this class the Lord began to reveal things that were buried deep in my soul.

One of the many things He began to reveal was an area of unforgiveness I had toward myself. I began to have memories of some of those times when my daughter was little. Emotional pain, shame and guilt began to spring up. I was praying for myself and asking the Lord why was this happening.

My Pastor said to me that, "what we bury alive stays alive." I realized that it was actually the work of the Holy Spirit putting his finger on a tree network in my mind / soul that needed healing. I knew I needed help to deal with this.

My friend, Pat, and I had gone through much of our emotional healing together as we ministered to each other. So I sat down with her and by the time I did I was deep into an intense grieving process over the loss of those precious years with my daughter. Pat said to me, "You know Donna that you have to forgive yourself." I said, "Well then we are done because I can't."

In that moment Pat had a rhema word that set me free. She said, "Did you set out on purpose to have a child and then not be there emotionally to meet all of her needs?" I said, "No, of course not!" In my next breath I said to her, "Oh that was good!" I could see it, I could see where she was taking me! She reminded me that hurting people unintentionally will hurt other people.

As she counseled me, I understood that when I had my daughter, even though I was twenty one years old, I was still emotionally only sixteen on the inside. And that wounded sixteen year old girl was still looking to get her needs met at the expense of her child's needs.

It is the knowledge of truth that makes us free and that night I was made free from a network of thorny dendrites and a pocket of emotional pain that I had buried alive. At that moment I was able to truly, from my heart, forgive and release myself from every expectation I had in me to be a better mother, to have known better and done better in that season of my life.

If you need to forgive yourself then ask yourself the same question Pat asked me, did you on purpose set out to do whatever it is you did with the intention to cause harm? Or were you acting out of a pain, laboring under a generational curse, perishing for lack of knowledge, etc? Choose to see the whole picture through the Father's eyes and not your perception through limited understanding. Then take the appropriate action to gain freedom.

So all of these areas of offense and unforgiveness need to be repented of and released in order to find freedom. Surprisingly we never even knew we took the bait of Satan. There are so many Christians that are waiting on God for an answer to prayer yet they are offended. They come to the altar for prayer from the Pastor after they have gossiped and bad mouthed him all week. In Mark 11:25 Jesus said, *"And when ye stand praying, forgive, ... "*

While writing this book I ran into a girl at the grocery store. I did not recognize her but she was excited and happy to see me, in fact she kept me talking with her for some time. After a few moments of talking I realized who she was.

In high school, just after my parents had separated and I was an emotional wreck, she had her boyfriend call me and pressure me to go out with him. He said they had broken up and he needed to talk to me. I was sixteen and didn't know how to say no. That night he forced himself on me, although it did not go all the way thank God, it was far enough for me to be upset and uncomfortable.

It turned out the whole thing was a set up. They had not broken up and she used that to spread rumors about me and get all the mean girls to hate me. That was a very traumatic time for me and made going to school and learning difficult.

So needless to say once I realized who she was I got a "thing." But the Lord used it to expose a thorny root hidden beneath the surface that had power to hurt me. I was kind and gracious to her and then I left the store that day and took care of it. I rooted out the offense, released her and moved that fracture out of my soul removing its power over me!

You will notice as you go through this book that the Lord will remind you of hurts or problems you had forgotten. Maybe they are not in your conscious memory but they are still in your soul and He loves you so much He wants to cleanse and heal you from the inside out.

X-RAY YOUR SOUL

1. Do you get a "thing" when you are about to see someone? Do you want to avoid them?

2. Do you still rehearse the incident and what you could have said?

3. Do you think of things you can do to retaliate? Like ignoring them, not cooking, doing laundry, or worse?

4. Are your thoughts tormented?

5. Are your prayers being answered? Are you praying in agreement with God?

6. Do you have physical problems, aches and pains that have no cure?

7. Do you condemn and accuse yourself? Remember, Satan is the accuser of the brethren.

8. Are you tormented with thoughts of all your shortcomings and failures?

9. Is your sleep disturbed? Do you have unrest? Are you troubled with dreams?

Our posture in life needs to be continually examining ourselves and looking for wrong attitudes in our heart / soul. For example, examine all of your relationships with the people in your life. What do you think of them? How do you treat them? Or how do they treat you? Perhaps you are identifying that someone may be offended with you.

In Matthew 22:37-39 *"Jesus said unto him, Thou shalt love the Lord thy God with all thy heart, and with all thy soul, and with all thy mind. This is the first and great commandment. And the second is like unto it, Thou shalt love thy neighbor as thyself."* The law of love is a direct order from our Father in heaven and it is not optional.

I Peter 4:8 in the Amplified Bible says, *"Above all things have intense and unfailing love for one another, for love covers (conceals, hides, and keeps a secret) a multitude of sins forgives and disregards the offenses of others."*

I Corinthians 13:4-8,11 says, (I personalized this for you from the Amplified Bible. I suggest copying it and memorizing it!) The love of God in me endures long and is patient and kind. This love is never envious nor boils over with jealousy, is not boastful or vainglorious and does not display itself haughtily. It is not conceited, arrogant and inflated with pride; it is not rude, unmannerly and does not act unbecomingly. God's love in me does not insist on its own rights or its own way, for it is not self-seeking; it is not touchy, fretful or resentful. I will take no account of the evil done and pay no attention to a suffered wrong. I will not rejoice at injustice or unrighteousness, but I rejoice when right and truth prevail. The love of God in me bears up under anything and everything that comes my way. I am ever ready to believe the best of every person; my hopes are fadeless under all circumstances; I will endure everything without weakening, for love never fails. When I was a child, I talked like a child; I thought like a child; I reasoned like a child – selfishly. Now that I have grown up spiritually, I am done with childish ways and have put them aside. I choose to walk in the love of God. When this is our posture we will keep our dendrites clean from thorns and our life healthy!

STEPS TO TAKE

We must recognize that our sense of justice has been defiled. We have a perverted sense of justice because of the sin nature resident within our soul. What our sense of justice is and what God's sense of justice is are two completely different things. Only God's opinion counts and He will administer justice His way, not ours.

1. Acknowledge to the Lord that we are hurt.

2. Make sure that we are not listening to the voice of our soul that is perpetuating the injustice.

3. Take these thoughts of anger, hurt and betrayal and apply II Corinthians 10:5. The verse says to take every thought captive that wants to nurse, protect and give attention to the hurt, thereby silencing the voice of our soul.

4. Purpose to see the one that hurt us or maybe even see ourselves through the eyes of God and understand that soul issues cause bad behavior. "Hurting people hurt people."

5. Focus on our own sin and not the sin of others. We have to purpose to keep our heart right before God.

6. Make a conscious choice to set our will to maintain an attitude of forgiveness.

7. We must release others from every destructive judgment, opinion and everything we think they owe us. They don't owe us anything, not even an apology (although it would be nice and the right thing to do).

8. Recognize that others may not live up to our unrealistic expectations. Release them from all expectations we may have had in them.

9. Examine our response to what has upset us. Perhaps a trigger ripped a scab off a wound in our own soul. Examine why we respond the way we do.

Jesus taught us exactly what to do with the overwhelming sense of injustice, wounds, hurts and betrayals that come our way. He said in Matthew 5:44, *"But I say to you, love your enemies, bless those who curse you, do good to those who hate you, and pray for those who spitefully use you and persecute you."*

As we begin praying for the people who have hurt us, our prayers will be short and without any passion, but it is our obedience to the Lord's instruction that is the only way to get released.

After the act of forgiveness, we must take some time alone before God and use our image center to see ourselves loving and blessing those who have hurt us. Now we are practiced in using our imagination for retaliation or what we would like to say. But I want you to practice using your imagination for good. WW JD? (What would Jesus do?)

This time will allow love to be worked in our heart for them. Declare to yourself that you will never act or think any other way towards them. Once we have done this from afar, then we may be ready to see them. When we do, we may have to stand against the symptoms of unforgiveness that our feelings may be experiencing. Our soulish reasoning may say, "Oh God, I thought I forgave them." We did. This is just our soul responding in a familiar way. At this point we need to stop that familiar process in our soul and enforce our act of love, faith and obedience.

Romans 12:18-21 gives us great instruction; it says, *"If it be possible, as much as lieth in you, live peaceably with all men. Dearly beloved, avenge not yourselves, but rather give place unto wrath: for it is written, Vengeance is mine; I will repay, saith the Lord.*

Therefore if thine enemy hunger, feed him; if he thirst, give him drink: for in so doing thou shalt heap coals of fire on his head. Be not overcome of evil, but overcome evil with good."

"Coals of fire" is an Old Testament expression for divine judgment (Proverbs 25:21-22 and Psalm 140:9-10). Hot coals were used to melt

metal and bend it into a different shape or object. Likewise, when we sow love and kindness, it can bend the hardest of hearts. It also has the implication of bringing shame, which one can experience when we overcome evil with good. We have to think like this on purpose it doesn't come naturally. Pray and ask the Lord how you can bless the person who has offended you.

Ask what you can do to show the devil he is not going to get you down. The Lord might tell you to just pray for them, not tell anyone about what happened, or send a gift. Remember the story I shared about my girlfriend and the money she owed me? I sent her a gift of a bag of clothes and gave her not only the clothes but the money she owed me. That released me from feeling owed.

Proverbs 15:1-2 says that, *"A soft answer turneth away wrath: but grievous words stir up anger. The tongue of the wise useth knowledge aright: but the mouth of fools poureth out foolishness."*

We are only accountable for our own heart and actions. We have to purpose to keep ourselves obedient to God. He can clearly see how we have been wronged. He sees the truth of the whole picture. We only see through a glass, darkly filtered through wounds and perceptions on our soul.

I remember one morning I was running around the house while getting ready for work. I had lights on in every room. Mark must have been in a bad mood that day because as he went through each room he was complaining that every light was on in the house. I was in the bathroom doing my hair and I could hear his murmuring. I became mad that he was complaining about the lights. My mouth wanted to say something sarcastic to him but I heard the voice of the Lord in my spirit telling me to go love him. Oh that was not a pleasant thought at the time! I would much rather have bit his head off for his behavior.

He was in the kitchen about to go out the back door and I ran down the hall into the kitchen and said lovingly, "Bye babe, love you." He stormed out of the house and I went back to the bathroom mirror. Now I was the one murmuring sarcastically mocking what I said to him, "Bye babe, love you"- yuk. I said, "Lord that felt horrible."

My only consolation at the time was that coals of fire were being heaped on his head. I did not have the right understanding of that verse so I literally wanted whatever coals of fire meant to be heaped all over him, in a bad way, of course. When he came home from work that day he was pleasant and everything was gone for both of us. In times past that could have turned into a "thing" and we would have been cold and distant with each other. But because I obeyed the Lord those hot coals melted and bent his hardened heart and my soft answer turned away his wrath and mine!

Matthew 5:23-25 Jesus taught in the Sermon on the Mount… *"Therefore if thou bring thy gift to the altar, and there rememberest that thy brother hath ought against thee, leave there thy gift before the altar, and go thy way; first be reconciled to thy brother, and then come and offer thy gift. Agree with thine adversary quickly, whiles thou art in the way with him; lest at any time the adversary deliver thee to the judge, and the judge deliver thee to the officer, and thou be cast into prison."*

We have all been the source of an offense at some point in our lives. If we know someone is offended, hurt or upset with us, we must go to that person and make it right. It is more important for us to reconcile one with another for if we don't, we both end up doing emotional jail time.

Pray before you go, listen to the instruction of the Holy Spirit. Search your heart for wrong thinking and the behaviors that may stem from strongholds and soul ties. The Holy Spirit may even instruct you to ask what you did to upset other people.

I find it best to express your love and concern for the relationship. Ask what the other person is thinking and feeling so you can identify your sin and wrong thinking and speak to them in a way that will be received.

The scripture says, "Agree with thine adversary quickly." We can speak the truth in love. If that person cannot receive from us, it is better to just agree with them. We can express our sorrow over the strife and hold back from defending ourselves. This will release them from holding an offense that would imprison us both.

James 3:17 says, *"But the wisdom that is from above is first pure, then peaceable, gentle, willing to yield, full of mercy and good fruits, without partiality and without hypocrisy."*

Matthew 18:15 Jesus' instructions are, *"Moreover if your brother sins against you, go and tell him his fault between you and him alone. If he hears you, you have gained a brother."*

God has given us the ministry of reconciliation and has committed to us the word of reconciliation - II Corinthians 5:18-21. Our heart needs to be motivated out of love and reconciliation. So do what's right and do it because it's right!

NOW WE ARE READY TO BEGIN

1. Get alone with the Lord.

2. Ask Him to reveal to you people with whom you are offended or hold judgments. You may even be offended at an organization as a whole; like your place of business, the government, school districts, religious communities.

3. Ask Him who may be offended with you? You may have to humble yourself and go to someone you have offended.

4. Forgive and release each one personally. Say out loud ,"I release that person from every expectation I had in her / him." Remember, *"Whose soever sins ye remit (forgive), they are remitted unto them; and whose soever sins ye retain (hold on to), they are retained."* - John 20:23.

5. Forgive and release yourself.

6. Cancel the debt owed to you. Say, "I release that person. I remit the sins against me." Pray for those who have sinned against you, and that the Lord will bless them and lead them into a closer relationship with Him.

Father, I repent for holding onto unforgiveness and offense in my heart. As an act of my will I choose to forgive everyone who has ever hurt me or any of my loved ones. I choose to forgive everyone who has ever taken from us in any way.

I repent for judging them, criticizing them and speaking against them. I ask You, Lord, to forgive me as I forgive them. And I stand in the gap as Jesus did on the cross and ask You, Lord, to forgive them also, for they know not what they do.

I also choose to release them. I release them from every expectation I had for them to behave differently and to have made better choices. They don't owe me anything, not even an apology. I release and remit their sins against me.

I pray that Your forgiveness will come to those who have sinned against me and against You, that You will bless them and lead them into a closer, more personal relationship with You. I ask You, Lord, to give me ways of blessing them that I may overcome evil with good.

Lord, I also ask You to show me my part in any of these offenses and to show me anyone that is hurt or offended by me. Expose my sin to me, show me wrong attitudes, behaviors and wrong words that I have spoken. Lord, show me if there is anyone I need to go to and repent and ask for their forgiveness.

I pray that You would open the eyes of my understanding that I might see where my behavior may have caused someone to lash out at me. If this hurt I feel is a result of something that I opened the door for, I am willing to accept responsibility for my own actions and behavior.

I pray that You would give me Your perspective on this whole situation so I can see clearly through the eyes of Your understanding and not through the filters on my soul. I choose from this time forward to take my thoughts captive and prune my mind. I will not rehearse this anymore, if it ever comes up to me again I will turn it to prayer for them and not meditate on the wrong done to me. If I see that person I will be quick to bless them.

Words

The Blueprint For Life

You will learn how to change the internal image and blueprint for your life so you can see yourself the way God has destined you to be. As death and life are in the power of your tongue, you will learn how to use your words effectively in prayer to find the perfect will of God for your life.

Chapter Five

We have come to understand that the salvation, healing, deliverance and wholeness of our soul is not only progressive but it is our Christian responsibility to pursue. In this chapter we will begin to learn what *The Answer* is for the restoration of our soul. We will learn how to take the Word of God and begin the maturing process of how to live life from our spirit and find healing for our soul.

THE FATHER'S WORD

Ephesians 1:18 says, *"The eyes of your understanding being enlightened."* Enlightened is the Greek word *photizo* which means; photo, or to let light in. This is where the word for photograph comes from. For instance, when you take a picture, the shutter opens, light comes in and an image is imprinted on the film. In the same way, the shutter or veil over our soul / understanding must open so we can be "enlightened," and receive a revelatory image that makes an impression on our understanding.

Psalm 119:130 tells us that, *"The entrance of Thy words giveth light (illumination); it giveth understanding (instruction) unto the simple."*

Here is how that happens, there are three Greek words used to describe the word for *"word"* in scripture: The first is the word rhema (*hray'-mah*) which are spoken or quickened words. For example when the Holy Spirit quickens a word or scripture to you, that is a rhema word. Ephesians 6:17 says, *"...the sword of the Spirit, which is the word / rhema of God."* That is the rhema word the Holy Spirit gives us to speak out in prayer or in a time of need.

The second word for 'word' is graphe (*graf-ay'*); the written words in scripture. In Matthew 22:29 Jesus said, *"Ye do err, not knowing the scriptures / graphe, nor the power of God."* This is the Greek word from which we have gotten the word for graphics and engrave.

The third word for 'word' is logos (*log'-os*) that is the logic that the word is conveying. It embodies a conception of the revealed will of God becoming logical to you. It is not talking about the wisdom of man being logical in a natural sense, but a revelation from the Word that is now revelatory logic to you. In Matthew 7:24 Jesus said, *"Therefore whosoever heareth these sayings / logos of mine, and doeth them, I will liken him unto a wise man, which built his house upon a rock."*

Jesus was saying that if we hear His words and they are logical to us, we have gotten a revelation and conceived an image on the inside. Then we will be a doer of that word and our house will be built on upon a rock!

Many people can read the written words and those words may just be *graphe* / graphics on paper. They did not become a *'logos / word'* a logical revelatory word. They did not conceive an image inside of them, therefore they did not act on that word and their house was not built upon a rock.

James 1:21 tells us, *"Wherefore lay apart all filthiness and superfluity (abundance) of naughtiness, (talking about a work within our soul as a result of a sin nature) and receive with meekness the **grafted word** (logos), **which is able to save** (Greek word sozo meaning to - heal, deliver, and make whole) **your soul**."*

We have come to understand that our soul needs healing, deliverance and wholeness. We have had a life time of bad impressions built up in our soul. *The Answer* is found when the Word becomes logical / *logos* to us; it has to make an impression on us, having "the eyes of our understanding being enlightened," letting the light in, which then lifts the veil over our soul. This in turn allows an image to be imprinted into the dendrites of our soul / image center.

When this happens, we get revelation and understanding; and the logical message of what is being conveyed becomes revealed and grafted knowledge to us. That means it will germinate and grow; then the fruit it produces will be the salvation, healing, deliverance and wholeness of our soul.

Jesus explained the way to do this in John 8:32 when He said, *"If ye continue (abide, remain) in My Word / logos, then are ye My disciples (a pupil, doer) indeed; And ye shall know (understand) the truth, and the truth (that is logical to you, that you have gotten revelation from) shall make you free."*

Just having heard truth does not make us free. Many Christians sit in church for years hearing truth and have no real freedom.

I have come to realize that most Christian believers are not disciples. The Bible doesn't commission believers to go into the world and make converts or get decisions.

We are commissioned to make disciples; teach them how to 'do the Word.' The difference between being a believer and a disciple is that a disciple will abide and remain in the *logos*. It is the restoration process for our soul. It is *The Answer* that brings maturity and saves *psuche* / your soul - I Peter 1:9.

Too many Christians try to get around being a disciple by running from counselor to counselor, or being the first one at the altar for prayer for the same need every Sunday.

Unfortunately, most Christians do not do the abiding process for themselves. We want a counselor and a little bit of prayer to change us. God has designed the only way to change the damage in our soul / *psuche*.

James 1: 22-25 says, *"But be ye doers (a performer) of the word / logos, and not hearers only, deceiving your own selves. For if any be a hearer of the word, and not a doer, he is like unto a man beholding his natural face in a glass: For he beholdeth himself, and goeth his way, and straightway forgetteth what manner of man he was. But whoso looketh into the perfect law of liberty, and continueth therein, he being not a forgetful hearer, but a doer of the work, this man shall be blessed in his deed."*

Every morning we get ready for our day by looking in the mirror. If I were to ask you how many freckles, lines or eyelashes you have on your face you probably could not answer me. But yet you look at your face every day, maybe several times a day. The reason you don't know the answer is that you didn't look in the mirror with the intention of finding that information. If you ever took the time to count the freckles, lines or eyelashes it would be a number you would always remember.

When we look in the mirror, what we see is the overall frame of our face; we are not looking for details. We, as Christians, have been looking into the Word of God and yet we only know the overall frame of the Word. But if we will look into the word with the intention of finding out what it says about our situation or need, then the word would become logical and revelatory to us. We would be able to conceive an image of our answer, and now the word has become a perfect law of liberation to us!

Now I am not talking about reading our Bible two hours a day. I am saying we need to abide, continuing to look into that mirror of the Word. Let it become logical to us as a lifestyle. Let the entrance of the Word bring illumination, letting the light in, which then lifts the veil over our soul, allowing an image to be imprinted in our understanding. As this happens, the logical Word will be making an impression on us, changing our thinking as it tears down thorny, toxic strongholds and heals the damage in our soul.

In order to do this, we have to start a process of meditating, chewing, rehearsing and pondering. The word *meditating* is likened to a cow chewing its cud. She swallows and brings it back up again, over and over, getting all the nutrients she can out of it.

As we meditate on the written Word by speaking it, chewing on it, pondering or rehearsing it, the Holy Spirit is quickening and revealing the truth of that Word to our understanding and we are becoming enlightened. The nerve pathway of our dendrites, the internal image we have had and the blueprint for our life will begin to change.

As this word is becoming *logos* / logical to us, it is penetrating our soul. It is then going to do a destructive, as well as a constructive work in our soul, through this meditating and abiding process. It is going to destroy deception in our perception and the thorny filters we have in place. Then it will construct an image of who we are in Christ, creating a new nerve pathway and blueprint for our lives.

Hebrews 4:12 tells us exactly how this happens. It says, *"For the word / logos, (not rhema or graphe) of God is quick (actively alive), and powerful (active, operative, effectual to work and full of energy), and sharper than any two-edged sword, piercing even to the dividing asunder (difference between) of soul and spirit, and of the joints and marrow, and is a discerner of the thoughts and intents of the heart."*

Hebrews is saying that when the word becomes *logos* / logical to us it is powerful and full of life. Once deposited in our spirit, it is full of His energy and it begins toiling and working within us. His words are operative and effectual words that are sharper than any two-edged sword, executing judicial punishment on the thorny strongholds, soul ties and wounds, penetrating and channeling themselves through the various chambers of our soul and spirit. His words are discerning and judging the thoughts and intentions of our heart. The Word of God will attain its desired goal within us, which is wholeness! Dr Caroline Leaf says that, "Faith based chemicals are stronger than fear based chemicals. Repenting and coming out of agreement with wrong thoughts removes the thorns. Then you can build a new faith based thought over the existing dendrite. Science has actually proven this in the laboratory. It is a bio chemical fact that this actually happens."

The abiding process will cause the Word of God to penetrate the area of our soul that it needs to, filling it with life. At the same time, it invades a negative stronghold / belief system to dismantle and tear down a destructive image or to permeate a wound with the healing love of God

We have to abide in the logical / *logos* Word because as the Word penetrates the soul it meets up with resistance by an exalted *psuche* / soul which does not want to change. This process of abiding will change our soul progressively. It doesn't happen instantly. As the *logos* begins to penetrate our soul, depending on the strength of the stronghold, it may take awhile to dismantle it. If you are purposeful in removing the thorny belief system and deliberate in changing your mind by replacing wrong thoughts with right ones, Dr Leaf says, "It will take just 4 days to change the chemical structure of your brain. Within twenty-one days of right thinking you will create a new nerve pathway and begin to heal!"

God intended His Word to divide, make a separation or distinguish between the soul and spirit. Once the logical Word gets in our soul, it passes judgment and discerns or critiques areas of sin, weakness, strongholds, soul ties or wounds. It then starts the healing process.

This is God's only designed method of transforming our soul / *psuche*. We must abide and remain grafted in the vine. Our answer doesn't lie in just reading generic scriptures every day. In other words, if we need vitamin C, don't take vitamin A. If we need inner healing, don't meditate prosperity scriptures.

We have to find scriptures that pertain to our need. Then begin to meditate, chew, rehearse and abide in them on a daily basis until they become revelation and logical to us. As they do the dendrite structure, internal image and blueprint for our life will begin to change. You will begin to see yourself the way God sees you. You will begin to see yourself doing and being what God has destined you to do and be. As you do, those words will become grafted, meaning they will germinate, grow and produce fruit in your soul.

The truth we now understand is what makes us free, transforming *psuche*. If we need wisdom, security or peace, for example, find scriptures on these subjects and begin meditating on them. Use your imagination, God gave you this image center as the creative part of you to help you shape your destiny. We need to be very practical and organized about this. I got a promise book and began chewing on scriptures that pertained to my areas of need. The following are a few of the scriptures I used to remove the thorns off my dendrites and change my internal image. As I meditated on them they created a blueprint for my new life in Christ.

Ephesians 1:17-23; Colossians 1:9-11 and Psalm 91. I suggest that you copy these, so you can meditate on them regularly.

ABRAHAM

Father God's relationship with Abram is a perfect example of His designed method of grafting the Word in our hearts.

Genesis 15:2-6

2 *And Abram said, Lord GOD, what wilt thou give me, seeing I go childless, and the steward of my house is this Eliezer of Damascus?*

Now let me ask you, what was Abram seeing? The answer is, that he was seeing himself childless. His inner-image, all of his thoughts, his internal agreement and the blue print for his life was childless.

> **3** *And Abram said, Behold, to me thou hast given no seed: and, lo, one born in my house is mine heir.*
>
> **4** *And, behold, the word of the LORD came unto him, saying, This shall not be thine heir; but he that shall come forth out of thine own bowels shall be thine heir.*
>
> **5** *And he brought him forth abroad, and said, Look now toward heaven, and tell the stars, if thou be able to number them: and he said unto him, So shall thy seed be.*
>
> **6** *And he believed in the LORD; and he counted it to him for righteousness.*

When God speaks to Abram He promises him an heir from his own bowels. Then He shows him the stars and says, "So shall thy seed be." God was trying to change Abram's internal image and blueprint for his life.

You have to understand, Abram didn't have the written Word of God. He couldn't find scriptures that pertained to his need. So God had to create a blueprint by showing him the stars to help change his imagination and create a new dendrite structure. As Abram looked at those stars he could begin counting children, grand children, great grand children and so on. What was God's intention in showing him the stars? It was for the purpose of getting the Word of God "So shall thy seed be," grafted in his soul.

Like Abram, many of us don't have an inner image and blueprint based on God's covenant promises and provisions. We have ignorantly agreed with wrong thoughts causing our dendrite structures and inner image to be defiled.

It is important to examine what we see in our image center as it is the blueprint for our lives. What you are seeing is what you will be doing because that is impregnated in you.

You should easily be able to figure out what your filled with. Close your eyes, what do you see? What are you dreaming? What is causing you fear?

Can you see right now why people's lives are the way they are? They spend more time programming their image center with all the wrong stuff and that is the fruit they produce in their lives.

The reason why worry is a sin is because worry is a negative form of meditation. The devil will sow thoughts of worry so your image center will be pregnant with the wrong thinking. Then you will give birth to what you worried about because *"as a man thinketh in his heart so is he"* - Proverbs 23:7. Job found this out the hard way and then said, *"For the thing which I greatly feared is come upon me, and that which I was afraid of is come unto me."* - Job 3:25

In actuality, the enemy is using your God given authority and your imagination, to produce his works in your life. Instead of you having dominion in your life, he is dominating your creative systems and using them to bring about what he wants produced in your life - the kingdom of darkness in the earth.

What you are seeing in your image center is the only thing that can be - because that is what is impregnated in you.

- What are you seeing? That is the only thing that can be - because that is what is impregnated in you.

- What do you see your self doing? That is the only thing you can do - because that is what is impregnated in you.

- What do you see yourself having? That is the only thing you can have - because that is what is impregnated in you.

What you are seeing is what will BE. Abram and Sarai saw themselves childless. He was seventy five years old when God told him he would have a child. Eleven years went by and still no child. So look at what happens.

Gen 16:2 and 15 - *"And Sarai said unto Abram, Behold now, the LORD hath restrained me from bearing: I pray thee, go in unto my maid; it may be that I may obtain children by her. And Abram hearkened to the voice of Sarai... And Hagar bare Abram a son: and Abram called his son's name, which Hagar bare, Ishmael."*

Obviously, Abram stopped looking at the stars and started looking at the maid. Uh Oh!

Right here is a good place to determine if you have stopped looking at the Word and Covenant promises of God and started looking at something else.

Make sure that you are not looking at your past, the world, the news, or the behavior of your loved ones. What are you allowing to influence the blueprint you have on the inside?

If God can use the stars to create an image and graft a word inside of Abram's heart, then imagine what the enemy can do using other people, the news, talk shows, and movies to graft an image within us. The enemy knows that what you are seeing is the only thing that can be – because that is what is impregnated in you.

Thirteen more years go by and now Abram is ninety-nine years old and the Lord appeared to him in Genesis 17:4-5, 15-16 and said, *"As for me, behold, my covenant is with thee, and thou shalt be a father of many nations. Neither shall thy name any more be called Abram, but thy name shall be Abraham (father of a multitude); for a father of many nations have I made thee."*

Genesis 17:15-16 -*"And God said unto Abraham, As for Sarai thy wife, thou shalt not call her name Sarai, but Sarah shall her name be. And I will bless her, and give thee a son also of her: yea, I will bless her, and she shall be a mother of nations; kings of people shall be of her."*

Abram, a ninety-nine year old man, has to say to his people, 'My name is no longer Abram for it is now Abraham. I am the father of a multitude. Sarai's name has also been changed and she shall now be known as Sarah, a mother of nations.'

Every day when he got up Sarah would say, 'Good morning Father of Nations,' and he would reply, 'Good morning Mother of Nations.' Their people would say to them, how are you Father and Mother of Nations? Can you see what was happening? God not only had to change what was in their image center, He had to get their words to line up as well.

The image you carry will shape your words. The words you speak will create an image. You see they work together. They influence each other.

Some of you need your name changed. Some of you have been named failure and you need to be named success. Maybe you see yourself as a victim; then your name needs to be changed to victor! Do you see yourself broke or sick? Then change your name to rich and healed!

There is an image in a name. There is vision in a name. There is destiny in a name. Don't let the world name you what God has not named you. Don't let your past or your circumstances name you. You have to get an image of who you are in Christ and change your name. Use the "I Am" list I gave you in the first chapter to help you.

Within three months of Abraham calling himself a father of a nations Abraham's wife Sarah conceived. The promised child, Isaac, was born one year after their names were changed.

I want to show you what the New Testament has to say about this in Romans 4:17-22.

Verse 17 says: *"(As it is written, I have made thee a father of many nations,) before him whom he believed, even God, who quickeneth the dead, and calleth those things which be not as though they were."*

The Amplified Bible says:

> **17** *God...Who gives life to the dead and speaks of the non-existent things that [He has foretold and promised] as if they [already] existed.*
>
> **18** *Who against hope believed in hope, that he might become the father of many nations, according to that which was spoken, So shall thy seed be.*
>
> **19** *And being not weak in faith, he considered not his own body now dead, when he was about an hundred years old, neither yet the deadness of Sarah's womb:*
>
> **20** *He staggered not at the promise of God through unbelief; but was strong in faith, giving glory to God;*
>
> **21** *And being fully persuaded that, what he had promised, he was able also to perform.*
>
> **22** *And therefore it was imputed to him for righteousness.*

Did you get that? God's way of doing things is to speak of non-existent things as if they already existed. In Isaiah 46:10 God says, *"He declares the end from the beginning..."* In Genesis chapter one we know God saw darkness and called it light.

As Abraham and everyone around him was confessing father and mother of nations their internal image and blueprint was changing, faith was coming by hearing and hearing the Word of God. We just read in Romans 4:22 that God calls this behavior *"righteousness."*

"According to that which was spoken, So shall thy seed be."- Romans 4:18. The word according means to be in agreement with. Abraham against all hope came into agreement with the word of God changing the dendrite structure of his brain. He developed fully persuaded faith and created a new nerve pathway. What you are in agreement with is what you really believe and what you speak day to day. We must let the Word of God become logical and make an impression on us to the point that our internal blueprint is pointing us in the right direction. The word has become grafted and then like Abraham we will have developed fully persuaded faith.

Here is what was happening physically for Abraham and Sarah. When we speak what we hear, a sound wave gets converted into electricity and goes through the same process of building the trees of our mind. So saying something positive will construct a healthy brain dendrite. There is a constant conversation going on in our mind body connection. There is a whole symphony of electromagnetic chemicals moving through our body. Your chemical factory will translate your thought life into a physical state. All the appropriate physical changes were taking place as they began to "call things that be not as though they were" and what they had conceived in their image center was then conceived in Sarah's womb!

Abraham did this again in Gen 22: 5: *"And Abraham said unto his young men, 'Abide ye here with the ass; and I and the lad will go yonder and worship, and come again to you.'"*

As soon as God told Abraham to sacrifice his son he immediately went to work on a new image. The same way his son was conceived was going to be the same way his son would rise from the dead. He got an image of returning with his son and he said so.

The book of Hebrews tells us in Chapter 11:

> **17** By faith Abraham, when he was tried, offered up Isaac: and he that had received the promises offered up his only begotten son. **18** Of whom it was said, That in Isaac shall thy seed be called: **19** Accounting that God was able to raise him up, even from the dead; from whence also he received him in a figure.

Abraham had a vision through an inner image. Scripture says, *"He received Isaac raised from the dead in a figure."* Abraham knew how to create an image for faith to fill.

Similarly, when we want to build a house, we order blueprints and then follow those images to build our house. Abraham had an image of returning with his son. God taught him how to use his image center to create a blueprint and then use his words to declare it to BE.

As men and women of God, we must develop an inner image, a blueprint of who we are in Christ. Allow that image to become grafted in our soul and change our name. Begin "calling things that be not as though they were" in our lives, having developed fully persuaded faith that staggers not at the promises of God. This way we may be established in righteousness.

See how the law of thought works both physically and spiritually throughout the Bible. The Lord told Moses to send a leader from each tribe to search the land of Canaan. Moses sent out the twelve men to spy out the promised land. They saw a land that flowed with milk and honey. They also saw walled cities, and men of great stature. When they returned, Caleb said, *"let us go up at once, and possess it; for we are well able to overcome it."* No thorns on those dendrites! The other men brought up an evil report saying, *"...we were in our own sight as grasshoppers, and so we were in their sight."* - Numbers 13: 30-33

Caleb's image was, "we are well able;" the other men, "we are as grasshoppers." The fact that the majority of the men saw themselves as grasshoppers and assumed that the people of Canaan saw them as grasshoppers as well, prevented them from receiving the promises of God. Had they gone to overtake the land with that thorny mentality they would have been destroyed. God had to wait for that generation to die off before giv-

136

ing them this opportunity again. Too often as believers we have been more like the spies with the evil report and we have failed to receive because of it. Our image center is not to be used for imagining worry and fearful thoughts.

If you don't like where you are in your life I suggest you start working on your dendrite blueprint and begin to see yourself in light of the Word of God. Then nothing will be restrained from you and nothing shall be impossible for you. You can make your way prosperous and have good success!

I can tell you these things but you have to be willing to do them. What if the doctor gives you a bad report? Do you come into agreement with that word and begin using your image center to enforce fear and continue to create the illness? Or do you take the Word of God that says in 1 Peter 2:24, *"by whose stripes ye were healed"* and start working on a blueprint for healing?

If you are experiencing health issues, I would like to remind you what I quoted earlier from Dr. Leaf. She said, "What you think affects your whole body; 87% of mental and physical illness that we experience comes from our thought life. There is a constant conversation going on in our mind body connection."

I suggest you start using your image center and the authority in your words to change the structure of your brain and begin to heal. If you have seen something bad in your image center that doesn't mean that you have to give birth to it. You can change your thoughts, removing the thorns. You can break the power of the wrong words you have spoken and begin meditating on the promises and provisions of God through His Word.

Just like as an architect makes time to go into the office to draw blueprints, you need to be the architect of your life, devoting your time to creating an image that is in agreement with the Word of God. Then this is all you should do, all you should see and all you should say until the image of the Word becomes grafted in the neuro-networks of your mind and becomes more real to you than your present situation or circumstance.

What you are seeing is what you will be doing because that is what is impregnated in you. So what are you seeing? What is your vision?

How to constructively use our image center is something that the enemy never wanted us to know. This is how he has gotten our authority over the earth and used it to prosper the kingdom of darkness. I encourage you to begin using your mouth as an instrument of life and use it to surround your loved ones with life and blessings, regardless of what you see them doing. What really matters is what you see in your image center and what you create with your words.

Let me ask you, is the enemy your god? Then why should you have to receive from him? Jesus said, *"I am the good shepherd; and I know my sheep, and am known by my own.... And the voice of a stranger they will not know or follow"* - John 10:14, 5. Say this out loud right now, "Devil, you are not my god and I refuse to receive from you any longer! I refuse to believe wrong thoughts; I refuse to say wrong words. I choose to change the blueprint of my mind!"

THE WORD OF GOD IS ALIVE WITH CREATIVE POWER ENFORCING THE RESULT FOR WHICH IT WAS SENT!

Isaiah 55:11 is one of my favorite scriptures on the power of the Word of God. It says, *"So shall my word be that goeth forth out of my mouth: it shall not return unto me void (empty, ineffectual), but it shall accomplish (create) that which I please, and it shall prosper in the thing whereto I sent it."*

Jeremiah 1:9,10,12 confirms Isaiah by saying, *"Then the LORD put forth his hand, and touched my mouth. And the LORD said unto me, Behold, I have put my words in thy mouth. See, I have this day set thee over the nations and over the kingdoms (of darkness), to root out, pull down, and destroy, to build, and to plant (the Kingdom of God) for I will hasten (watch over) my word (coming out of your mouth) to perform it."*

This is how I learned to pray. I understood that we are to destroy the workings of the kingdom of darkness in the earth and we are to build the

Kingdom of God by using the Word of God. Like I said in the chapter on Strongholds, the course of this world, where sin, sickness and curses flow, has carried our lives in the natural direction of the kingdom of darkness. That is the whirlpool effect.

Jesus came preaching, *"...the Kingdom of God is at hand"* - Mark 1:15. He also said that, *"...the kingdom of heaven suffereth violence and the violent take it by force"* - Matthew 11:12. Jesus brought us the Kingdom of God and it is suffering violence here on the earth. The Greek tells us that means a forceful pressure is coming against it, i.e. - the flow of that whirlpool.

However, we as believers have the ability to overcome the kingdom of darkness in our lives by being violent and forceful ourselves. We are to press against that whirlpool pressure by going in another direction.

We do this by first meditating on the Word for our situation. This will create an inner image and blueprint of who we are in Christ and change the dendrite structure of our minds. We will know what our covenant provisions are and create a new nerve pathway. Then we can begin "calling things that be not as though they were" by praying the Word of God. This will cause us to rise up with violent faith that roots out, pulls down and destroys the workings of darkness, and establishes the Kingdom of God in every area of our life. The Word of God will not return unto us void (empty, ineffectual), but it shall accomplish (create) that which we please, and it shall prosper in the thing whereto we sent it." The Word of God is alive with creative power enforcing the result for which it was sent!

BE IT UNTO ME ACCORDING TO THY WORD

L uke 1:30-38,

30 *And the angel said unto her, 'Fear not, Mary: for thou hast found favor with God.*
31 *And, behold, thou shalt conceive in thy womb, and bring forth a son, and shalt call his name JESUS...'*

34 *Then said Mary unto the angel, 'How shall this be, seeing I know not a man?'*

35 *And the angel answered and said unto her…*

37 *(from the Amplified Bible) 'For with God nothing is ever impossible and no Word from God shall be without power or impossible of fulfillment.'*

38 *And Mary said, 'Behold the handmaid of the Lord; be it unto me according to Thy word.'*

Like Mary, our faith must speak and come into agreement with the Word of God. When it does, then *"No Word from God shall be without power or impossible of fulfillment,"* - Luke 1:37.

The Word of God, which is a seed, can be lodged in the womb of our spirit. Once it enters, the eyes of our understanding will become enlightened, the *rhema* / spoken word becomes logical / a *logos* word full of revelation. Conception will take place and we will be pregnant with the image of that Word. If we will hold fast to that Word, it will become flesh and dwell among us and a miracle will be born - John 1:14.

Conception always starts on the inside. Likewise, once we have a vision of who we are in Christ, no circumstance can tear us down. Once we plant the Word in the womb of our spirit, we should never allow anything to remove it.

Jesus warned us in Mark 4:15 that the enemy would try to steal the Word that was sown in our heart. The enemy's tactic is to get other people to push our *psuche* buttons thereby ending the process of its work within us.

We have all seen a cartoon or picture of a person with a good angel on one shoulder and a bad angel on the other. That is an image that will help you to understand what is happening in the spirit realm so that you can make a clear choice in which direction you should be going.

If we yield to the enemy's tactics instead of holding fast to God's Word, then we have just allowed him to perform a spiritual abortion. When we find ourselves under emotional heartache or attack that is when we must press harder against the circumstance by keeping God's Word before our eyes and ears and coming out of our mouth. The image of what the Word says about us must become more real in our spirit, more real than any circumstance in our life or any filter on our soul.

THE WORDS OF THE SONS OF GOD

(That's us!)

In Genesis Chapter One, verses 1,3,31 say: **1** *"In the beginning God created the heaven and the earth."* **3** *"And God said, 'Let there be light:' and there was light."* (Nine times God spoke something into existence.) **31** *And God saw every thing that He had made, and, behold, it was very good...*

God saw everything He made because what He said MANIFESTED! In Genesis 1:26 He continued creating: *"And God said, 'Let us make man in our image after our likeness: and let them have dominion...'"*

God said, *"...man in Our Image..."* we know that within every seed there is a blueprint to produce after its own kind. We were produced by the incorruptible seed of the word of God. We were made in His image and likeness with a spoken word.

Just as there is creative (active, operative, effectual) power in God's Word, because we are made in His image and likeness there is creative (active, operative, effectual) power in our words as well.

God told Adam to subdue and have dominion over the earth. Who was in the earth that Adam had to subdue and dominate? Satan. God gave Adam His Word to dominate Satan and his kingdom. It was all he needed.

The words *subdue* and have *dominion* mean to have supreme sovereign authority, to rule over, to tread down, to conquer by force, to prevail against, and bring into subjection by superior power. This is who we were created to be in His image and likeness and what we were created to do!

Satan has no creative power within himself. He saw that Adam was created in God's image and likeness with the same authority to rule, and the same creative power in his words that the Father has.

Satan knew he had to get Adam's God-given creative authority over the earth and be the source of man's influence to perpetuate the kingdom of darkness in the earth. Unfortunately for the whole human race, Satan was successful at this when he got Adam to switch lords in the Garden of Eden.

At that point, the soul of man became independent of the spirit and the influence of God and became infected with the sin nature. In order for the kingdom of darkness to operate in the earth, all the enemy has to do is make suggestions to our minds.

As soon as we accept or come into agreement with his suggestion then the image center of our soul will begin to develop it, then what do we do? We speak it using our God given creative (active, operative, effectual) power and authority to speak and we have perpetuated the kingdom of darkness.

Deuteronomy 30:19 says, *"I call heaven and earth to record this day against you, that I have set before you life and death, blessing and cursing: therefore choose life, that both thou and thy seed may live:..."* We can see that our words activate life or death blessings or curses and they affect us and our seed.

Proverbs 18:21 agrees with Deuteronomy, saying, *"Death and life are in the power of the tongue: and they that love it shall eat the fruit thereof."*

Paul showed us exactly how to overcome the cycle of death and cursing, when he revealed that operating the law of the Spirit of life in Christ Jesus (from our spirit), would make us free (from perpetuating) the law of sin and death (with our words) - Romans 8:2.

We know that there are two kingdoms operating in this earth envelope; I want you to see that what we do with our mind and mouth determines which of these two kingdoms we agree to give our creative authority.

Matthew 6:25,27,31: Jesus said, *"Therefore I say unto you, Take no thought for your life / psuche, what ye shall eat, or what ye shall drink; nor yet for your body, what ye shall put on. And who of you, by worrying and being anxious, can add one unit of measure to his stature or to the span of his life? Therefore take no thought, saying..."*

142

As soon as we 'take the thought' of worry or fear and accept what the enemy has suggested to our thought life a dendrite thorn and inner image is created, then we confess it with our mouth. That is why Jesus said here, 'don't take the thought and say it.' Satan has gotten us to use our God-given authority to imagine, and speak words. In our ignorance, the words we have been speaking have perpetuated the kingdom of darkness, not only in our physical life but in the earth.

- Your thoughts determine your emotions.

- Your emotions determine your actions.

- Your actions determine your behavior and habits.

- Your behaviors and habits determine your character.

- Your character determines your destiny.

And it all started with a thought that you authorized.

When we speak words that are not in agreement with the Word of God, demons hear those words of darkness and quickly go to work to bring them to pass. Instead of using the spiritual law of words to dominate him, we have allowed Satan to use our words to dominate us.

When we speak we have just placed an order, whether for good or bad. Right words obligate Jesus as our High Priest to bring those words to pass - Hebrews 3:1. Wrong words authorize the kingdom of darkness - Deuteronomy 30:19, Proverbs 18:21.

James 3:3-6 is a great illustration of how this works; it says, *"Behold, we put bits in the horses' mouths, that they may obey us; and we turn about their whole body. Behold also the ships, which though they be so great, and are driven of fierce winds, yet are they turned about with a very small helm, withersoever the governor listeth. Even so the tongue is a little member, and boasteth great things. Behold, how great a matter a little fire kindleth! And the tongue is a fire, a world of iniquity: so is the tongue among our members, that it defileth the whole body, and setteth on fire the course of nature; and it is set on fire of hell."*

In Verse 3, James is equating the bit in the mouth of a horse with the tongue in the mouth of a man as a means of turning of the body. He is saying that if we can control our tongue, we can take words and control not only our whole body, but the course our life will naturally take! Did you get that? We can take words and control our body but it all starts with a thought!

Neurologists say that the speech center in our brain has dominion over the central nervous system as well as the whole body. For instance, when you say, "I am weak" all the chemicals in the body adjust themselves to weakness. What would happen if we began saying, "I am strong in the Lord and the power of His might?" This is why *as a man thinketh in his heart, so is he:"* - Prov 23:7. Medical science is proving the Bible!

Right now we all are living in the 'course' our thoughts and mouth have taken us naturally. Look how great a matter a little fire of some wrong thoughts and words has kindled in our life. This law of words is a spiritual law and it works for whosoever will put it to work. Remember that words are vibrations and have frequencies. As we hear them, sound waves get converted into electricity and reinforce the whole creative process.

In Verse 4 it goes on to say that it doesn't matter how big the ship or the storm, the rudder will turn the ship, but it's "whithersoever the governor listeth." We are going to have to make a quality decision to be the governor over our tongue which is the spiritual rudder of our life, or we will never be able to weather a storm!

In Matthew 12:33-35 Jesus was teaching that we *"either make the tree good, and his fruit good; or else make the tree corrupt, and his fruit corrupt: for the tree is known by his fruit. O generation of vipers, how can ye, being evil, speak good things? For out of the abundance of the heart (what you think and imagine) the mouth speaketh. A good man out of the good treasure of the heart (of his image center) bringeth forth good things: and an evil man out of the evil treasure (of his image center) bringeth forth evil things. "*

Did you notice who Jesus said causes the manifestation of good or evil to be brought forth in our life? We do. What we say "bringeth forth" good or evil. Whether good or evil comes out of our mouth, they both get results. We are either being influenced by the kingdom of darkness and the world around us; or, if we have been abiding in the Word, we are being influenced by the Kingdom of God. When we agree with thoughts from either kingdom and speak them, we have authorized them to be established. We have just placed our order!

The enemy knows that his ability is limited as to what he can get us to agree with and authorize with our words. Now we can't keep thoughts from coming, but if we don't speak them, they die un-born. Dr. Leaf says, "the wrong thoughts that you reject get released as heat energy or hot air out of our bodies." This is when it would be ok to be full of hot air! Out of the good treasure of our heart we bring forth good things. We can create a different and better environment and world around us by using our image center in alignment with the Word of God and speaking faith filled words.

Dr. Masaru Emoto is a Japanese author and entrepreneur known for his claim that if human speech or thoughts are directed at water droplets before they are frozen, images of the resulting water crystals will be "beautiful" or "ugly" depending upon whether the words or thoughts were positive or negative. Emoto claims this can be achieved through prayer, music or by attaching written words to a container of water. Since 1999 Emoto has published several volumes of a work titled *Messages from Water*, which contains photographs of water crystals next to essays and "words of intent." If you go to youtube.com you can view many of Dr. Emoto's experiments.

I did one of Dr. Emoto's experiments myself. I placed the same amounts of cooked white rice in jars and sealed them. On one jar I placed a label that said life. On the other jar I placed a label that said death. I kept the jars on the island in my kitchen. Several times a day for thirty days I would pick the jars up and speak to the rice. To the jar I labeled life I would say, "I speak life to you, I love you, you're beautiful, you will live long and prosper." To the jar I labeled death I would say, "I hate you, die, I curse you, you're ugly, rot, grow mold, you're worthless." I took pictures of the jars and recorded the process. By day eleven the jar labeled death began to turn brown and develop black mold spots. The jar I labeled life was still white and fluffy. By day fourteen the jar labeled death was getting darker brown and growing mold fur all over. The jar labeled life was still white and fluffy. At the end of thirty days the jar labeled death was completely brown and moldy. The jar labeled life was just beginning to look a little tan in color.

This experiment only reinforced my belief in the Scriptures regarding the authority of the believer and the power of our thoughts and words. To the friends and family that visited my house and saw the changes in the jars, it made believers out of them! I highly suggest using these experiments to teach your children.

Romans 10:10 is another great example; it says, *"For with the heart man believeth unto righteousness; and with the mouth confession is made unto salvation."*

It is a spiritual law that with the heart man believes or imagines either righteous or unrighteous thoughts; then with the mouth he confesses what he has imagined and those words will make or create just what he has spoken. Your mind and your mouth work together to create either kingdom.

Let's dissect Romans 10:10. The Greek word for salvation is *soteria* and it literally means - healing, deliverance, prosperity, soundness, protection, preservation from danger, rescue, safety, wholeness.

The Greek word for confession is *homo-loge* - Homo means the same as. Logos means logical, to hold or say the same thing.

So what Romans 10:10 is saying is that with the heart man believeth (uses his image center) unto righteousness; with the mouth *confession makes* our healing, deliverance, prosperity, soundness, protection, preservation from danger, rescue, safety, wholeness.

With righteousness as our blueprint and God's word being authored from our mouth, what we say will not return unto us void (empty, ineffectual), but it shall accomplish (create) that which we please, and it shall prosper in the thing whereto we sent it – Isaiah 55:11. What we believe and confess makes our provision according to Romans 10:10. This is a spiritual law that can change the course your life has naturally taken, as well as heal your body. Oh God is so good!

Who will we employ with our words? It will either be the Kingdom of God or the kingdom of darkness. Whether you believe it or not, there is power in your words and they have no expiration date; they are in operation until you break their power.

Jesus said, *"For verily I say unto you, that whosoever shall say unto this mountain, be thou removed, and be thou cast into the sea; and shall not doubt in his heart, but shall believe that those things which he saith shall come to pass; he shall have whatsoever he saith."* - Mark 11:23 Jesus Himself said that we have what we say.

ANGELS AND DEMONS GET THEIR MARCHING ORDERS FROM OUR WORDS

Hebrews 1:13,14 says, *"But to which of the angels said he at any time, Sit on my right hand, until I make thine enemies thy footstool? Are they not all ministering spirits, sent forth to minister for them who shall be heirs of salvation?"*

Psalm 103:20-21 says, *"Bless the LORD, ye His angels, that excel in strength, that do His commandments, hearkening (responding, obeying) unto the voice of His word. Bless ye the LORD, all ye His hosts ye ministers of His, that do His pleasure."*

Angels are ministering spirits that have been sent forth to minister on our behalf. They do His commandments; they hear, respond and obey the voice of His Word coming out of our mouth! Our responsibility is to frame our life with the Word of God and the Angels were created to obey that word. So speaking God's Word employs angels to bring that Word to pass.

Since this is a spiritual law, the law of reciprocals must be applied. Speaking the words of the god of this world employs demons to bring that word to pass.

This confirms what Deuteronomy 30:19 and Proverbs 18:21 say; that life and death, blessing and cursing are in the power of the tongue: and they that love it shall eat the fruit thereof. When we speak, we give our God-given authority to create either to the Kingdom of God or to the kingdom of darkness.

WE ARE KINGS AND PRIESTS HOLDING COURT!
WHO WILL WE EMPLOY WITH OUR WORDS?

Think of it this way, we are a King on this earth with God-given authority and we are holding court. The angels of God are on one side and demons are on the other side. They are all looking at us waiting for their marching orders. Those orders for life or death, blessings or curses come out of our mouth!

Let's look at Isaiah 54:17. In the course of teaching all about our covenant provisions it says that, *"No weapon that is formed against thee shall prosper; and every tongue that shall rise against thee in judgment (to pass sentence) thou shalt condemn (declare to be wrong). This is the heritage of the servants of the LORD, and their righteousness is of Me, saith the LORD."*

We have been learning that words have power, and they are active, operative, effectual to work, full of energy, and they come to pass. Wrong words come to pass as a weapon formed, whether we spoke them or someone else spoke them against us. Weapons will be formed, but they don't have to prosper.

Words which are formed or spoken rise against us in judgment. That judgment can either be exercising the law of life and producing the blessing or exercising the law of sin and death and producing the curse.

We all have a life time of speaking wrong words, to our kids, our spouse and each other. Remember it is what we have believed that has caused an inner image. We have agreed with that image and then we speak it.

Dr. Phil says it takes five hundred 'good girl' or 'good boy' praises to undo the damage of one negative comment made to someone.

In every situation we have the power to decide what we will think. What you say to yourself in your own mind is just as powerful as what you speak. For out of the abundance of your heart (your image center) your mouth speaks.

What do you say to yourself? Do you tell yourself that nothing ever works out for you? Do you say, "I can't do anything right" or "I am so stupid?"

Even if you hold your tongue and don't say it you are doing immeasurable damage by believing the lie and allowing it to shape your image center.

We need to monitor our thought life and the way we talk to ourselves as carefully as we monitor the words we speak out loud. A negative thought pattern will lead to a negative attitude, which leads to negative speaking, which leads to a negative, defeated life. The more you dwell on the negative, the bigger it becomes, even if you don't want it to, because you already set your blueprint for the course your life will naturally take. You can change that pattern right now by making a quality decision to refuse to focus on the negative and begin to take your thoughts captive.

I Peter 3:10 says, *"For he that will love life, and see good days, let him refrain his tongue from evil, and his lips that they speak no guile;..."*

Now don't get scared about all your wrong thoughts and words. Isaiah 54:17 said, every tongue that rises against us in judgment, to pass sentence on us, we have the authority to condemn. This means we can declare that word empty and powerless over us. This is a part of our covenant heritage.

I know that we all have an image center that has been defiled; so we get a lot of thoughts that are not good. We cannot keep thoughts from coming, but we can refuse to come into agreement with them and we can refuse to say them. If you don't agree with them and speak them they will die unborn.

INNER VOWS

Vows can be either positive, like marriage vows, or negative. It is the negative vows that open the door for the enemy in our lives and bind our souls. People make vows in an effort to either set up self-protective boundaries or because of a judgment we have placed on ourselves or someone else. We say things like I wish I were dead, I will never forget or I will never do this or that, they will never change, I will never lose weight, I will never make any more money than this...., etc. Once in place we have employed the kingdom of darkness, and the vow hinders God from being able to move in that area of our lives.

In the chapter on Strongholds we discussed vows. Numbers Chapter 30 describes vows in great detail for us. I suggest reading the chapter for yourself right now. What we can see in this chapter is that when we vow a vow, we bind our soul and that vow can be forever established in our lives. If vows are not broken, we will bear the iniquity of them.

If we make a negative vow, or we hear someone else make a negative voe, words have been spoken authorizing the kingdom of darkness to steal, kill and destroy in our lives. In both cases we have the responsibility as well as the authority to overrule, disallow and break the power of destructive vows.

At this point I think we should stop and pray to break the power of wrong words and vows.

PRAYER

Father, I am so grateful that You created me in Your image and likeness; so that I too have the power to create with my words and all of heaven backs up the right words that I speak.

Father, my ignorance has caused me to use my image center and my words incorrectly, thereby enforcing the kingdom of darkness to work against me. I come out of agreement with every wrong thought, vain imagination and vow that has bound my soul. I ask You to forgive me and cleanse me from the defilement of these wrong thoughts, words and destructive vows.

I stand on Isaiah 54:17 and declare that no weapon formed against me shall prosper and every tongue that has risen against me in judgment, even my own words in ignorance, I condemn. I break the power of all these wrong words.

I bind every evil spirit that has been empowered by these wrong thoughts, words and vows. I cancel their assignment against me in Jesus' name.

Father, I choose to have my image center be in alignment with the mind of Christ. I am Your sheep and I hear Your voice and the voice of a stranger I will not know or follow. I want to see through Your eyes and hear what Your Spirit is saying to me. I choose to think righteous thoughts and speak right words. Thank You Lord for the ministry of angels that have been given to enforce those words, establishing my covenant of peace. Thy Kingdom come on earth as it is in heaven.

THE HOLY SPIRIT'S WORDS

As we begin to look at the Holy Spirit's words in the eighth chapter of Romans, I suggest that you go read the whole chapter in your Bible first. As you will see, the whole chapter is the Apostle Paul talking about our walk in the spirit versus our walk in the flesh / soul and the struggle it creates for the child of God. I want to pick up Paul's discourse in verse 26 as Paul begins talking about how to pray through this spirit / flesh (soul) struggle.

Romans 8:26-28:

> **26** *Likewise **the Spirit** also helpeth (Greek - takes hold together with us against) our infirmities (**comes to our aid** and bears us up in our weakness): **for we know not what we should pray for as we ought (in our soul / mind): but** the Spirit itself maketh intercession for us with groanings (unspeakable yearnings and groanings too deep for utterance) which cannot be uttered..*
> **27** *And He that searcheth the hearts knoweth what is the mind of **the Spirit** (what His intent is), because He **maketh intercession for the saints according to the will of God.***
> **28** ***And we** know **(are assured** that God being a partner in their labor) **that all things (we just prayed out in the spirit) work together (and are fitting into a plan) for good** to them that love God, to them who are the called **according to his purpose.** (KJV and Amplified Bible combined.)*

Did you notice that some of the words above are in bold text? The reason for that is to help you see the content better. In class I have my students go back with me and we read just the bold text out loud. For the reader I am going to rewrite just the bold text, so you can see where I am taking you.

The Spirit comes to our aid, for we know not what we should pray for as we ought (in our soul / mind); but the Spirit maketh intercession for the saints according to the will of God. And we are assured that all things we just prayed out in the spirit work together and are fitting into a plan for good, according to His purpose.

ALL THINGS WORK TOGETHER FOR GOOD

In an attempt to bring comfort I have often heard Christians say, "All things work together for good." Perhaps you have used this scripture that way as well. I want to put this verse in proper context for you.

Paul was saying in your area of weakness when you don't know how to pray, *"The Holy Spirit comes to our aid He takes hold together with us and bears us up in our weakness. For we do not know what prayer to offer or how to offer it worthily as we ought. But the Spirit Himself goes to meet our supplication and pleads on our behalf with unspeakable yearnings and groanings too deep for utterance."*

He who searches the hearts knows what is in the mind of the Spirit and what His intent is. The Holy Spirit intercedes and pleads before God on behalf of the saints according to and in harmony with God's will. So we can be assured and know that God being a partner in our labor *"all things that we just prayed out in the Holy Spirit are fitting into a plan for good"* for those who love God and are called according to His purpose.

Can you see in context that Paul is not saying that 'all things' ie, all bad things, all difficult situations, all evil that comes your way, will work together for your good. No. He said all things that we prayed out in the spirit will work together for good. That is quite different from the way I hear people minister this scripture.

I know we were raised in our Christianity hearing this passage misused. What I have come to understand is that we hear so many scriptures being misquoted that it confuses our belief systems about God. I like to line up what we believe with what the Word of God actually says, instead of what we hear others say.

Did Adam handing over the earth to Satan work for good? NO! God intended earth to be like heaven. There are millions in hell today, that was not the will of God and it certainly hasn't worked out for their good. Do murder, hate, and violence work together for anyone's good? No. Millions live in peril, heartache and pain never finding any freedom. So then, we cannot rightly say, "all things" work together for good because clearly "all things" don't.

If I think about my life and all I have gone through; the wrong decisions and bad choices, they did great damage to my soul. It has taken years to undo that damage in me, none of it has worked for my good. None of it was the plan of God for me. In fact God's will for me was to make right choices so I wouldn't have had to reap the harvest that I did.

It has been a manifestation of the curse that mankind has had to learn the hard way. This was never God's designed method of child rearing. That is why we try so hard to protect our children from learning the hard way as well.

It is imperative that we understand this spiritual law, *"Be not deceived; God is not mocked: for whatsoever a man soweth, that shall he also reap. For he that soweth to his flesh shall of the flesh reap corruption; but he that soweth to the Spirit shall of the Spirit reap life everlasting."* - Galatians 6:7-8

With divorce running in my family, my parent's divorce and ultimately my divorce came as a result of sowing wrong thoughts and reaping a failed relationship. None of these divorces have worked together for good for any of us, they were all painful and devastating for everyone involved. They left scars that have effected four generations, many of which still need healing. The forces of a spiritual law had been set in motion and once in motion continued until I learned how to stop it.

There is a better way in which we as Christians can describe the Lord's redemptive, restorative ability and it is this: in every wrong choice we have made, in every bad thing that we have ever gone through, God knows how to re-weave every situation, deliver and heal us from them all!

In Genesis 50: 19-20 it says, *"And Joseph said unto them, Fear not: for am I in the place of God? But as for you, ye thought evil against me; but God meant it unto good, to bring to pass, as it is this day, to save much people alive."* The word *mean*t means – to weave like a fabric. It was not implying God's intent for evil against Joseph in order to bring about good. God, through foreknowledge, knows every right and wrong decision we will make. He knew that Joseph would end up in Egypt. The scripture is showing us that even though Joseph went through hard times because of seeds sown, God was able to re-weave Joseph's situation and use it to bless many people.

When we read this passage of scripture, to the soulish ear it does sound like God meant for evil to happen for Joseph's good. However that is not what this scripture is saying. This is why we need to rightly divide the Word of Truth.

What you need to understand is, not every abuse we have suffered or every loss in our life will work for our good. No! Those painful things that happened to us were not the will of God, nor were they by the hand of God. The painful things that we have been through hurt us, many who go through pain like this never recover and the damaging affects go on to defile generations, none of which was ever God's plan. These are all manifestations of the curse.

However, if we will look to the Lord for our 'answer', God can take the tattered fabric of our life and re-weave it into a beautiful tapestry. You can find yourself healed from your past and even using those experiences to minister to others.

The next time you hear someone say, don't worry, *"all things work together for good"* or *"God meant it for good"* please don't feel that you need to correct them, unless they are teachable, of course. I went through this lengthy clarification for your sake, so none of these belief systems would hinder your freedom. Scripture tells us to *"Study to show thyself approved unto God, a workman that needeth not to be ashamed, rightly dividing the word of truth."* - II Timothy 2:15

Understand that if you can rightly divide the Word you can also wrongly divide it. And unfortunately we have had people use scripture incorrectly to minister to us, leaving us with incorrect thinking about who God is and why 'things happen.' I suggest you take what you hear people say about God and line it up with the spiritual laws you are learning and what the Word of God is actually saying. People have come to these inaccurate conclusions by trying to understand God in light of their circumstances. We should be understanding our circumstances in light of the Word of God, His truths and spiritual laws. Once you do, everything will make sense.

These were important scriptures for me to clarify. I need you to see the context of where I am taking you, so you can understand the Words of the Holy Spirit.

Going back to what Paul was saying in Romans 8:26-28, in your area of weakness, when you don't know how to pray *"the Spirit comes to our aid for we know not what we should pray for as we ought in our soul / mind, but the Spirit maketh intercession for us according to the will of God. And we are assured that all things we just prayed out in the spirit are fitting into a plan for good according to his purpose."*

I want to add another scripture to this foundation from I Corinthians 14:2; it says, *"For **he that speaketh in an unknown tongue speaketh** not unto men, but **unto God**: for no man understandeth Him; howbeit **in the spirit he speaketh mysteries.**"*

Again I am going to rewrite just the bold text for you. *"**He that speaketh in an unknown tongue speaketh unto God, in the spirit he speaketh mysteries.**"*

What I want you to see is that according to I Corinthians 14:2 and Romans 8:27, when we speak or pray in the Spirit, in other tongues, with yearnings and groanings too deep for utterance, we are speaking directly to God and we are praying the perfect will of God.

Did you get that? Praying in the spirit is praying *"the perfect will of God!"* Wow! Have you ever wanted to know the perfect will of God, especially in a difficult situation? Sometimes we just don't know how to pray. Praying in the spirit is *The Answer*!

Anything beyond what we can comprehend has naturally been a mystery to us. We all have been limited as to what we can understand due to the issues and limitations of the soul.

Do you realize that *The Answer* for every situation, circumstance, and trouble in our life is a mystery to us? It is above what any of us can ask or think to pray. So just think, no limits would exist in our life if we knew how to pray out the mysteries.

How can God heal your broken heart, bring life to a dead relationship, increase your income, reach your children, save your entire family? These are all mysteries to you.

MOST HOLY FAITH

I want to add another scripture to this foundation and that is Jude verse 20 it says, *"But ye, beloved, building up yourselves on your most holy faith, praying in the Holy Ghost."*

God calls praying in the Spirit our most holy faith because it is the Holy Spirit Himself that is praying through us. The Holy Spirit knows how to make intercession for the saints according to the will of God. He is our Comforter, Counselor, Helper, Advocate, Intercessor, Strengthener and Standby – Romans 8:27; John 16:7 (Amplified Bible.)

The word *Holy* means – something that is set apart, consecrated, sacred, not to be defiled.

The reason Jude is calling it our most holy faith is because our limited soulish thinking is not able to contaminate or defile it. If we knew what we were saying, our soul could rise up with doubt and unbelief and hinder the perfect will of God from being manifested in our lives and in the earth.

The Holy Spirit knows and speaks the mind, of the Father and the Son. Praying in the Spirit bypasses our rational mind, prevents it from defiling righteous thoughts and communicates directly with our spirit, thereby making it most holy - I Corinthians 2:11.

I want to share one of my testimonies with you of how this has worked for me. Years ago we lived in a house right across the street from our church. I loved that house, but I also had desires for a home that could not be met there. Mark wanted land, privacy and barns. I wanted to stay in the same neighborhood where I was centrally located near church, shopping and my family.

We would often pray for financial increase and talk about the home we imagined. Every week I would get out the John Deere tractor and cut the grass. We had an acre of land and it would take me a good hour to circle the house on that tractor. For ten years I would use that time to pray. As I was circling the house I would pray in other tongues, believing God for things that were above what I could ask or think.

In January of 1999 I went to Kenneth Copeland's Ministers conference. Kenneth and Gloria are my spiritual parents and I have grown tremendously from my relationship with them. That year, there was a special offering for Kenneth and Gloria, and those who wanted to could bless them for all they had imparted into our lives. I couldn't wait to sow. I grabbed a hundred dollar bill, which was a huge offering for me to sow. I went up to Kenneth and said to him, "my prosperity has come out of your mouth." As I walked back to my seat, I named that seed for my house.

In May of 1999 I sowed another hundred dollar seed to my Pastor, still believing for my house. The next day I went to a prayer meeting at church and when I got home Mark said to me, "You better sit down." He said a realtor had come to the door telling us that someone wanted to buy our house to access the land behind us. They were offering us twice what we paid for our home. Our house was not on the market! The realtor gave us a two thousand dollar bonus check, we signed the papers and the ball was rolling. He said we would close in November of that year. November came and went and we never heard from that realtor. I was disappointed but I thought 'Well Lord, you blessed us with two thousand dollars.' It's not every day a stranger knocks on your door and gives you two thousand dollars. I kept praying in the spirit about this situation, which was the only way I could pray because it was completely above what I could ask or think with my natural mind.

Eleven months later in October of 2000 that realtor knocked on the door again. He presented us with another offer on the house and this time gave us another bonus check for two thousand dollars. He said we would close in April of 2001, we signed the papers and the ball was rolling again. April came and went and we never heard from that realtor again. I was disappointed but I kept praying. There was no way I could pray this situation out in my understanding, tongues was the only prayer that could handle it.

On December 23rd 2001 I had a dream about a realtor coming and wanting to buy the house again. Three days later the realtor called and said, "The deal is back on and they want to close in February 2002." Again they gave us our third two thousand dollar bonus check.

This time, we did in fact close on February 2, 2002, the date was 02/02/02! We didn't have to move out of our house yet or pay any rent until September of 2002, we lived in the house seven months rent free. This whole ime Mark and I had discussed that we would pick the house up and move it to the vacant lot across the street right next to our church. In March as we made plans to do so every door was shut on us.

I was really upset, now where were we going to live? I did not want to leave my neighborhood. Mark did not want to live on a tract. He said if we have to buy another house, he wanted an empty one that we could gut. He wanted to strip our house of all the new doors and windows we had put in and use them in another house. After all, they were going to tear our house down if we didn't move it. That night at midnight I was on the internet and found a house that fit both our needs and it was less than a mile down the road. The next day I drove to see it. It was empty; what were the chances of that!

We got in to see the house and it was in really bad shape. But we had great vision; we knew exactly how to tear down the walls down and re-shape the house to be our dream home. We brought all our family through the house and they thought we were nuts. They could not see our inner image or share in our vision, but we had a blueprint in our minds. We drew it out on paper and knew exactly what we wanted to do. The asking price on the house was $140,000. It had 1½ acres of land that backed to woods, two barns, a four car garage, a shed and a greenhouse. Mark's dream! Once gutted and re-built it would be my dream too. The house was empty because the owner had accepted a deal for the full asking price, purchased another house and moved a great distance away.

Then his deal fell through and he was stuck with two houses. So we came in with an offer of $95,000 and he rejected it. What? Rejected it! Oh no, now what were we going to do? We had to move in six months. So we continued to pray and look for the house God wanted us to have. I gave this completely over to the Lord, I had gotten my hopes up and I was very disappointed but He didn't bring us this far to let us down, I knew He had a plan. But that plan was really above what I could ask or think. It was a mystery to me how any of this was happening. The next day I called the realtor and asked her to show us more houses. She called the owner back and told him we were moving on and there wasn't going to be a counter offer on our part, so then he decided to accept our offer!

Let me tell you, there was an anointing on us to work all day, and come to the new house and work at night. We literally had twenty weeks to de-construct our old house and re-construct our new house using those items, all the while living in the house we were tearing apart. We moved into our new home in September of 2002!

Now I said all of that to say this: do you think I could have prayed any of that out in my own understanding? What if, while I was driving that tractor around my house across from the church I began praying, "Lord, will you send a realtor to my door and have him give me a two thousand dollar bonus to sell my house at twice its value? Then will you let the deal fall through twice so he has to come back and give me a total of six thousand dollars just in bonuses? Or, what if I prayed, Lord, will you send someone to offer the asking price on the house we want to buy so that owner will move away? Can the house be sitting empty so we can gut it and remodel it before we move in? Then will you make the deal fall through so we can by the house at a much lower price?

You know, this was above what I could ask or think in prayer. It was a mystery how God was going to fulfill our inner image and blueprint for the home we wanted with all our desires of location, privacy, barns and land. If I had tried to pray any of this out in my understanding, doubt and unbelief would have risen up and defiled my faith.

This is why Jude called it praying in your "most holy faith!" Remember the word holy means – something that is set apart, consecrated, sacred, not to be defiled.

Jude called it our most holy faith because limited, soulish thinking is not able to contaminate or defile what is being prayed out in other tongues. If we knew what we were praying, our soul could rise up with doubt and unbelief and hinder the perfect will of God from being manifested in our lives.

The Holy Spirit knows and speaks the mind of the Father and the Son. Praying in the Spirit bypasses the rational mind of our soul man and communicates directly with our spirit man. What an amazing provision the Lord has provided for us - I Corinthians 2:11.

I want to add another scripture to this foundation, in I Corinthians 2:7-8 it says, *"But **we speak the wisdom of God in a mystery**, even the hidden wisdom, **which God ordained before the world** unto our glory: Which none of the princes of this world knew: for had they known it, they would not have crucified the Lord of glory."*

Praying in the Spirit brings the Will of God from the place of being a mystery and hidden from us, to the place of being wisdom to us. So the wisdom of God for any given situation comes to our understanding as we are praying in the Spirit. - Romans 8:27, I Corinthians 14:2

The wisdom of God has been hidden from the enemy. The princes of this world, the demonic realm, cannot understand our prayer in the Spirit! Had they known the fullness of the plan of God, they would have never crucified the Lord of glory. God established this provision for us from before the foundation of the world. He always makes the way of escape! – Ephesians 1:4, I Corinthians 2:8 and 10:13

Paul has a lot to say on this subject of praying in the spirit. Let's continue.

I Corinthians 2:13 saying, ***"Which things also we speak,** not in the words which man's wisdom teacheth, but which the Holy Ghost teacheth; comparing spiritual things with spiritual."* (Amplified Bible says - combining and interpreting spiritual truths **with a spiritual language**.)

Once more I am going to rewrite just the bold text from I Corinthians 2:7, 8 and 13 so you can see where I am taking you. It says, **we speak the**

wisdom of God in a mystery, which God ordained before the world, which things also we speak with a spiritual language.

Can you see that God has ordained before the world a way in which to receive the deep things of the Spirit, which things also we speak as we are praying in our most Holy Faith?

Let's continue with Paul's teaching in I Corinthians 2:14-16, I combined the KJV and the Amplified Bible to bring out the full meaning to you. It says:

14 *But the natural, non-spiritual (soulish) man does not accept or welcome into his heart the gifts and teachings and revelations of the Spirit of God, for they are foolishness (moronish, meaningless nonsense) to him; and he is incapable of knowing them (of recognizing and understanding them), because they are spiritually discerned.*

15 *But he that is spiritual judgeth (he examines, investigates, inquires into, questions and discerns) all things, yet he himself is judged of no man.*

16 *For who hath known the mind of the Lord, that he may (be united in association together with) him? But we have the mind of Christ and do hold the thoughts, feelings and purposes of His heart.*

Obviously Paul had encountered soulish Christians who did not want to hear about spiritual things. This is why he spent so much time teaching on the subject. He is showing us that the natural, soulish man will not accept the gifts, teachings and revelations of the Spirit.

Have you ever noticed that if you start talking to a soulish person about spiritual things like praying in the spirit, their soul / *psuche* will rise up against what you are saying? They just can't relate to it. The things of the spirit are foolishness (moronish) to them. This is how you can tell if you are talking to a spiritual person or a soulish person.

When I was young in the Lord and just learning these things, there were people who said to me that speaking in tongues was of the devil, it passed away with the last apostle, it's not for today, etc. I understand now exactly what Paul was saying, a soulish Christian can not understand spiritual things, soulish people cannot accept these Bible truths. We know the enemy operates in the soul realm and he has caused them to believe a lie and have deception in their perception. He does not want us to understand this powerful truth because he is powerless against it. So he has hidden it from everyone he can.

The best way to deal with a fellow believer that cannot receive these Bible truths is to agree to disagree and perfect your love walk. The worst thing you can do is argue with them and separate yourself. The Lord wants unity in His Body and not division. We don't have to all agree on everything. What is important is that we walk in the revelation we have and never argue over the Word. Believers are at all different places in their level of maturity in the Lord. That is okay with God, let it be okay with you.

What the spiritual believer will understand is that the Lord made a way for us to bypass the issues (of fear, unbelief, lack of faith, religion, etc.) in our natural / soul and have the mind of Christ flowing from our spirit so we can pray effectively and bring the will of God into the earth. - Romans 8:26, 27 and I Corinthians 2:13, 14, 16

Too many Christians live their lives subject to every wind the devil can blow their way, when the Lord has already made our way of escape - I Corinthians 10:13. He made a way for us to stay ahead of the enemy, a way to be above only and not beneath, the head and not the tail. He created us to subdue and have dominion with our words and some of those words are in other tongues!

All the things we have prayed out in the Spirit or in tongues, the mysteries, hidden plans and perfect will of God, are going before us and working together, fitting into the plan of God for our good. - I Corinthians 2:7; 14:2, and Romans 8:28

The Holy Spirit Himself, who is within us and knows the mind and will of God, is making intercession for us according to the will of God, bringing us the mind of Christ, as we pray in the Spirit - our most holy faith! - Romans 8:27 and I Corinthians 2:16

The Holy Spirit sees to it that God's will is carried out even in areas where we do not know how to pray. He searches the heart and knows the mind of the Spirit. - Romans 8:26, 27 and I Corinthians 2:13, 14

In other words, when you pray in tongues you are not praying mentally limited prayers. You are praying beyond your own limited knowledge. You have moved beyond your natural understanding and into the place where the Holy Spirit can reveal all things.

Do you realize that neither our past nor our present is hidden from us? What is hidden is our future. God knows exactly what the obstacles in our future are. So when we pray in the spirit concerning our future, we can know that we are praying out His perfect will for our lives - Romans 8:26,27. So then when obstacles appear, we have world (kingdom of darkness) overcoming faith in operation for our breakthrough. We have already prayed out our provision - I John 5:4. What an amazing God we serve!

This is why the enemy has tried to hide this truth about praying in the spirit from the Body of Christ and has caused so many denominational divisions over this subject – because he is powerless against it!

Paul says, "Though I speak with the tongues of men and of angels..." I Corinthians13:1. According to this scripture, we speak not only with tongues of men, but we also speak with tongues of angels! Just as English is the voice or language of our mind, praying in tongues is the voice or language of our spirit. Scripture shows us that angels understand both languages. The ministry of angels is to hear, respond, and obey the voice of the word by bringing it to pass and minister on our behalf. - Psalm 103:20; I Corinthians 13:1 and Hebrews 1:13,14

We just read that when we speak in an unknown tongue, we speak to God. Now we can see that angels are bringing to pass the words we pray in the Spirit as well as the words we pray in our understanding. Paul said in I Corinthians 14:15, *"For if I pray in an unknown tongue, my spirit prayeth, but my understanding is unfruitful. What is it then? I will pray with the spirit, and I will pray with the understanding also: I will sing with the spirit, and I will sing with the understanding also."*

So it is important to pray in your understanding as much as you can.

Make prophetic declarations, pray the Word, use your authority and take the dominion for which you were created. Then spend time praying in your most holy faith, as you do you can direct your tongues toward a particular situation or person by thinking in that direction.

While praying in the spirit, release your faith on purpose, knowing that you are praying out the perfect will of God. Take time to thank God like you would if you were praying in your understanding. Say, "Thank you Lord, I believe, I receive that!"

It is my sincere hope that you can clearly understand why the Apostle Paul spent so much time teaching on this subject. He has given us several strong exhortations, for example:

"Pray always with all prayer and supplication in the Spirit, and watching thereunto with all perseverance and supplication for all saints;..." - Ephs 6:18.

He said, *"I thank my God, I speak with tongues more than ye all;"* - I Cor 14:18.

He also said, *"Let a man so account of us, as of the ministers of Christ (the anointing), and stewards (distributors, managers and overseers) of the mysteries of God."* - I Cor 4:1

Did you get that? We are ministers of the Anointing and stewards of the mysteries of God.

"...forbid not to speak with tongues." - I Corinthians 14:39. The Greek word *forbid* means - we should not hinder, prevent, restrain, stand in the way of or withhold tongues.

I encourage you to be a good minister and steward of the mysteries by placing the same value over your prayer language that the Apostle Paul and the Holy Spirit do.

I want you to find comfort in knowing that, even though the answer to overcome situations, circumstances, and trouble in our life is a mystery to us and above what we can ask or think; we are told in Ephesians 3:20 that, by the action of the Holy Spirit's power that is at work within us (our spirit), He is able to carry out His purpose and do super abundantly, far over and above all that we can dare ask or think infinitely beyond our highest prayers, desires, thoughts, hopes or dreams (in our soul)! (I amplified and personalized this for you).

It is important for you to understand that I have been talking to you about the "devotional side" of tongues which is your prayer language by the Holy Spirit. I am not talking about the "ministry gift" of prophetic tongues and interpretation in a church service. If you want to know more about the ministry side of tongues, Kenneth Hagin Sr. wrote some very easy to understand books on the subject.

HOW DOES TONGUES WORK?

Many people over the years have said to me that they have prayed for the baptism of the Holy Spirit to receive their prayer language, but never got it. I want to tell you that when you asked the Holy Spirit to come to you He did. We have a misconception about receiving our prayer language. You should not be waiting for an overwhelming sensation to just come over you and cause you to start speaking differently.

Jesus said, *"And all things, whatsoever ye shall ask in prayer, believing, ye shall receive."* Matthew 21:22. Once you have prayed, believing - you should consciously receive. It's yours now.

This is where we have missed it. We keep begging until we see manifestation - that's called unbelief. If you received when you prayed you would talk and act like you have it now. Remember Abraham, he called things that be not as though they were.

God made speaking in tongues very simple, but we have complicated it. How did you teach your children to speak your language? Well here in America we taught them at a young age to say words like, 'ma ma or da da'. Once they learned some simple two syllable words we added some harder words like 'please mommy' or 'no thank you mommy'. They heard us speak and they copied us.

In class, as well as in altar ministry, I have taken people who wanted their prayer language and taught them to repeat after me. I spoke a couple of syllables in my prayer language and I had them repeat after me. Or

165

sometimes I would encourage them to just begin saying hallelujah over and over. I would tell them to break that word down and say hallel a few times, then hallel - jah and keep repeating those words until they felt comfortable letting their tongue roll. The point is to let yourself and your tongue go. Many of my students tell me they use their shower or driving time to get comfortable praying in the spirit.

We haven't seen manifestation of our language because we think something has to forcefully come over our mouth and make us speak. That is not true. That wasn't true when we learned to speak any other language. We always have to consciously open our mouth, form our tongue and push sound out when learning a new language.

It doesn't really matter if you are saying la la la or ba ba ba. What matters is that you are releasing sound by faith believing that the Holy Spirit and the ministry of angels are at work on your behalf. Once you get comfortable letting your tongue go, you will develop a language. It may only be a few syllables to begin with, but the more comfortable you get with it, the more developed your language will become.

I want you to understand the simplicity of this law. We were created in God's image and likeness. We were given authority over this earth and we were given words with which we release our authority.

Man is a spirit with a physical body. Only spirits with physical bodies can legally function in the earth realm. This explains why demons need our words and bodies to function. This also explains why Jesus needed a physical body to redeem us from the curse of the fall. We can see all through scripture that God works within the boundaries of these laws and does not violate them.

Adam's sin cut off the flow of the blessing in the earth realm. God is trying to get blessings and provision back to us, but He is bound by the laws He established, just as we are. When you release sound, by faith, God is able to get blessings flowing.

According to the laws of creation and words, we need to authorize words with our mouths so creation can take place. Then angels can respond and we can enforce the Kingdom of God on earth as it is in heaven.

Since we don't always know what or how to pray, especially concerning mysteries, then we are unable to access our provision. So God, in His divine wisdom, prepared a way for us before the world unto our glory; He gave us a language the devil couldn't understand and that we don't have to understand. We just have to open our mouths and release our authority by faith and through sound. When we do, it authorizes God and His angels to move on our behalf; bypassing the hindering forces of the kingdom of darkness. If you didn't understand this, I suggest you read it over and over again until you do, it's that important! - I Corinthians 2:7, 8; 13:1 and Romans 8:27

The reason others have received their language easily is that they believed by faith and were willing to open their mouths and just begin to speak. If you haven't done that then unbelief is hindering you. You are too concerned with how foolish you sound and that is your soul stopping you. You are to release this prayer from your spirit, which means you must bypass what your soul is saying and just do it.

Remember that the devil cannot understand your prayer language. If he can't understand what you are saying, then he can't go before you and hinder what you're creating. It renders him powerless, this is why he has made such a denominational division over this subject. He does not want you to have the ability to speak something that is the perfect will of God, above what you could ask or think in your natural understanding. - Romans 8:27 and Ephesians 3:20

I always tell my students that they will get a thought that says, "That's not the Holy Spirit speaking, that's you." Well guess what? It is you! The devil is trying to stop you with that thought. So now you know it's coming and you won't let it stop you.

Legally it has to be you, a spirit with a physical body, releasing sound by faith. That is what is required of us. Is it you speaking when you're praying and using your God-given authority in your birth language? Yes, it is always us doing the speaking, but the Holy Spirit and the angels of God understand what you are putting forth - that's the difference.

Don't let the devil fool you, he is a soul devil who operates in the soulish realm. The point is, just start speaking by faith, using your God given authority as a believer. Over the years I have noticed my language changing. I have heard myself saying Hebrew words that I didn't know with my understanding. I later found out what they meant.

I can add several more pages to this book if I were to include all the testimonies from my prayer language. I am only going to share one more. I was a fairly new babe in Christ and at that season of my life, I was heavily into intercession for the salvation of my family and friends.

One morning while getting ready for work I felt an urgency in my spirit. It was like a nervous feeling of pressure to pray and pray now. I had no idea who I was being led to pray for, I just yielded to the Holy Spirit's promptings. Many times we will sense this prompting and not know it is the Holy Spirit Who needs our voice of authority in the earth on behalf of a need somewhere. We will ignore this prompting in our ignorance; I want to point out that the Holy Spirit is always faithful to do His part to get our attention, the failure is always on our part.

So that morning I was praying in tongues as I was getting ready for my day. If I remember the time correctly, it was around 11:15 am as I was driving to work and my prayer became extremely intense. I began screaming and crying and saying, "Now Lord, do it NOW!" Let me tell you that you can not conjure this kind of prayer up on your own. This is entirely Holy Spirit led. It comes on fast and hard like labor pains and lifts just as fast once you have delivered. You may never know what happened but you gave birth to something. You just know you were obedient to be used by the Holy Spirit to bring God's perfect will into a situation somewhere.

So anyway I am driving, crying, screaming and praying and then it was gone, all of that pressure just lifted. When I got home from work that day my mom told me that my best friend's father was killed in a car accident. I was in shock, I said, "What time?" She said, "11:15 this morning." That was the time that the urgency came and I began screaming, "Now Lord!"

I had spent much time in prayer and intercession for my friend and her family, my heart was very tender for all of them. The Lord used my prayer that morning and at the time of her father's death to usher him into the Kingdom. I am sure of it. You may be asking yourself, why then did he die if I was praying? Why didn't my prayer stop the accident? The answer is complicated, he had his own issues, laws were in motion, and seeds had been sown. The important thing is at some time before he left his body he had an encounter with the Most High God! Jesus takes the sting out of death. Just because he died doesn't mean my prayer wasn't answered. My friend's father is very much alive, at peace and living in eternity until we are all joined together as one.

Jesus said, *"But whosoever drinketh of the water that I shall give him shall never thirst; but the water that I shall give him shall be in him a well of water springing up into everlasting life."* - John 4:14. The Spirit of God is a well of living water inside of you, springing up. A well is for personal use. God's ultimate purpose is that other thirsty souls can partake of that water. He desires to pour out of His Spirit from the inside of you through intercession. *"He that believeth on me, as the scripture hath said, out of his belly shall flow rivers of living water."* - John 7:38

If you have never asked the Holy Spirit to come into your life, then the time is now. Just as you asked Jesus to come into your heart and received eternal life, you can ask the Holy Spirit to come into your heart as well. The Holy Spirit will come to your aid and bear you up in areas of weakness; He is your Comforter, Counselor, Helper, Advocate, Intercessor, Strengthener and Standby. John 14:26; 16:7 Amplified Bible and Romans 8:26 says, *"...he will teach you all things, and bring all things to your remembrance,"* You need Him!

PRAYER

Holy Spirit, I ask You to baptize me and fill me with your presence. I believe I receive my prayer language, my ability to pray in my most Holy Faith. I give You permission to make impressions in my understanding so that I will know the mind of Christ in every situation.

I am grateful that Your power that is at work within me is a well of living water that is able to do superabundantly, far over and above all that I can ask or think in my natural mind, infinitely beyond my highest prayers, desires, thoughts, hopes or dreams. I give you permission to use me to pray out Your will on earth, as it is in heaven. Teach me to be sensitive to your promptings and teach me to pray.

Generational Curses

The sins of our forefathers have imbedded a stream of weakness into our DNA structure. I will show you exactly how iniquity works and how to stop iniquity in your family line. Galatians 3:13 says that Christ has redeemed us from the curse of the law; unfortunately too many of us are still laboring under a curse not knowing how to get free.

CHAPTER SIX

We have been learning about how the kingdom of darkness operates in our unsurrendered soul. Our lack of knowledge about the soul and the kingdom of darkness has given the enemy an easy way to gain access into our lives. In this chapter we are going to see how not only our sins, but the sins of our fathers have opened the door for an embedded stream of weakness known as a generational curse in our family line.

This inherited weakness has controlled past generations and has the ability to affect present and future generations. It has gone undetected in our lives and prevented us from receiving the fullness of our covenant benefits.

Deuteronomy chapter 28 verses 1-14 describe the blessings that will come on us and overtake us when we walk in obedience. Verses 15-68 describe the curses of disobedience that will come on us and overtake us. I suggest that you read this chapter so you can see what their manifestations look like in your lives.

Psalm 112:1-3 puts the blessing in a nutshell, *"Blessed is the man who fears (reverences and honors) the Lord, who delights greatly in His commandments. His descendants will be mighty on the earth; the generation of the upright will be blessed (empowered to prosper). Wealth and riches will be in his house, and his righteousness endures forever."*

In Exodus 34:7 God is talking with Moses saying that He *"Keeps mercy for thousands, forgiving iniquity and transgression and sin, and that will by no means clear (cleanse) the guilty; visiting the iniquity of the fathers upon the children, and upon the children's children, unto the third and to the fourth generation."*

The word *sin* means falling short, erring, missing the mark. The English word for sin comes from the Greek used in sport archery. The archer would draw the bow and send the arrow toward the target. If he missed the mark the overseeing official would yell, "Sin."

The word *transgression* means more of a willful deviation from the laws laid down by God; therefore, it is rebellion. This means that sin is committed out of ignorance, but transgression is done with full awareness.

The word *iniquity* means to have a lawless nature; it is a deformity of the soul. It is a driving force within our nature; the tendency to sin that we inherit. Iniquity also means a perversion of character, to be bowed down under the weight of something, to be twisted, bent or crooked and going in a wrong direction. We must know that these inherited weaknesses are open doors for demonic influence and activity, not only in our soul life, but also in our bloodline.

Have you ever felt like you were bowed down under the weight of something and couldn't get free? The idea of generational curses is expressed in the familiar sayings, "like father, like son," "like mother, like daughter" or "the apple doesn't fall far from the tree." They may be identified by looking for patterns such as unfortunate events. We all have seen patterns of behavior or natural tendencies in our family line and just accepted them as normal.

The reason we have these patterns and tendencies in our nature is because of the access our ancestors gave the enemy.

A curse or iniquity is a "driving force within our nature" that gives us the tendency to do wrong. This iniquity causes us to be bent in a certain direction. It is imbedded in the nature of our unsurrendered soul from unmet needs, unhealed hurts, unresolved issues, strongholds, soul ties and offenses.

When we sin and don't repent, it is equivalent to sowing a seed that will bear the fruit of an iniquity thorn. The harvest on that fruit will defile our character. Thought patterns and emotional conditions can become ongoing and get deeply imbedded within us altering the DNA in our family line.

Evil spirits that were given entrance by our ancestors or by us, if not evicted, will travel down though generations. These are called familial spirits because they travel among members of a family. They make us think it's just heredity.

HOW INIQUITY WORKS

We are very aware that we naturally inherit things from our family. For example, the first time we go to a doctor, we are asked about our family history. It's understood that if there is a history of heart disease, diabetes, cancer, arthritis, mental illness, etc. that we should be watching for similar symptoms. We know this through the knowledge of genetics. These things are hereditary and are passed down through our DNA bloodline.

The same way we inherit illness from our family, we also inherit our looks and behaviors, both good and bad. Spiritually speaking, we inherit generational blessings as well as curses, as these are passed on through our DNA as well.

We learned that we all have been raised by people, who were also raised by people, who had their own *psuche* / suitcase full of baggage. Now we are learning that part of that baggage is the "stuff" we inherit. These impressions and imperfections in our family tree have marked not only the bloodline, but the souls of generations.

A quick internet search on the subject of curses is eye opening. Ranging from family curses and movie curses, to curses on Egyptian Pharaohs and Presidents. The number of Kennedy family tragedies have led some to believe there must be a curse on the whole bunch. You decide:

JFK's brother Joseph Jr., and sister Kathleen both died in separate plane crashes in 1944 and 1948, respectively. JFK's other sister, Rosemary, was institutionalized in a mental hospital for years. John F. Kennedy himself, America's 35th president, was assassinated in 1963 at age 46. Robert Kennedy, JFK's younger brother, was assassinated in 1968. Senator Ted Kennedy, JFK's youngest brother, survived a plane crash in 1964. In 1969, he was driving a car that went off a bridge, causing the death of his companion, Mary Jo Kopechne. His presidential goals were pretty much squashed after that. In 1984, Robert Kennedy's son David died of a drug overdose. Another son, Michael, died in a skiing accident in 1997. In 1999, JFK Jr., his wife, and his sister-in-law died when the small plane he was piloting crashed into the Atlantic Ocean.

Understanding this has forced me to examine the way my life was marked by the sins of my ancestors. Particularly, on one side of my family, I knew of incest, sexual abuse, abortion, traumas and divorce. There were third and fourth cousins that came from this side of my family who owned dirty book stores and massage parlors in our city. My grandfather, who lived with us, used to work at one of those stores and sometimes I would see the magazines he brought home.

Like I said in an earlier chapter, my parents got divorced when I was sixteen. I got married when I was twenty-one years old and my daughter was 1½ years old when I left my husband. Right there I could see the bend in my family towards divorce. I could see a pattern of divorce, aborted relationships, aborted plans, dreams and purposes in my family for generations; there were seven divorces in my immediate family alone. All the men on this side of the family died tragic deaths, aborting their destinies. I was able to identify all of this as iniquity.

Through these family connections to perversion and smut, I was given a stack of free passes to a strip club that had male dancers on Friday and Saturday nights. Entrance to the club was five dollars but I was able to get in free and go as often as I liked. I went with a group of women in my family a couple of times and that's all it took to hook me. I had a blast and wanted to continue going every weekend. Over time I went from just hanging out and partying, to actually working there. I began by working at the front door checking ID and running the cash register. I tended bar, ordered the liquor, stocked the bar, cleaned during the day, booked weekend reservations and private parties. I basically did everything but strip. I made friends there and actually found a false sense of identity.

During this season of my life, while my divorce was being finalized, I had a divine encounter with Tony C; he was the Christian dad of an old friend.

God had spoken to him and told him to wait in the lobby of an office building downtown, because there was someone who needed ministry. He was standing in the lobby for about a half hour when I walked in. Neither one of us could believe we were seeing the other. He took me to lunch and told me about Jesus. As he brought me back to the building, we prayed and He led me to the Lord. I was excited and told everyone at the club about Jesus!

However, my life did not change right away. I was already involved with one of the male dancers at the club. I was in my early twenties, newly divorced with a little girl, looking for this man to meet my needs. I remember his response when I tried to tell him about Jesus he said, "I used to know Jesus years ago, now I know Satan." That should have stopped me dead in my tracks but it didn't, because I already had an unhealthy emotional tie with him and with my friends at the club.

Looking back, I can see how receiving those free passes opened the door to that club, and exposed the perversion in my family line that was able to grab me and cause me to bend in a perverted direction.

Being a Christian was really hard. I had one foot in the church and one foot in the world. I used to watch the 700 Club every morning and I called them frequently for prayer. I felt the war within my members, I was trying to be a Christian and still have my boyfriend, my social life and my job. The internal pressures were too great and I wasn't mature enough in my Christianity to know the difference between my soul and spirit. I didn't know how to get free from all the junk in my trunk. There was a driving force within my nature, causing me to be bowed down and bending in the wrong direction. I spent five years of my life bound in this place.

I remember one night in particular. As I was tending bar, I looked up at the almost naked men dancing and I heard the voice of the Lord say, "This is disgusting to me." I remember literally saying out loud to that voice, "Really?" I know now that seeing my grandfather's magazines as a child had desensitized me to the club and what went on there. Yet through it all the Lord was faithful to keep drawing me.

177

During these years I used to go out into the alley behind the bar; and I'd notice a church across the parking lot with a large cross on top of the steeple that was all lit up. I would look up at that cross and say, "Lord, help me!" I could see no way out of the mess I had made of my life. One day I was cleaning the bar and I stopped to eat lunch; I literally laid my hands on the bar and spoke out loud, "I command this place to be closed down in Jesus' name." Where did I get that from? No one ever taught me to do that. Looking back I could see it was the Holy Spirit leading me. At that time I believed that the bar closing down was my only way out.

A couple of years went by and I continued to live in this mess of a life and cry out to God for help. Then on July 17, 1984 at 10:45 am, on a clear blue summer day with not a cloud in sight, I was in the car with my friend Rhonda when I noticed a single little cloud in the sky. It was right above our car with the word **"yes"** in perfect cursive dark blue handwriting inside of the cloud.

We both stared at that cloud in shock. We were looking at the cars next to us and saying to one another, how is it no one else can see this cloud? We thought there would be an accident if anyone else on the road saw this cloud. We stared at this 'yes cloud' for about five minutes as it stayed over our car. Even as the expressway curved around, the cloud stayed above the car. Our eyes were fixed on this miracle until the letters seemed to slowly fade away. It was unmistakable!

When we got home I grabbed a piece of my daughter's paper and a crayon and drew out what we saw. I had no idea what it meant. I kept asking God, "Yes what?" I had been praying for so much I wasn't sure which part He was saying yes to. I had a little pocket Bible and I drew the 'yes cloud' inside the cover of that Bible. I was so excited I showed it to everyone, but they thought I was nuts.

Then in April of 1986 a very handsome man named Mark Fiorini came into the bar. He was a friend of one of my co-workers and he came in to bring us our drugs for the evening. We soon became friends and he, along with his cousin, ended up moving into the apartment upstairs from where I lived.

Because Mark was right upstairs we would hang out together all the time and within two weeks we were dating. One day when my daughter Jenelle was with her father and I was home alone, I had snorted ¼ gram of coke and had a buzz. I was sitting by myself on my front porch enjoying a beautiful spring day when the phone rang.

It was a prayer counselor for the 700 Club. She said she was going through a stack of names and numbers and the Lord told her to call me! I proceeded to tell her how I was a backsliding Christian and that I had just gotten high. She began to tell me that God loves and forgives me; then she prayed for my life to be turned back over to Jesus and immediately my high left me. I hung up the phone, ran upstairs and told Mark what just happened. I told him my high was completely gone and we had to give our lives to Jesus.

Two months later the bar was forced to close down. Shortly after that, Mark got a call from his mom. When he hung up he said to me, "They know I have been dealing drugs, I'm done."

Now that the club was closed I was out of a job, so Mark's mom, who is a strong Christian, hired me to paint all the windows inside her house. She knew I was a divorced, young mother who was dating her son and she wanted to get to know me. As I was painting she would spend time with me telling me her testimony and all about Jesus. Now that I was free of the club and its influence I was genuinely able to let Jesus be the Lord of my life. It turns out that Mark's parents went to the same church as my mother. His family knew my family and shared mutual friends. What a small world, here was my mom and Mark's mom praying for their wayward children in the same church. Was this a coincidence? I think not. More like a God - incidence!

In October Mark asked me to marry him. We were wed on December 13, 1986, a mere six months after we met. When I think of it now, it all happened so fast, Mark and I stand amazed at what the Lord has done in both of our lives. After we were married I got a letter from the 700 Club asking for testimonies. I wrote out what the Lord had done and how He used that prayer minister to call me. After receiving my testimony, the 700 Club contacted me again because they wanted to film my testimony. It aired many times over for several years in the late 1980's.

I want to encourage you if you are praying for a lost loved one; God knows how to reach them. He is speaking to them; He knows how to bring other Christians into their path. When I think back now, I see all the ways the Lord tried to get my attention even while I continued to make bad choices. He sent Tony C. to me (who led me to the Lord) because He was trying to pull me out of that club before I got in too deep. On top of that He showed me the cross up on the church steeple causing me to cry out for help, He gave me many dreams during this season, and He gave me my "yes" cloud. Finally my future husband walked into the darkness of that bar. My friends tried to protect me from Mark because they didn't want to see me get involved with a drug dealer. But God re-wove that situation and then set both of us free! I could see that these were all divine encounters and answers to prayer. I think the Lord was in hot pursuit, drawing me unto Himself.

Looking back I could see not only the faithfulness of God to reach down and touch a broken life, I could also see how my life was marked by the sins of my ancestors along the way. I can see that the enemy knows exactly how we were raised, the belief systems that were sown and what iniquities lay in our family lines. He uses his vast knowledge of every weakness in our DNA as an arsenal against us. He tries to keep the iniquity flowing through our generations by influencing our circumstances and environment, as well as other people's behaviors to affect us. Given just the right pressure, events or circumstances, he is counting on us to agree with wrong thoughts so we will bend in the wrong direction, securing his "place" of influence in the next generation. The damaging effects of iniquity in my family were not as tragic and obvious as the ones in the Kennedy family, which only made them harder to detect.

What we really need to understand is that when we sin and are quick to repent, be cleansed from the unrighteousness and never do it again, we have stopped that seed from bearing fruit. However, if we leave that seed in the ground, it produces a thorny harvest on our dendrites that will shape the blueprint of our mind, perpetuating the iniquity. Ecclesiastes 10:8 says, *"He that diggeth a pit shall fall into it; and whoso breaketh a hedge, a serpent shall bite him."* As soon as we position ourselves outside of righteousness, we can count on being bitten by a serpent.

Galatians 6:7 warns us, *"Do not be deceived; God is not mocked; for whatever a man sows, that shall he also reap. For he who sows to the flesh will of the flesh reap corruption, but he who sows to the Spirit will of the Spirit reap everlasting life."* We cannot sow toxic thinking without reaping a thorny pattern on the trees of our mind that will produce a toxic life.

The Hebrews in the Old and New Testament were well aware of iniquity. They fully understood that the fathers passed the tendency to sin on to their children. This is why David said, *"...in sin did my mother conceive me."* - Psalm 51:5

We can see a great example of this in King David's life; he committed adultery with Bathsheba and then had her husband murdered. The prophet Nathan was going to kill him, but David repented. The prophet told David that his sins were forgiven but the sword shall not depart from his house. Although David was forgiven, his sin still produced fruit. David's children became the very sin David had committed. They were immoral, violent, and murderers. - 2 Samuel 11:3-17; 12:1-10

A curse may also be a result of a demonic force brought to bear upon a person, family, organization, territory, object or heirloom, etc., by speaking wrong words, coming into wrong agreements, sinful actions or participation in the occult and witchcraft. Seeking information from things like a Ouija board, astrology, psychics, etc., give the enemy legal entry into your family line.

The most infamous possession movie *Poltergeist* is afflicted with Hollywood's most infamous curse: four deaths are associated with the trilogy, which was premised around destructive spirits who inhabited a house. The film's young star, Heather O'Rourke, died at only 12 years old of septic shock, and her onscreen sister, Dominique Dunne, was strangled to death by her distraught boyfriend. Julian Beck, who played an evil spirit, died of cancer, while Will Sampson, who played a good spirit, died after a heart-lung transplant. All the deaths occurred within a six-year period.

Many people have come for prayer seeking help for things like; mental confusion, fear, torment, and strange manifestations. In those instances I have found that there has been some sort of attraction to horror movies or dabbling in the occult, either by them or someone in their family.

The effects of a curse are not limited to an individual. They are passed from generation to generation unless they are canceled. They don't happen by accident. They work because of the spiritual law of cause and effect - sowing and reaping. We will cover this more in the next chapter.

We have learned that demons will enter where they are given legal right through open doors of sin. Then they perpetuate the iniquity and curses through our lives and the lives of our descendants for generations.

An Old Testament example of how generational curses happen is Exodus 34:7 - *Keeping mercy for thousands, forgiving iniquity and transgression and sin, and that will by no means clear the guilty; visiting the iniquity of the fathers upon the children, and upon the children's children, unto the third and to the fourth generation.*

John 9:1-3 is a great example of a New Testament proof that generational curses were a common part of Hebrew beliefs and culture, *"And as Jesus passed by, He saw a man which was blind from his birth. And His disciples asked Him, saying, 'Master, who did sin, this man, or his parents, that he was born blind?' Jesus answered, 'Neither hath this man sinned, nor his parents: but that the works of God should be made manifest in him."*

The Eastern mindset understands these things naturally, but our Western mindset is ignorant of them. They asked Jesus, *"Master, who did sin, this man, or his parents, that he was born blind?"* - John 9:2. They knew that a generational curse could be manifested in a physical affliction like blindness, either from the man's sin, or his parent's. In his case, it was neither, but their questions prove that a generational curse *could* have been the source of his affliction.

182

Jesus' answer was neither, because it didn't have to be that man or his parents who sinned. It may have come from several generations earlier. The point is that Jesus was going to manifest the works and will of God to them by healing the man.

We have all seen handicapped people and I don't think our first thought is whose sin caused that person to be born handicapped. We are western minded and we just accept things for what they are. The eastern mindset understands spiritual laws, that's why the disciples asked Jesus this question. If we would see things through the understanding of spiritual laws we might look around and ask, "What caused addiction to run in this family, or what caused infirmity in that family?"

We can all see traits running in family lines. To a lesser degree we may see things like adultery, pride, laziness, bitterness, depression, anger, lying or poverty. To a greater degree we can see things like tragedies, handicaps, mental illness, deadly diseases, incest, abuse, etc.

Many have said things like, "I will never be like my mom or dad." Yet if the curse isn't dealt with, they often find that they have repeated the same transgressions and have become just like their parents. This is easily identified as a bitter-root judgment bearing the thorny fruit of iniquity. This is why we will often see a parent struggle with things like alcohol or drug abuse and then their children have the same addictions. We see rebellious, angry, violent parents spawning rebellious, angry, violent children. We see things like poverty, sickness and divorce running rampant in families. The whirlpool cycle just continues until someone knows how to stop it.

It's painful when we see our children demonstrating the same traits that we hated in ourselves. We don't want them to make the same mistakes we did. We have prayed for our children to be saved, delivered and healed; yet it may be that our repentance is the key to their deliverance. Confessing your faults is the first step in closing the door, then you can break off the iniquity and cleanse the bloodline.

We can find comfort and trust in the Lord, knowing He has delivered us, and He knows how to reach our children. If you haven't had children yet, I suggest you repent for your sins as well as the sins you see in your family and cleanse the bloodline so your children will not inherit iniquity.

183

WORD CURSES

Curses can also be set in motion as a result of the words that we speak. Deuteronomy 30:19 declares, *"I call heaven and earth to record this day against you, that I have set before you life and death, blessing and cursing: therefore choose life, that both thou and they seed may live:"*

We have learned that speaking wrong words employs demons to bring those words to pass, establishing curses. Since words have no expiration date we must break the power of the wrong words we have spoken to cancel their curses - Isaiah 54:17. Participation in the occult and witchcraft will open doors to generational curses as well. We will cover this more in the next chapter.

Numbers 23:8 says, *"How shall I curse, whom God hath not cursed? Or how shall I defy, whom the LORD hath not defied?"* It's important that we don't get in fear over other people cursing us. Curses cannot just land on us. They must have a legal right for an entry point. These things function by spiritual law. Ecclesiastes 10:8 says to us, *"He that diggeth a pit shall fall into it; and whoso breaketh an hedge (enclosure, fence, wall), a serpent shall bite (strike, sting, oppress) him."* The hedge was put in place by God; it is the wall of His Blessing. It is activated through our obedience and deactivated through our disobedience. Our disobedience causes us to "give-place" to the enemy, then he can secure his position in our lives, homes and families for generations. When we walk in obedience, the kingdom of darkness, curses and demons have no authority over us. Our protection is in walking righteously before God, and understanding the power of the blood of Jesus.

HOW TO STOP INIQUITY

James 5:16 encourages us to, *"Confess your faults one to another, and pray one for another, that ye may be healed."* Let's look at the phrase, *"Confess your faults."* The Greek word for *faults* means an unintentional or willful error, transgression, offense or sin - something that has landed upon you.

These faults or weaknesses may be the result of seeds we have sown or something that landed upon us because of seeds someone else has sown. These faults or weaknesses can be likened to the faults or cracks beneath the surface of the earth. When enough pressure comes, the earth convulses and quakes.

We may not even know that the fault / iniquity is within us until the pressure causes us to react, and we feel a weakness; a tendency in our nature, a driving force within us that bends us in a wrong direction. I didn't know going to a male strip club would cause me to bend in that direction. None of the friends I brought to the club bent in the same direction I did. They didn't have the same weakness in their nature.

In Luke 23:34 when Jesus was hanging on the cross, He said, *"...Father, forgive them; for they know not what they do."* Jesus was showing us a spiritual principal; He repented for the sins of others. We too must confess the sins of our forefathers, breaking the power of their sin from affecting our lives.

I strongly suggest repenting and confessing your sins on a daily basis, as well as standing in the gap for your loved ones and repenting on their behalf. This is a maintenance program as seeds of sin are sown daily, they must be pulled up daily so they don't take root and produce fruit.

It is important to understand how the laws of seed time and harvest operate. Seeds of iniquity bloom in different seasons just as natural seeds do. As some seeds bring forth fruit in winter, spring, summer or fall, so do the seeds within us bring forth fruit in different seasons of our life.

For instance, maybe your grandmother developed an illness in her sixties, then when your mom was in her sixties, she began to develop the same illness. Now you're entering your sixties and your body is beginning to develop similar symptoms. The season of life in the sixties produced a fruit that you didn't previously see in an earlier season. Take an inventory of your family and pay attention to the patterns you see, they are an indication of an embedded root producing that fruit.

I have found twenty-two Biblical references (so far) for someone standing in the gap and repenting for the sins of others. The most notable are:

Nehemiah confessed his sins, the sins of his father's house, as well as the sins of the Children of Israel - Nehemiah 1:58.

Daniel confessed the sins of the kings, princes, the fathers as well as his own sins - Daniel 9:3-20.

Moses prayed to pardon the iniquity of the people and the Lord responds to him saying, *"...I have pardoned according to thy word:"* - Numbers 14:19-20. I love this one because the Lord said He pardons according to our repentance! We can have confidence that when we hear our loved ones speaking curses, binding themselves with an oath, or opening a door to sin, we can stand in the gap and repent on their behalf and the Lord will pardon them according to our word.

We have accepted Jesus as our Savior and we know that He died so our sins could be forgiven and they are. In our ignorance we have not known how to be free from curses; and therefore we've still labored under the fruit those sins produced.

Forgiveness and eternal life are but two of the threads that make up the fabric of our redemption.

REDEEMED FROM THE CURSE

Thank God as believers, we are forgiven of our sins and when we die we can go to Heaven. Much of the church focuses only on forgiveness and eternal life. Jesus' death purchased so much more than that for us. He wants us to live the blessed life and experience all of His Covenant benefits in the here and now.

Galatians 3:13 declares, *"Christ hath redeemed us from the curse of the law, being made a curse for us: for it is written, Cursed is every one that hangeth on a tree."*

I want to break this scripture down and help you to fully understand the power of the cross and all that Jesus' death and resurrection purchased for us. Let's begin with:

"that hangeth on a tree"

Why a tree? The first Adam sinned when he partook of the forbidden fruit on a tree. The second Adam, Jesus, became the fruit of God for our salvation and had to be hung on a tree to reverse the effects of the curse. Adam took the fruit of God off the tree. Jesus came as the fruit of God and was put back on the tree.

I want you to see the spiritual law in action here. Jesus had to undo what Adam did in order to reverse the effects of disobedience. In the first chapter we learned that in the beginning before the fall, there was the law of life and everything was righteous and right in the world. When Adam fell he handed over his authority to the enemy. Luke 4:5-6 tells us that all the kingdoms of the world were delivered unto Satan, establishing the law of sin and death. (Because he offered them to Jesus meant they were his to give away.) Everything became unrighteous and wrong in the earth.

With the separation of man's spirit from God's, the law of life in this earth was severed and perverted. It became the law of sin and death - Romans 8:2. All of the blessings God had designed for man to live in were perverted, in the hands of Satan they became a curse.

Jesus had to come to earth as a human spirit with a physical body so that He could legally nullify the law of sin and death in His body on that cross. All the sins that could ever be committed, and the effects of those sins, came on Jesus as He hung on that cross. In so doing, Jesus' obedience reversed all the effects of the curse from Adam's disobedience.

"Hath redeemed us"

The word *redeemed* means - to purchase back, to ransom, to free from captivity or bondage, to free from any obligation or liability to suffer. Jesus ransomed us back to the original state Adam and Eve had in the garden before the fall! They sinned and iniquity was passed down to all of mankind. Did you get that? Jesus death on the cross was so complete that it restored mankind back to his "original state" in the Garden of Eden. That means all power and all authority that Adam had given to the devil was restored back to us. That means that we have the power and ability to live like God intended us to live in the beginning. That means that sickness, disease, poverty and every manifestation of the curse have no more legal right over us. By taking a look at the Body of Christ today you can see that they don't know this. Most believers really do not understand this or how to enforce it.

"Christ"

Did you know that Christ is not Jesus' last name? Christ is a Greek word that was never translated into English. It means - anointed, to smear or rub with oil; to consecrate. It is the Hebrew word Messiah. We can find further definition of Christ the anointed in Isaiah 10:27, it is talking about the Messiah, the Anointed One when He comes, it says, *"And it shall come to pass in that day, that his (referring to Satan's) burden shall be taken away from off thy shoulder, and his (Satan's) yoke from off thy neck, and the yoke shall be destroyed because of the anointing."* So we can see then that the anointing is burden-removing and yoke-destroying power! Jesus the Messiah "the Christ" is anointed with burden-removing yoke-destroying power. (With that definition in mind you should meditate on what "Christ in you" truly means!)

Let's re-read Galatians 3:13 with the amplified definitions - *"The Anointed One, with burden-removing yoke-destroying power, hath redeemed us from the curse of the law removing Satan's burden from off our shoulder, and his yoke from off our neck. He purchased us back, paid the ransom, and freed us from every bondage or liability to suffer; He ransomed us back to the original state Adam and Eve had in the garden before sin entered in. Being made a curse for us; His body literally absorbed the effects of those sins on the cross. For it is written, cursed is everyone that hangeth on a tree."* Jesus the Christ became the fruit of God for our salvation; He was hung on a tree to reverse the effects of Adam's sin, removing the burden and destroying the yoke that was created when Adam took the fruit of God off the tree. Selah.

Romans 6:23 shows us that, *"the wages of sin is death;"* We understand that the wages (payment or harvest) of our sin perpetuates the death cycle of the kingdom of darkness. It brings spiritual and physical death in our lives, marriages, families, finances, health. When we sow sin we reap death somewhere.

Romans 5:19 says, *"For as by one man's disobedience many were made sinners, so by the obedience of one (Jesus) shall many be made righteous."*

Jesus paid that price for us with His death on the cross. He became sin with our sin so we can be made righteous with His righteousness. When we receive Him as Savior, the burden of our sin is removed and we can obtain forgiveness, but the curse is still in effect and has been hindering us from receiving all of our covenant blessings and benefits. Too many in the Body of Christ have not known how to appropriate being redeemed from the curse and have only received the forgiveness side of our redemption.

Jesus is not just the burden-remover of our sin. He is the yoke-destroyer of the curse. When we commit a sin, we are a slave to the moral liability of that sin, which is our yoke or iniquity. When you are in a yoke you are bound to go where you are being driven. Our lack of knowledge has allowed inherited weaknesses to drive the course our life has naturally taken.

"OUR COVENANT OF PEACE"

Jesus' death purchased the New Covenant and it's called our Covenant of Peace.

Isaiah 53:4-5 describes what Jesus did to purchase that covenant it says, *"Surely He hath borne (suffer punishment; pay the penalty for; carried away) our griefs (sicknesses and diseases) and carried our sorrows (pains and afflictions): yet we did esteem Him stricken, smitten of God and afflicted. But He was wounded for our transgressions; He was bruised for our iniquities: the chastisement of our peace was upon Him; and with His stripes we are healed."*

I am going to break down verse 5 to amplify what it is saying.

He was *"Wounded for our transgressions,"* a wound is bleeding you bear on the outside; it refers to when someone has transgressed or trespassed against you or you them. For instance, a wound can be received by someone speaking against you, breaking their word to you, defiling or abusing you. This portion of the scripture speaks of spiritual healing and is related to the forgiveness of sins.

189

He was *"Bruised for our iniquities,"* a bruise is bleeding on the inside, it also implies to be misshapen or deformed. It is what you carry on the inside (in your soul) - inherited generational weaknesses, sicknesses and behavior patterns on the trees of your mind within your damaged soul. These issues cause us to bleed emotionally and to be deformed in our soul. This is where curses dwell and can even alter our DNA structure. This portion of the scripture speaks of emotional healing for your soul / mind, will and emotions.

"Chastisement" This word means correction. It was the correction to reverse the curse of Adam's disobedience that was needful to obtain our Covenant of Peace.

"Peace" is the Hebrew word *shalom*. When we think of peace we may only think of an absence of war or a calm feeling. But this Hebrew word means so much more than that. It means healing, deliverance, prosperity, soundness, wholeness, preservation from danger, favor, rest and restoration of things stolen, killed or destroyed. It literally means to have nothing missing and nothing broken anywhere in our lives; it means complete wholeness! Can you see that Jesus death purchased all of this for us? I think we should receive it and enforce it don't you!

"With His stripes we are healed" This refers to healing for the physical body.

So lets re-read Isaiah 53:4-5 and amplify what it is saying, *"Surely Jesus hath borne suffered punishment; paid the penalty for and carried away our griefs, sickness and disease, He carried our sorrows, pains and afflictions. Yet we did esteem Him stricken, smitten of God and afflicted. He was being wounded for our transgressions; for every sin we could ever commit. He was bruised, crushed and destroyed beyond recognition for our iniquities; for all inherited curses and every manifestation of the curse of the law. The correction needful to reverse the curse and obtain our new covenant of peace, healing, deliverance, restoration and wholeness was upon Him; and with the stripes He bore on His back we are healed in our physical body."*

If we really believe this scripture then we must stop accepting things like: pain, affliction, grief, addictions, sickness and disease. Our position needs to be one of resisting these things that Jesus bore for us and enforcing our covenant benefits. To learn how to enforce these benefits you might want to read the chapter on Words again.

In addition to the crucifixion, every place Jesus shed His Blood, more of our redemption was purchased.

THE SEVEN PLACES JESUS SHED HIS BLOOD

1. In the Garden of Gethsemane – In preparation for the cross Jesus sweated great drops of blood in the Garden of Gethsemane. In the Garden of Eden Adam essentially said, Father, not Your will but my will be done as he disobeyed God. Four thousand years later in the Garden of Gethsemane, Jesus (the second Adam) said, *"Father, not My will but Thy will be done."* This reversed the curse of what the first Adam did. Jesus purchased back the independent, sin-infected soul of man - Luke 22:44. So today, whatever your soul is suffering, there is power in the Blood that Jesus shed; and we can apply it over our soul in times of need.

2. By His stripes we are healed – I have heard biblical scholars say that there are thirty-nine roots to all diseases known to mankind. Jesus was whipped thirty-nine times. Every time he was whipped blood flowed. That blood reversed the curse of every sickness and disease for us. So when you are experiencing any kind of ailment, plead the blood and release your faith for healing. Be assured that affliction has no legal right to you so enforce your victory.

3. The crown of thorns – When Adam and Eve sinned in the Garden of Eden, God told them, *"Because of what you have done, now thorns and thistles shall the ground bring forth and by the sweat of the brow shall thou eat bread."* - Genesis 3:17-19 Instead of the blessings and prosperity flowing naturally as they had known, they now had poverty and lack. They had to toil for their food and prosperity.

While purchasing our redemption Jesus, the second Adam, bore a crown of thorns around the cortex of his mind and was hung on a tree. The crown of thorns that was placed on Jesus' head had three-and-a-half-inch razor sharp spikes. It represented the thorns that hindered prosperity in the ground of the earth as well as the prosperity in the ground of our minds. When they pressed that crown of thorns into His brow, blood came out. That blood reversed the curse of mental and natural poverty for us. There is power in pleading the blood of Jesus in prayer over our minds as well as our financial needs, as we do we are enforcing our covenant provisions for a prosperous life.

4. The spikes in Jesus' hands – When Adam sinned, he handed over our God-given authority and Satan became lord and god of this world, establishing the kingdom of darkness in the earth. Luke 4:5-6 tells us all the kingdoms of the world were delivered unto Satan, establishing the law of sin and death. Hands are the symbol of authority. Jesus shed blood in both His hands to buy back our authority. He said, *"The Kingdom of God is at hand, heal the sick, cleanse the lepers, raise the dead, cast out devils: freely ye have received, freely give. "* - Matthew 10:7,8. *"As My Father has sent Me, so now I send you."* - John 20:21. He said this because He purchased our God-given authority back. All that we put our hands to shall be blessed once again - Deuteronomy 28:8.

5. The spikes in Jesus' feet – When Adam sinned, mankind's ability to walk uprightly with God became afflicted. The blood Jesus shed from His feet reversed the curse for us so that we can walk righteously with God once again. Everywhere the soles of our feet shall tread is the land that the Lord has given to us, so we must take it and be possessors of our promised land - Joshua 1:3.

6. The spear in Jesus' side – Out of His side poured blood and water - John 19:34. Doctors say that the reason the water and body fluids were released is because it is a physical symbol that His heart burst. In Luke 4:18, Jesus said, *"I have come to heal the broken-hearted and bind up their wounds. "* The word broken hearted means - maimed, crippled and ruptured. Jesus' heart burst as a result of separation from the Father. That is what killed Him, not the crucifixion. Now we have a way that has been made available for us to have our broken hearts healed, so plead the blood over every place you hurt!

7. Bruised for our iniquities – A bruise is bleeding on the inside. Iniquity is an inherited weakness within man's DNA that affects his body and soul nature. This is the driving force within our nature. This is why Jesus said, *"I have come to set the captives free."* - Luke 4:18. This is not referring to self-control but to blood-bought power on the inside, delivering us from the driving force of habitual sin lodged in our soul.

Jesus purchased a complete redemption for our entire spirit, soul and body so that there would be nothing missing and nothing broken anywhere in our lives. Religion reads these scriptures with no real understanding. Once you see every step that Jesus took to redeem us, it becomes a violation of our covenant privileges not to accept and enforce every bit of it.

You see there was a judgment written on the cross of Calvary. That judgment says the consequences of Adam's sin have no legal authority over our lives any longer. The kingdom of darkness only has the authority that we give it. We must execute the judgment of Calvary. If we have only executed the forgiveness side of what Jesus died to purchase for us, then forgiveness is all we will receive.

Unfortunately much of the Body of Christ has only executed forgiveness and has forsaken the bulk of our provision.

We must execute our complete redemption from the curse. We are responsible to enforce and put into effect our healing, deliverance, prosperity, soundness, wholeness, restoration, safety and rest in our life. Have you noticed these provisions don't come automatically? They must be obtained and enforced. The chapter on Words is the way to do that and another very significant way we can execute our redemption is by taking communion.

COMMUNION

I Corinthians 10:16 says, *"The cup of blessing which we bless, is it not the communion of the blood of Christ? The bread which we break, is it not the communion of the body of Christ?"*

When we eat the bread and drink the cup, we are communing with the body and blood of Jesus. We are sharing and exchanging what we have for what God has. We come to Him with nothing but sin. He comes to us with all of His righteousness.

Ephesians 1:3 declares, *"Blessed be the God and Father of our Lord Jesus Christ, who hath blessed us with all spiritual blessings in heavenly places in Christ:"*

"All spiritual blessings" - They are all the blessings that God has provided for us that are ours legally, right now in the spirit realm. We have a covenant of provision that Jesus died to purchase for us. Jesus wants to get these provisions into our life. One of the ways to receive from Him is through the Bread and the Cup. Communion is a physical thing we have as a point of contact, or a conduit, for *"all spiritual blessings in heavenly places"* to be made manifest to us in this natural earth realm.

WHAT ARE POINTS OF CONTACT?

In the natural world electricity, for instance, can't be seen, yet we can place a demand on electrical power by plugging an appliance into the outlet in our wall. The outlet is a point of contact and power is released.

In the spiritual world an example would be the woman with the issue of blood - This woman was pressing through the crowd and pushing people out of the way, repeating, "If I just touch His garment I will be made whole." She had an inner-image of herself touching and receiving whole-ness. Touching Jesus garment was her point of contact. Immediately after being touched by her faith Jesus felt power go from Him, and she was healed - Mark 5:28.

THE FIRST PASSOVER
EXODUS 12:3-14

There are so many prophetic pictures and parallels in the Passover that are shadows of our redemption. I just want to point out a few.

The children of Israel were told to get a lamb for a house. They were told to eat the whole lamb and let none of it remain. We know that lamb was a representation of Jesus' death to purchase our redemption. Today in the church we are picking and choosing which parts of the Lamb's redemption we not only will believe in, but which parts we are comfortable with eating and digesting. The command was to eat the whole lamb! We should be eating, digesting and partaking in all of what Jesus died to purchase for us.

They were told that the blood was to be a token upon their houses which would cause the destroyer to pass over them. There was no power in the slain lamb or its blood. It was merely a point of contact by which protection was made for the people. There is however much power in the Blood of Jesus. I plead the Blood of Jesus over myself and my family daily. I highly suggest reading the book *The Blood and the Glory* by Billye Brim for greater understanding of the power of the Blood. That night in Egypt, when the children of Israel by faith and as a point of contact applied the blood of a slain lamb over their houses, the death angel had to pass over them. How much more would the Blood of Jesus the Lamb of God applied over our lives protect us? There is power, power, wonder working power, in the Blood of the Lamb!

The children of Israel left Egypt, with their silver and gold and there was not one feeble person among their tribes - Psalm 105:37. Do you realize they were slaves, they worked in the mud all day, and they had been beaten and abused? Their physical bodies were a mess. But that night they ate the whole lamb and appropriated its blood. In so doing, they were completely made whole, not one feeble among them. They had an inferior covenant; we have a better covenant! - Hebrews 8

Taking the bread is a point of contact - There is nothing magical about taking communion. It is only a point of contact. However, when we partake we are to release our faith in what Jesus purchased for us on the cross with His body and receive our needs being met. I know before I understood the power of communion I only partook in communion as a religious act. Now I partake with purpose and receive the benefits!

Drinking the cup is a point of contact - When we drink that cup, the provisions and blessings of God that Jesus purchased with all seven places that He shed blood, now flow through that point of contact into our life, releasing blessings to every area of our life that we apply it.

The act of taking communion places a demand on God's power and blessing for our life. As we partake of communion, there is a point of contact. Then "...*All spiritual blessings in heavenly places...*" are being released - Ephesians1:3.

The point of contact is a conduit by which power flows from the spiritual realm to this natural realm. This understanding takes communion out of the realm of being just a religious tradition. Taking communion actually has a purpose and a benefit for believers.

THE CUP AND BLOOD OF JESUS

Matthew 26:27-28 says that Jesus, "*...Took the cup, and gave thanks, and gave it to them, saying, 'Drink ye all of it; For this is My blood of the New Testament, which is shed for many for the remission (freedom, deliverance, forgiveness, liberty, pardon) of sins.'*" Did you notice that Jesus said to drink *all* of it? Think of all the places Jesus shed blood and what that purchased for us. When we drink of the cup we are to receive *all* that the blood provided.

Jesus being born of a virgin was an awesome miracle! The reason He had to be born of a virgin was so the sin-infected blood of man would never touch His blood. His blood had to remain absolutely pure so that it could take away the sins of the world!

Jesus came into the earth to deal with the sin-infected areas of our lives, our bodies, marriages, families and finances. However, He had to die to take the infection of sin out of the body and come up in newness of life. That's why Isaiah 53:4 says, *"He carried them away."* Now you can fully see the judgment that was written on the cross of Calvary, how Christ redeemed us from the curse of the law.

THE BREAD AND BODY OF JESUS

Matthew 26:26 says that, *"And as they were eating, Jesus took bread, and blessed it, and brake it, and gave it to the disciples, and said, 'Take, eat; this is My body.'"*

Take, eat this is My body - This word *take* is very interesting it literally means - to violently seize. When we take communion we should be violently seizing by faith what Jesus died to purchase for us. Pressing against the whirlpool pressure of the kingdom of darkness and violently enforcing by faith the blessings of the Kingdom of God.

Partaking of communion should not be viewed as a magical formula that will work like taking two aspirins for a headache. It is a spiritual act and must be reverenced as one. It must be received in faith and not in unbelief. It is also important to understand that partaking of communion must not become a lifeless routine that is done without true spiritual significance. If we allow it to become that, we are in spiritual danger.

I Corinthians 11:28-31 admonishes us by saying, *"But let a man examine himself, and so let him eat of that bread, and drink of that cup. For he that eateth and drinketh unworthily, eateth and drinketh damnation to himself, not discerning the Lord's body. For this cause many are weak and sickly among you, and many sleep. For if we would judge ourselves, we should not be judged."*

I am going to break this portion of scripture down for you. I want to begin by looking at the word *unworthily*, it means - irreverently or unfit, taking communion and not understanding its importance. I think we have all been guilty of this at one time or another.

Verse 28a says, *"But let a man examine himself."* Before we partake in communion we should ask the Holy Spirit to reveal to us if we are about to partake in an unworthy manner. Ask Him to reveal every area of sin and help you search for areas of offense, unforgiveness, inner vows or judgments you may have towards yourself first.

Examine if you judge and condemn yourself, do you deem yourself unfit because you believe negative things about yourself? Examine the inner-images and internal blueprints you have about you. If you are seeing yourself in a negative light, then you need to change your mind and come out of agreement with every deception in your perception. Pray for the Lord to give you revelation so that you no longer see yourself as unfit or unworthy; so you no longer live under the judgments and condemnation that you have heaped upon yourself. Then ask the Holy Spirit to help you develop a godly blueprint of who you are in Christ. Make a decision to see yourself through the "Father's Eyes."

After examining ourselves verse 29 says, *"For he that eateth and drinketh unworthily, eateth and drinketh damnation (judgment, condemnation) to himself, not discerning the Lord's body."* We are the "Body of Christ" so before partaking in communion we must also examine our hearts to see if we are harboring strife, offenses, unforgiveness, anger, bitter-root judgments, word curse or unhealthy soul ties toward anyone else. If any of these exist in us we must repent before partaking in communion. We are commanded to love one another with a pure heart - I Peter 1:22.

Eating and drinking unworthily in the past has caused us to damn ourselves to those ungodly judgments we have held. Remember that I Corinthians 11:30 says, *"For this cause many are weak (diseased, sick, feeble) and sickly among you, and many sleep (died as a result of the disease and sickness)."*

Many times our blessings, healing, deliverance and even our finances have been hindered because of these issues. There is a spiritual law in operation here. The same word of truth that sets a man free when he believes will condemn a sinner who will not believe - Mark 16:16.

Verse 31 tells us, if we would judge ourselves, we should not be judged. Doing this self examination before partaking in communion will close the door to the enemy and cut off any legal right he has to you.

If you have been taking communion for years and it has just become a religious tradition for you, I believe that the eyes of your understanding have been enlightened to the fullness of our redemption. Now you can begin to create generational blessings that will be passed down through your family line.

198

I encourage you to partake of the Lord's Supper not only when you have a spiritual, physical, emotional or financial need, but also as part of your act of worship together with friends and family. Release your faith as a point of contact, stand on the promises in His Word enforcing your God given Covenant provisions.

PRAYER

Father, I come before you to humble myself and pray, and seek Your face. I confess my sins and the sins of my ancestors, those that I know of and those that I don't. (Do this now.)

I ask You to forgive them for their sins for they knew not what they did. I stand on Your Word that You are faithful and just to forgive us and to cleanse us from all unrighteousness and heal the land of my family line.

I repent for holding onto unforgiveness and offenses in my heart. As an act of my will, I choose to forgive everyone that has ever hurt me or my loved ones, and I release them from every expectation I may have had in them.

I repent for any bitter-root judgments against them, criticizing them and speaking against them. I ask you, Lord, to forgive and release me with the same measure I forgive and release them.

Lord, expose my sin to me; show me wrong thoughts, attitudes, behaviors and wrong words that I have spoken against others as well as myself. Show me ungodly inner-images and internal blueprints that I have about myself as well. I am willing to repent and come out of agreement with all of them. I pray that You would give me Your perspective on every situation so I can see clearly through the eyes of Your understanding and not through the filters on my soul.

I plead the power of the blood of Jesus over every sin, transgression and iniquity in my soul and in my family line. I break the power of every curse; and I loose myself and my children from any and all inherited curses, curses from others, witchcraft or voodoo assignments, curses from my bloodline and culture. I break and renounce every judgment and wrong word spoken against my family or me by others or by myself in my own ignorance, in the name of Jesus.

I break all charms, hexes, spells, psychic powers, bewitchments, witchcraft, sorcery, incantations, impartations or assignments that have been put upon me or my family line as a result of participation in the occult, from any person or persons, living or dead. I break any occult or psychic sources, including a familiar spirit assigned to me at my birth to try to lead me astray during my life. I repent where my own sins have brought this on me. I rebuke all connected and related spirits and command them to loose me and my family in the name and by the blood of Jesus.

Father, I bind my body, soul and spirit to Your will and purposes for my life. I acknowledge and thank You for what the body of Jesus purchased for me, that His body was anointed to remove my burdens and destroy my yokes. His body absorbed every manifestation of the curse of the law so my body wouldn't have to.

I receive the benefits of the body of Christ as I partake of communion. I execute the judgment written on Calvary's cross. I enforce my covenant provisions as I partake of the bread, the representation of the body of Christ; I do this in remembrance of You. (Take bread)

Father, I acknowledge and thank You for what the blood of Your Son, Jesus purchased for me, that every day I can overcome the enemy by the Blood of the Lamb and the word of my testimony. I plead the power of the blood of Jesus over my family and me. I bind healing to our bodies and souls. I acknowledge that the Blood is the cup of blessing, which I bless. It is the cup of all the spiritual blessings in heavenly places in Christ Jesus.

As I partake of it, I am placing a demand on those blessings, moving them from the spiritual realm and causing them to be made manifest in this natural physical realm. I do this in remembrance of You. (*Take drink*)

SCRIPTURE REFERENCES:

II Chronicles 7:14; I John 1:9; Luke 23:34; John 20:23; Ephesians 1:18; Isaiah 53:4,5; 54:17; 10:27; Galatians 3:13; I Corinthians 10:16

Spiritual House Cleaning

Many people experience things like feeling a presence, movement, or strange occurrences in their homes. You will discover why these things happen, how to identify cursed objects and how to cleanse your home.

CHAPTER SEVEN

Iactually considered not putting this chapter in my class. However when I was laying out the workbook to teach from years ago, the Holy Spirit showed me that it would be an injustice to the process of wholeness if I left this material out.

So here it is, we have spent time dealing with the many areas of our soul that needed some cleaning up, it is time to turn our attention to our home in order to cleanse it also. We have come to understand that through the open door of sin, demons have been able to stake a claim to particular areas in our lives. This also includes objects in our possession, our home and the land we live on. We will see in this chapter that the enemy not only gains access through sin, but then has a legal right to be there until the sin is repented of and we evict him.

This seems to be a "hush-hush" subject in the body of Christ. It isn't talked about very much among believers. Before I was a Christian I had several disturbing experiences. One day I told a friend what was happening and she looked at me as if I were crazy. I knew right then, this is something you just don't discuss.

I think that is a common belief system among people, no one talks about this. By not exposing it we are leaving a door open for the enemy to have more room to torment us. Not knowing what to do about this subject has been another area where we are perishing for lack of knowledge - Hosea 4:6.

Several years ago I took a class on spiritual warfare. The teacher asked to see a show of hands for all the people who had experienced either movement, a presence, a feeling of not being alone, or strange unexplained occurrences. The majority of the room raised their hands. I was astonished. It seems that most Christians do not know what to do about this subject. One of the women who raised her hand was Jude, she had taken my class several times. I later asked her how it was that she was having symptoms in her home and had not dealt with them yet. Her answer was, "You know I guess it never dawned on me before, the stuff that happened was so familiar, the noises, feelings, etc, that I just accepted them as normal."

I have found when you talk about this subject with people it can bring up fear, so before we go any further I want to disarm the spirit of fear. Fear has no right, dominion or authority over the child of God.

II Timothy 1:7 says, *"For God hath not given us the spirit of fear; but of power, and of love, and of a sound mind."* When our mind is sound, there should be no fear or negative emotion. Being established in the perfect love that casts out fear will ground your heart and mind. - I John 4:18

The enemy can't do anything to you apart from fear. He needs you to agree with and operate the spiritual force of fear, so he can move. Likewise God needs us to agree with and operate the spiritual force of faith, so He can move on our behalf. These are spiritual forces and laws in operation. Fear operates the kingdom of darkness and faith operates the Kingdom of God. So the choice always comes back to us as to which kingdom we will operate.

Scripture warns us that we are to, *"Be sober, be vigilant; because your adversary the devil, as a roaring lion, walketh about seeking whom he may devour:"* - I Peter 5:8. You see just because he is walking around seeking whom he may devour doesn't mean that he 'may' devour you or me. So be grounded in your belief system - that he may not devour you!

James 4:7 says, *"Submit yourselves to God. Resist (stand against and oppose) the devil, and he will flee from you."* We all have this responsibility to resist the enemy, however many times we find ourselves not resisting, but unknowingly submitting.

Ephesians tells us that we are to be strong in the Lord, and in the power of His might. His might has been deposited within our born again spirit. We must access that might and stand against the wiles (methods of scheming and crafty deceit) of the devil (our false accuser). *"For we wrestle not against flesh and blood, but against principalities, against powers, against the rulers of the darkness of this world, against spiritual wickedness in high places."* - Ephesians 6:10-12

Did you ever hear the acronym for the word "fear?"

F - false
E - evidence
A - appearing
R - real

That's exactly what fear is, false evidence. We falsely believe that these things are more powerful that we are. Fear does not come from God; it is from the enemy. Being in fear is having more faith in the enemy's ability to harm you than God's ability to protect and bless you. God has given us power to tread over all the power of the enemy - Luke 10:19. Everything on this earth is subject to change if we will use our faith and operate the law of life in Christ Jesus. Say this out loud, "I'm as strong as I need to be to accomplish anything I place my attention on. I'm a creative genius, a child of my Father the Creator, therefore, I have in my possession all of the DNA, anointing and ability I need to tread over all the power of the enemy and nothing shall by any means harm me. I am able to fulfill my God-given destiny."

OUR RESPONSIBILITY

Genesis 1:26 tells that we have a God-given responsibility over this earth, it says, *"And God said, 'Let Us make man in Our image, after Our likeness: and let them have dominion over... all the earth..."*

The word *dominion* means to - tread down, prevail against, reign, rule over, and take.

God placed man on earth and commissioned us to have dominion; to tread down, and prevail against the enemy. We saw in the first chapter that Adam didn't do very well with his dominion and as a result of his sin man has lost ground not only in our soul lives, but in our home and on our land as well.

When we walk in our rightful authority and begin to take dominion, we can take back what the enemy has stolen from us and reclaim the ground we have lost. This begins by being a good steward over our soul, bodies, lives, relationships, family, etc. As we have learned, when we are not a good steward evil can gain a foothold through our sin and neglect.

Ephesians 4:17–27 gives clear instruction on what is required of us,

> **17** *This I say therefore, and testify in the Lord, that ye henceforth walk not as other Gentiles walk, in the vanity (emptiness) of their mind / soul,*
> **18** *Having the understanding darkened. Being alienated from the life of God through the ignorance that is in them, because of the blindness (stupidity) of their (hardened) heart:*

We are being commissioned here to not walk as other people walk in the emptiness of their darkened understanding.

In the first chapter on the Fall of Man we learned that when Adam sinned he lost his God given spiritual vision and the eyes of his soul / understanding became darkened. We can see this is the condition of the human race. Paul is telling us not to walk like that any longer.

> **19** *Who being past feeling have given themselves over unto lasciviousness (pressures of the flesh), to work all uncleanness with greediness.*
> **20** *But ye have not so learned Christ;*
> **21** *If so be that ye have heard Him, (and we have) and have been taught by Him (and we have), as the truth is in Jesus:*
> **22** *That ye put off concerning the former conversation (soul behavior) the old man, which is corrupt (defiled) according to the deceitful lusts;*
> **23** *And be renewed in the spirit of your mind;*
> **24** *And that ye put on the new man, which after God is created in righteousness and true holiness.*

This is *The Answer*. It is what we have been learning in every chapter so far: how to walk in the power of our born again human spirit, being led by the Holy Spirit who dwells with in us and release on purpose the DNA of our Father so we can walk in righteousness and true holiness.

> **25** *Wherefore putting away lying, speak every man truth with his neighbor: for we are members one of another.*

26 *Be ye angry, and sin not: let not the sun go down upon your wrath:*

27 *Neither give place to the devil."*

These verses in Ephesians are a great example of how we have given place to the devil. At the fall, man lost his spiritual vision and the eyes of his understanding became darkened. So through ignorance and darkened understanding we have yielded to pressures from the kingdom of darkness that have come our way.

Did you notice that when your old man (*psuche* - your soul) is in control, you are usually giving place to the devil?

The word *give* in Greek means - offer, yield, or deliver.

The word *place* in Greek means - a position.

To amplify what Ephesians 4:27 says, don't give, offer, yield to, or deliver up to the devil any foothold. Don't let him secure a position, or place, where he can steal, kill and destroy in our personal life as well as on our land. This is our mandate from God - *"Don't give place!"*

One area we probably have not recognized as 'giving place' is where it says, "be angry and sin not." This was a big problem for me. When I was angry I formed judgments, became offended and spoke sharply with people. I am sure I'm not alone in this. I have come to understand that to "be angry and sin not" means to keep my heart pure while I am upset. We do this by guarding our thoughts and emotions from developing a destructive stronghold or unhealthy emotional tie. Choose to see others and their actions through the Father's eyes and keep your heart clean. At times we will have righteous anger, that is to feel angry over the same unrighteous actions and injustices that make God angry, while we keep our hearts pure toward people by maintaining our love walk and keeping the mind of Christ in every situation.

The last verse says, *"Let not the sun go down upon your wrath: Neither give place to the devil."* I never thought of going to bed angry as "giving place to the devil." Now that our understanding has been enlightened about this it would be wise of us to give as much reconciliation as possible with the people we can. There will be others perhaps that we can't reconcile with before sun down. Then we must do what it takes to get our hearts right before we go to sleep.

Now that we know our responsibility it is essential that we put off the old man which is our soul nature and put on the new man which after God is created in righteousness and true holiness in our spirit.

SCRIPTURE WARNS US ABOUT OUR LAND BEING CURSED:

Leviticus 18:1-4, 24-25 gives great instruction, *"And the LORD spake unto Moses, saying, Speak unto the children of Israel, and say unto them, I am the LORD your God. After the doings (customs) of the land of Egypt, wherein ye dwelt, shall ye not do: and after the doings of the land of Canaan, whither I bring you, shall ye not do: neither shall ye walk in their ordinances. Ye shall do My judgments, and keep Mine ordinances, to walk therein: I am the LORD your God... Defile not ye yourselves in any of these things: for in all these the nations (people) are defiled (contaminated, polluted, unclean) which I cast out before you: And the land is defiled (contaminated, polluted, unclean): therefore I do visit the iniquity thereof upon it, and the land itself vomiteth out her inhabitants."*

The sins God says that defiled the land were: incest (vs 6-19), adultery (vs 20), divination (vs 21), homosexuality (vs 22), and bestiality (vs 23). These were the customs, behaviors and ways of the people.

The Lord is saying here that I brought you out of Egypt where you had observed the people's ways and customs. I am bringing you into Canaan where you can also see the ways and customs of these people. Both nations Egypt and Canaan have been defiled (contaminated, polluted, unclean) with iniquity as a result of the people's sins; their ways and ordinances have defiled them and their land is now defiled as well, vomiting out their inhabitants. I don't want you to be defiled by behaving like the people you have been observing. I want you to do My judgments, and keep Mine ordinances, to walk therein so that you can remain blessed.

Ezra 9:11b gives a warning as well saying, *"The land, unto which ye go to possess it, is an unclean land with the filthiness of the people of the lands, with their abominations, which have filled it from one end to another with their uncleanness."*

We can see that whether we have sinned or others have sinned on our land, the land becomes unclean and defiled as a result of the sin. The land has been delivered up to the kingdom of darkness which now has the legal right to secure a position, to bring stealing, killing and destruction. We then inherit all kinds of demons and the curses their presence brings because they have been given legal right to the land.

Perhaps you have never thought in these terms before. We all have sinned, so the land we sinned on, the house we sinned in, have been left with an unclean stain. We are so accustomed to sin we haven't realized the stain that sin has left, giving place to evil spirits and the curse their presence brings.

Genesis 4: 9-10 says, *"And the LORD said unto Cain, Where is Abel thy brother? And he said, I know not: Am I my brother's keeper? And He said, What hast thou done? The voice of thy brother's blood crieth unto Me from the ground."*

God even hears the cry of shed blood on the land. No wonder He told Joshua, *"Every place that the sole of your foot shall tread upon, that have I given unto you, as I said unto Moses."* - Joshua 1:3

God was saying Joshua, *I have given* - I have assigned this land for you to avenge, so that it can be healed, I want you to bring forth restoration and deliverance in this place. Don't look at the sins of the people, their customs or ways just avenge the land. This is still our mandate today.

We are seeing that the kingdom of darkness operates according to the course of this world (system - whirlpool,) according to the prince of the power of the air, the spirit that now worketh in the children of disobedience. - Ephesians 2:2

This is saying to us that when we live a lifestyle of disobedience we are giving place to the kingdom of darkness; the prince of the power of the air is at work not only in the children of darkness, but defiling the land as well.

Through all these chapters you can clearly see that evil spirits are given authority and place to operate legally through open doors of sin, word curses, trauma and the occult.

Ecclesiastes 10:8 explains clearly that, *"He that diggeth a pit shall fall into it; and whoso breaketh an hedge (enclosure, fence, wall), a serpent shall bite (strike, sting, oppress) him."* The hedge was put in place by God. It is activated through our obedience and deactivated through our disobedience. Our disobedience causes us to "give-place" to the enemy, then he can secure his position in our lives, homes and families for generations.

In his book, *Protecting Your Home from Spiritual Darkness*, Chuck D. Pierce records a list of sins and their symptoms along with instructions for cleansing.

SOME SINS THAT BRING DEFILEMENT ON LAND

1. **Idolatry** (Exodus 20:3-4) The worship of false gods curses the land.

2. **Immorality, fornication, sexual sins** (Leviticus 18:1-23)

3. **Bloodshed, abortion** (Genesis 4:11; Numbers 35:33-34; Psalm 106:37-39)

4. **Broken covenants with God or man, divorce** - a covenant-breaking demon can be affecting all new tenants of that land. Some of our homes have been built on land that was taken from Indians through broken treaties, giving the enemy a foothold to the land we live on.

5. **Anger** I am talking about unrighteous anger that can defile our land. Ephesians 4:26 tells us, *"Be ye angry, and sin not: let not the sun go down upon your wrath: Neither give place to the devil. Let him that stole steal no more:"*

Symptoms

1. Sudden, ongoing illness; constant sickness – may come from generational curses or you may be living in a house where a spirit of infirmity has place.

2. Continual bad dreams and nightmares – may be the result of your own or generational occult involvement.

3. Insomnia, can't rest peacefully

4. Behavioral or relational problems among adults or children such as constant fighting, miscommunication, strife

5. No peace

6. Unexplained illness and fatigue

7. Heightened bondages

8. Ghosts, spirits, movements

9. Foul, unexplained odors

10. Atmospheric heaviness, nausea, headaches

MY EXPERIENCES

In the early 1980's I was not walking with God, I was working at a strip club as a bartender, doing drugs and living it up, as they say. One particular night my boyfriend and I were in my bed together, wide awake. Suddenly we heard the sound of my electric curlers, which were on my nightstand, moving slowly as if they were being pushed. Then they went flying violently across the room with great force; there were curlers and clips all over the place. We were both in shock and couldn't believe what just happened, it was pretty scary. Having never experienced anything like that before, we stayed up for hours talking about it. What I didn't tell him that night was that my uncle had recently passed away and I ignorantly believed that he swiped those curlers off the night stand. I believed he was trying to show me that he did not want me with that man and that he was unhappy with me. The next day my mom came over to cut my hair. As she was trimming my bangs, I told her what happened and how I thought it was her brother that smashed my curlers across the room. When I stood up and looked in the mirror she had cut my bangs as short as a pixie almost up to the top of my head. I was horrified and so upset. I said, "What did you do to me!?" She yelled, "Why did you tell me Uncle Vinnie was here?" I upset her, and my hair showed it for quite some time.

You see when things like this happen we do think it's a relative. Let me tell you when grandma's rocker is rocking, it's not grandma! We think it is and so these manifestations become familiar to us and we begin to accept things in our homes that we shouldn't. Many have said things like: "But it gives me a warm feeling, I feel like they are protecting me, they smell just like the person used to smell," etc. So they don't want to accept the fact that these occurrences are not happening by their loved one. The truth is, to be absent from the body is to be present with the Lord for the child of God - II Corinthians 5:8. Spirits familiar with your family will mimic their smells, behaviors, walking the halls, and doing similarities like your lost loved one. It is not okay for that spirit to remain. Only the Holy Spirit is our comforter, protector, guide and helper.

One night I was waiting in the car while a friend went inside a house to buy drugs. While sitting in the car completely sober I could see figures, hundreds of them walking all around the car and the yard of the house. I kept staring at them almost in disbelief, I couldn't believe what I was seeing. I wasn't really afraid, I was thinking that they were the spirits of dead people roaming the earth and my eyes were being opened to see them. After that I had a great awareness of how we are not alone. I knew that there were crowds everywhere we just couldn't see them. Frequently I would see shadowy figures out of the corner of my eye, like someone had walked by; then I'd turn my head and no one was there. Of course now I now understand that what I saw were not dead people at all, but the Lord was opening my eyes to see the kingdom of darkness. He was so faithful to keep drawing me and revealing things to me. Even in my disobedience He never left me or forsook me.

I moved to a beautiful older home that used to be a convent right across the street from Holy Rosary Church. There were three apartments in that house and mine was on the first floor. It was common for me to be in my apartment and hear constant walking back and forth; all the while know-ing that no one was home upstairs. I heard it all the time. The people who lived up there moved out and my future husband Mark moved in on the second floor. He would be downstairs with me and we would both hear the walking. Many times we would go up and investigate only to find nothing was there.

Mark told me that when he lived with his parents his sister would hear walking in his room when he wasn't home. Mark's mom and sister believed it was from the record albums Mark had in his room.

While I was living in that old convent is when the 700 Club called me and I gave my life back to the Lord. From that moment on I never touched drugs again. I remember one day I was sitting in my living room praying and it felt like a faucet had been turned on in my heart and water was rushing through me. I felt like I was being filled with God. I called Mark's mom and told her what was happening to me and she told me about John 7:38 that said, *"He that believeth on me, as the scripture hath said, out of his belly shall flow rivers of living water."* That was exactly what I was experiencing, rivers of water pouring in my heart, what a sensation! She told me that I was just baptized in the Holy Spirit and I could now speak in tongues. We hung up, I went in my bedroom, got on my knees and did just that!

When I look back I can see that even thought I led a 'party girl' lifestyle, I only had these experiences when I was completely sober. They never happened when I was high. You'd think it would be the other way around but it wasn't.

When Mark and I got married in 1986, we were both baby Christians. We moved to a house in Hilton, NY. Mark worked nights at the Post Office and he would leave around 10:30 pm; it was just Jenelle and me at home. I hadn't had any manifestations in some time until we moved into this house. At that time we had a water bed, I would be laying there alone, reading or watching television when suddenly it was as if a very large dog came and jumped on the bed and ran up along side of me. The waves from the bed were very strong and as I was being tossed around on the bed, I could feel myself being touched. I felt a hand across my head and through my hair. A figure came alongside my body. I was gripped with terror. That was one of the worst and most personal manifestations I ever had. Jenelle was asleep and of course I was her only protection, so I just began calling on the name of Jesus until it stopped. I was still a new baby Christian, but I was forced to learn spiritual warfare and learn it quickly. I was really afraid. Before Christ I didn't have fear when these things happened. I had fear about everything else in life but not these types of things, why?

213

Perhaps because they had me? This thing jumping on my bed and being touched happened several times. Other times it sounded like there were toenails scratching the top of the dresser or the bathroom floor. I would call for someone to pray with me and they could hear the sounds as well. After prayer they always left. I didn't understand why they kept coming back?

One day Jenelle had her friend Melissa over and they were sitting on the front porch playing. Melissa told Jenelle that she heard dogs growling near her and Jenelle told her we didn't have any dogs. I told Mark and asked him where his albums were. He told me they were in the house but he didn't listen to them. I asked him if we could get rid of them. That night he put them in the car and was leaving for work. On his way to work he was in a car accident and the car was totaled. Thank God he wasn't hurt but all those albums got towed away with that car, good riddance to them.

After living in Hilton for a few years, we eventually did get a couple of dogs and some birds. They used to sleep in the spare bedroom next to ours. One night Mark was home and everyone was sleeping but us. It was a Friday night and we were in bed watching 20/20. They were talking about Shirley Maclaine's experiences, astral projection and then they interviewed a man who was a spirit guide. The interviewer asked the man to channel the spirit for the interview. When he did, that spirit came right through the TV and into our house. Immediately the dogs began howling. The bird cage was banging against the wall and you could hear the birds screaming and flapping frantically. It sounded like someone was in that room killing the animals. Mark reached into the headboard to get his gun as I was laying there frozen in fear and I said to him, "I don't think that is going to help." I reached for the phone and called his mom, she could hear the commotion and commanded that spirit to leave in the name of Jesus and immediately it left. That night I learned not to watch anything like that on TV because it gave it entrance to my house.

By this time in our lives we had just started attending New Testament Christian Church so I went to my Pastor and told him what was happening. The elders of the church came over to pray through our house and anoint the doors and windows with oil. They taught Mark and me how to pray together, therefore we began to do that every night before he left for work and all the manifestations stopped! On July 29, 1988 when Jenelle was 7 years old, we were sitting on the couch together watching a video tape of worship, when I heard her crying. I looked down and said, "What's the matter, why are you crying?" She said, "I just love God so much and I can feel water running in and through my heart!" Wow that's exactly what happened to me! So I told her what my mother-in-law told me. You are being filled with the Holy Spirit and now you can pray in tongues, and she did! I had never known of anyone getting baptized in the Holy Spirit with that kind of experience and now it happened to my child as well, hmm. (In the late 1990's I read a book by Smith Wigglesworth where he described having the exact same experience, so now I know three.)

I could tell that Jenelle was sensitive to spiritual things like I was, even though she was only 7. I remember one day while driving her to school she told me she could hear angels singing in the car.

We lived in that house in Hilton for five years and then moved to North Ave in Greece right across the street from our church. In our new home I was a much stronger Christian and quite a warrior, after unfortunately learning the hard way. I had prayed through this house and anointed the doors and windows with oil. But I began having a different kind of experience. Every once in a while I would be laying in bed watching TV, when I would see a dark figure flying through the door of the room from the hallway and headed right for me. I would scream, jump, run, duck under this figure and run out of the room, then I would continue on in warfare, not being as gripped with fear as I used to be. I felt I was being harassed, as this happened several times. One time we were at the cottage up in the Thousand Islands with Mark's parents. I was in bed, awake, the door was open, the hall light was on and my mother-in-law was standing in the bathroom right across from me. All of a sudden here comes this thing flying in the door headed right for me. Again I would scream, jump, run and duck under it, running right into Mark's mom. We prayed, commanded it to leave and I went back to bed.

One day my sister Jodie said, "You know I have this weird thing that keeps happening to me." She described exactly what was happening to me. Had she never mentioned it I would not have thought to ask anyone in the family if that ever happened to them. So now I was able to identify it as some sort of generational thing and war against it.

When we first got cable television as kids, my sister Jodie and I would watch the movie *The Exorcist* over and over in the dark. We had a Ouija board, it worked, we did séances with our neighbors and they worked; all of this we did as kids in ignorance, not realizing the danger and how it opened the door to the kingdom of darkness in our lives. After identifying its root; then breaking and canceling its power over us, it has never returned.

I now believe that my involvement with the occult as a teenager, participation with drugs as a young adult and my sinful life style all contributed in opening the door for many of these manifestations I experienced. For a while I didn't know if they followed me house to house, or if every house I lived in was haunted. I think it might have been a bit of both. Most importantly is that I learned how to get rid of it.

As I grew in my Christianity I learned that one of my gifts is discernment. I am very sensitive to atmospheric heaviness, changes, presences, etc. That is why even before coming to Christ, I was able to see and hear things that others could not. That helped me to understand why these things seemed to happen to me and not the people around me.

During these same years my dad lived in a historical cobblestone home that was part of the Underground Railroad in upstate New York. The house had a name and for the sake of protecting my family I will pretend the name of the house was "The Fields." So shortly after my dad and his wife moved in this house they began making changes, remodeling, painting, etc. They would begin sharing with us some strange occurrences that were happening in the house. My stepmom told me that one morning a wreath that had been hanging on the bedroom door was now laying in the bath tub. They would hear pots and pans clanging in the kitchen. They had a standing joke that anytime they made any changes to the house "The Fields" didn't like it and would act out. They were always making changes so there was a lot of activity.

On one Thanksgiving the whole family was there for dinner. My sister Jodie was sitting across the table from me. Suddenly she said, "Hey, something just smacked me in the head." As she looked to her husband sitting next to her, we could all see it wasn't him. It wasn't anyone (that we could see). Then my sister Marlo sitting to my left said, "Hey something just smacked me in the head." While everyone is laughing and saying it must be "The Fields", I went up to the bathroom and began spiritual warfare commanding that spirit to leave; then I came downstairs and sat down. Mark said, "I thought you guys got rid of your cats?" Dad says, "Yes we did." Mark and Marlo looked at me and asked, "What were you doing upstairs?" They both heard the sound of cat claws running over the plank wood floors. I laughed because they heard the spirits running out of the house! Every time I went to my dad's house I would stand in the gap and intercede, binding any spirit that was given place there and commanding it to go in Jesus' name.

The manifestations had stopped for years when one day my stepmother said, "They're back!" and she was laughing. I said, "Get out!" then proceeded to ask her what happened? She was getting up for work and dad was still sleeping when she heard voices downstairs (that was a new one). She said she went down to see and when she got to the family room the television was on, the lights were on, the pillows were thrown all over the couch, the drawers to the table were not only pulled out, but up on the table and the room was a mess. This was not at all like she left it. She laughed it off and said, "Oh, they are upset because your dad just painted the kitchen." I quickly asked the Lord, how is it that this happened again? Immediately He showed me the power of words unlocked them. There was a belief system in place and words spoken 'that every time we make any changes to the house "The Fields" don't like it and act out.' Well as soon as another change was made there was a new manifestation. This time I broke the power of those words so that could never happen again. I realized I could only go so far with that house. It didn't belong to me, however because it was my family I had some limited authority. My family doesn't understand spiritual laws so they could open a spiritual door I had closed and they would never know it.

A couple of years ago two very old sisters came to the house. They told my stepmom that they grew up in the house and asked if they could come inside. They walked through the house reminiscing and before leaving they asked if there were any strange occurrences in the house. They went on to tell their own stories of manifestations in that house. They heard violins playing, that was a new one.

The message God gave the children of Israel to go in and drive the giants out of their promised land is still our mandate today. Just as we have been learning to drive them out of the ground of our soul, so too we have to drive them out of the physical land that we live on.

Demonic forces that were given place will remain and continue to operate until we repent of the sin that opened the door and drive them out. Like words and curses they have no expiration date. Demons are not going to leave your house or land just because you moved in. You have to drive them out and take back the land by faith and by force.

Jesus commissioned us when He said, *"Behold, I give unto you power (super human delegated authority) to tread on serpents and scorpions, and over all the power of the enemy: and nothing shall by any means hurt you."* - Luke 10:19

I don't want you to be in fear over these things. Maybe you have never heard anything like this before. That is why I took the time at the beginning of the chapter to expose fear and build your faith. You must know who you are in Christ and that the enemy is under your feet if you'll keep him there.

ROBBIN'S STORY

Shortly after moving into a renovated historic school house in Hilton, NY., Robbin was diagnosed with lupus and multiple sclerosis. She would often come to the altar for prayer. She said that after prayer she would feel relief but it was temporary and the symptoms would come back. So while she was struggling with her health she began sharing stories with me of hearing walking in her attic at night. She said that both she and her husband had experiences of waking up in the middle of the night feeling like someone was on top of them trying to crush them. One weekend they went up to the cottage and her husband was attacked there during the night with a manifestation in the night of being crushed and suffocated.

218

One afternoon a bunch of us girls were at her house visiting and she was telling us of all the manifestations. So we began walking around the house and looking in all the rooms. We saw that her husband had an extensive collection of pewter dragons and castles that were very expensive. There were also some collections of demonic movies and books. So she put everything in several large garbage bags and put them out on the porch. When her husband came home from work she told him what we identified and asked if he would get rid of it. After much hesitation, he finally agreed.

However, the manifestations didn't stop. They made arrangements for the elders of the church to come pray. I was unable to be there when the meeting started and arrived about an hour later. When I arrived I just went and sat on the couch and began to pray. Immediately I was gripped with fear and felt very uncomfortable. After some time my friend Pat, who was leading the meeting, asked me how I was feeling. I told her I was being gripped with fear. She smiled in her yup-that-is-what-I-was-looking-for confirming smile. We continued to stand in the gap, repent, plead the blood of Jesus and pray, doing all that we knew to do.

Then Pat asked me to come with her over to the attic door. When we walked over there she asked me to touch the door and tell her what my impressions were. When I touched the door, a horrific scream came out of me and I was immediately doubled over on the floor in terror and travail. This was not something I made happen of my own accord. I was on the floor hysterical for some time as they were interceding around me. I guess Pat got the confirmation she was looking for. Everyone continued to pray and intercede.

As I mentioned earlier, I am extremely sensitive in the area of discernment which is why I can see and hear the things I do. My chest felt heavy and it was hard to breath. When it lifted, I was so very upset that this had happened to me that I shouted, "What the ___ was that?" "I don't ever want that to happen to me, ever again!" Pat told me that before I arrived they had been interceding and the Lord showed them a horrific crime that had been perpetrated against a little girl. Well it must have happened in that attic because when I touched the door, I literally felt what that little girl had felt. Robbin told us that her cat was recently found dead in front of the attic door.

By the time I calmed down Robbin's brother, Michael, had arrived. We didn't tell him anything that had happened and just asked him to walk through the house and pray and tell us of the impressions he was getting. After awhile he told us he too was gripped with fear upon arriving at the house. He went and walked through the basement and he said he could see shadowy figures moving and flying out the basement windows.

By the end of the evening I was still gripped with fear and did not want to go home alone. Pat prayed for me and all the fear was instantly gone! I like when it leaves that fast! I was able to drive home, Mark was gone for the evening and I had no fear being home alone. It was clear to us, that as we were praying, the spirits were leaving. However, we did not free that house from the demonic hold on it. Soon the manifestations were back. Obviously, we did not have enough information to accurately take back that land.

There were still areas where the kingdom of darkness had some legal ground, so Robbin and her husband put the house up for sale by owner. A woman came to see the house. After walking through the house she said to Robbin, "I love this house, there are spirits here." She bought the house and Robbin and her family moved out. Every manifestation of lupus and multiple sclerosis left Robbin's body and she was completely made whole!

In the example of Robbin's house, we can see how the sins of others had caused the land to become unclean and defiled. The land had been delivered up to the kingdom of darkness and given legal right to secure a position, to bring stealing, killing and destruction. That is why when Robbin moved into that house she inherited the curses and sickness. She wasn't aware of these dark kingdom entities in that new house and she had doors in her life that she had also opened through past behaviors.

JUDE'S STORY

I want to go back to a story I started in the beginning of this chapter. I told you that I went to another church to take a class on spiritual warfare. The teacher asked to see a show of hands for all the people who had experienced either movement, a presence, a feeling of not being alone, or strange unexplained occurrences. The majority of the room raised their hands. I was astonished because one of the women who raised their hand was Jude, who had taken my class several times. I later asked her how it was that she was having symptoms in her home and had not dealt with them yet. Her answer was, "You know, I guess it never dawned on me before, the stuff that happened was so familiar, noises, feelings, etc, that I just accepted them as normal."

After that night Pat and I set up a time to go to Jude's house and spiritually clean it. I remember it being a very hot summer day. Jude had her friend Joy there as well. We began talking and asked if her house had a story. Did she know anything about the previous owners? Jude said that the previous owners were two lesbian women and one of them killed herself by asphyxiation in the garage.

We began in the bedrooms, just walking, praying, using our discernment, anointing the doors and windows with oil. When we were in the spare bedroom there was an oriental temple on the dresser. Pat asked Jude, "Do you know this is a temple for the worship of a false god?" Jude said, "Oh, I guess you're right." See, to her it just looked like something pretty. She was willing to get rid of it, so we began praying and commanding the spirit of that false god associated with that temple to leave.

Suddenly the front screen door opened wide and slammed shut, hard. We thought Jude's husband just walked in the house. He wouldn't understand what we were doing so we all just casually walked out of the bedroom. Much to our surprise, no one was there. We realized that the spirit that went with the temple just left and it slammed the door on its way out. We had a nice laugh over that and kept praying.

When we got to the garage, the door was open so we went inside, but it was very hot and humid in there. Still, we stood there and began to pray again. We were doing identificational repentance for a lesbian lifestyle, breaking the power of agreements and words that were spoken in that house, canceling their assignments and commanding them to leave. Then we got to the spirit of death, we began repenting for the agreement with death and breaking the power of death that was released in that house to kill. We broke its power over Jude's family, etc.

As we did this, we all could feel the heaviness on our chest, it was hard to breath and we felt dizzy and disoriented. Once every door was repented of and closed, we commanded death out of that garage and off of that property. Suddenly a very cold wind went through the garage; it was so cold that we had chill bumps, then just as suddenly it was stifling hot again. We literally felt that spirit being whisked away and the house was clean. To top it off, we walked the property, pouring oil from a squeeze bottle to draw a blood line around the property by faith, sealing the work we had done

Here are some scriptures which show our God-given responsibility as a good steward over our home and the land that we live on:

Deuteronomy 7:25-26 admonishes us that, *"The graven images of their gods shall ye burn with fire: thou shalt not desire the silver or gold that is on them, nor take it unto thee, lest thou be snared therein: for it is an abomination to the LORD thy God. Neither shalt thou bring an abomination into thine house, lest thou be a cursed thing like it: but thou shalt utterly detest it, and thou shalt utterly abhor it; for it is a cursed thing."* Did you notice that when you bring a cursed thing into your house you become snared and cursed?

Deuteronomy 8:1 also says, *"All the commandments which I command thee this day shall ye observe to do, that ye may live, (means to - stay alive, be nourished, preserved from danger, restored to wholeness) and multiply, and go in and possess (occupy by driving out the previous tenants, seize and inherit with out fail) the land which the LORD sware unto your fathers."*

This needs to be our posture that by faith and by force we are possessing our promised land, driving out the enemy. Knowing who you are in Christ should cause aggressive faith to rise up in you, but too many Christians are passive and laying down under the kingdom of darkness.

There are several principles we need to observe in order to prepare ourselves to spiritually clean our homes. As we have learned while reading this book, it is important to search our heart daily for sin, including wrong words, attitudes, judgments, behaviors, ungodly soul ties and generational issues.

We know that repentance and the appropriation of the blood of Jesus brings forgiveness, cleansing from all unrighteousness, and subsequent liberty.

II Chronicles 7:14 is a perfect example of how to do this; it says, *"If my people, which are called by my name, shall humble themselves, and pray, and seek my face, and turn from their wicked ways; then will I hear from heaven, and will forgive their sin, and will heal their land."*

Having repented and aligned ourselves to the will of God, we are now positioned to tread on serpents and scorpions and over all the power of the enemy and nothing shall by any means hurt us - Luke 10:19. Jesus has already defeated the enemy and made an open show of him. We are only called to enforce the victory! The kingdom of darkness and every low-level devil have no right, dominion or authority over the born again child of God. No right to our homes, our families, our health, our finances or anything that is a God given provision, unless we give it to them. We must enforce our victory.

It is important to know that we must heed spiritual boundaries, submitting to authorities that are over us. (Women, if your husbands are not believers or not yet in agreement, do not remove any object without their permission. Do not press the issue if they don't understand.)

I don't want you to go grab all your husband's pornography, demonic movies, or drug paraphernalia and throw them out. But instead go lay hands on his stuff and pray. We know that pornography ties our minds and emotions as well as our bodies, with images, leaving the door open for perverted sexual spirits. So it is wise to bind the power of the enemy off the object, plead the Blood over his stuff, plead the Blood over his clothes, his pillow, etc. Cancel curses and bind any demon attached to it declaring that it can not influence your husband and it has to stay bound in Jesus' name. Then trust God to bring it to pass.

Avoid strife, for where there is strife there is every evil work. I see couples pick each other apart, put each other down, make little jabs in jest, when really it is a truth they are trying to drive home. This is all creating strife and opening the door for every evil work in your relationships, home, family, kids, etc. I see women do this more than men. Men are usually quiet and just ignore us. Women, you set the tone for the house, so you can change any environment if you use wisdom and are led by the Holy Spirit.

The cleansing of your home, like the cleansing of soul issues, is a process and may take some time. Allow the Holy Spirit to guide you.

Pray audibly and, if possible, in agreement with another family member or believer. Do it by faith. Believe you receive when you pray. Every house cleaning will be different because every home has a history and story to tell.

Sometimes on a Sunday afternoon Mark and I like to go to open houses. We are always looking and you never know what treasure you may find. On this one particular day, I have to admit, I was not walking in the spirit.

I was up in the master bedroom of an open house and Mark was downstairs. In the master bedroom I noticed there were weird pictures of Jesus, like I had never seen before. I began to get a bad feeling in this house. I was looking at the pictures of the family on the dresser and to be quite honest I was being a soulish Christian, not discerning the Holy Spirit at all. I thought, 'Well I think I better pray for these people.' My discernment was working, but not enough to show me not to touch the bed. I was ready to do spiritual warfare; not just a 'God Bless you' prayer. I laid my hands on their bed to pray, when suddenly I felt like I was electrocuted by hundreds of tiny bee stings all over my body. I jumped back and said, "Whoa."

Then I knew immediately how stupid I was. I had no authority in that house to bind any evil spirits. I passed Mark on the stairs going down. At the bottom of the stairs was the realtor who politely asked me, "So how do you like the house?" Honestly, I was so irritated, mad and carnal that my answer to her was rather harsh. I said, " I don't like the house." She said, "Really? What don't you like?" I said, "You don't want to know." She said, "No, really, tell me I want to know." This went back and forth a few times and out of frustration, because she wouldn't drop it, I blurted out, "This house is full of demons."

She looked at me wide-eyed and said, "Really? It's interesting that you should say that because the owner of the house is a witch, in fact she owns a psychic detective agency."

I thought to myself, "Wow, of course I got stung so badly. This wasn't just anyone, the owner was a witch and a high level one at that. I quickly said to her that I am very sensitive to these things, that's how I knew and didn't like the house. Mark and I left that house and when we got in the car I told him how stupid I was. I repented for being carnal and then pled the Blood of Jesus over us, cleansed us from all defilement or transference of anything that would try to follow after us.

This taught me a valuable lesson I pray I never forget. Demons are very territorial, they know where they have legal ground and they understand authority. Unfortunately for me I forgot that fact. Stay within the realm of your authority. You have authority in your own home. You have some authority in your families' homes, especially if they have given you a key to their house; you have some authority where you work. Some authority can go a long way but it will have to be maintained by you, because other peoples' behaviors can undo the good you've done.

Have you ever walked into an environment and felt "icky" or had a bad "vibe?" Have you ever walked into a room where there has been strife and even though no one is fighting in front of you the tension can be felt in the air? Have you ever left a place and felt like you needed a bath? That is discernment. Usually we just "feel" these feelings and we don't know why. Begin to pay attention to how you "feel" in certain places. Next time that happens stop and ask the Lord what He wants you to know, see, or do in that place. This is part of what intercession is about. When you have to be in an environment that is not peaceful, prepare yourself spiritually, be prayed up, keep your spiritual eyes open for areas where the Lord needs you to intercede.

There are no set rules for spiritual house cleaning, only guidelines. Here are some of those guidelines:

1. **Dedicate your home to the Lord.**
   Pray and invite the presence of the Lord into your home. Declare that as for you and your house, you will serve the Lord - Joshua 24:15.

Most Christians will do this because we do know a little bit. But we have left out the eviction process of the spirits that may be there.

2. Believe the Lord for strategy.

The Holy Spirit may lead you to:
a. Play praise music.
b. Read scriptures.
c. Plead the blood of Jesus over your family members.
d. Command the spirit to exit. (Be led by the Holy Spirit. You may want to anoint the entry points and beds with oil and plead the Blood.) The most important thing is to be sensitive to the Holy Spirit and do what He shows you no matter how silly you might think it is.

3. Take inventory.

Please take your liberty here and underline or make a separate list of all the things characterized below that pertain to you. So when you are ready to close doors and pray you aren't forgetting anything.

Satan looks for any way he can to find entry into your life and home. Some often neglected items are old love letters, memorabilia, cards, pictures or gifts from past relationships. Many times a spirit of lust may be attached to those things. There may also be an unhealthy soul tie keeping the door open for a spirit that is hindering wholeness in your present or future relationships.

Sometimes we have an item from a past relationship to which our soul is tied. If that item is hindering a future relationship in any way, even if it brings up fond memories of the past that hinders the maturing of a future relationship, then you might want to consider getting rid of the item.

One woman in my class had items from her dead husband. She loved and missed him so much. She was re-married and those items were hindering her heart from fully committing to her new husband. Once she got rid of them her heart was free.

If items are bringing up bad memories or triggering a trauma, you know for sure it has to go. These items can be an open door for a spirit to keep harassing you. So look specifically for items that trigger emotions, then examine the emotion. The Holy Spirit will show you what to do.

Other neglected items are our clothing. I suggest periodically going through your closet, identifying clothing that may represent painful periods of your life, or items that hold memories that you shouldn't be hanging on to, and get rid of them.

Your soul can be tied to memorabilia, pictures, jewelry, etc. Any "thing" that can bring up a negative emotion or pain is an unhealthy soul tie and may have demonic attachments. So consider getting rid of it.

HOTEL ROOMS

There is a lot of sin and immorality that takes place in hotel rooms. Because we have paid for the room, it gives us legal spiritual authority to cleanse our environment. It is always a good idea to stand in the gap and repent for any sin that was committed in that place before you rest there.

Take a few minutes and be sensitive to your environment, as the Holy Spirit may lead you to pray more specifically. Pay attention to the artwork and items in the room for anything that looks strange. Then command every spirit that has had legal right to be there to go. Plead the Blood of Jesus over the room and receive the filling of the Holy Spirit and ministry of angels in your new environment.

Every time I've taught this, I've asked my students for a show of hands to see who cleanses the hotel rooms they enter. The majority of my students have not done this.

In the early 1990's my mom and I went to a Christian retreat center in Virginia Beach. It was a beautiful hotel, the grounds were fabulous, and you could feel the presence of God in this place. But that night in the hotel room I was awakened by a man's face leaning over mine, staring at me. It was so real, so vivid and frightening that I screamed a horrible sound and jumped out of bed, scaring the heck out of my mother. I couldn't understand why that happened to me in such a wonderful Christian place. I was still pretty ignorant of spiritual things back then. But again, I learned the hard way and I never stay in a room without cleansing it first.

Following is a list of some things to look for in your house. This list comes from the book, *Portals to Cleansing* by Dr. Henry Malone, pages 24-28.

MEDIA

Look over all music, videos, books and games that have Satanic, New Age, psychic, horror or occult themes or that deal with murder, pornography, perversion or inappropriate sexual material; all games associated with Wizards of the Coast, including Pokémon, Dungeons and Dragons and Dragonball Z; other games with high violence ratings that promote anger, rage or murder. Other less obvious things may catch your attention, such as comic books, posters, movies, books and magazines devoted to fantasy or music with demonic, violent, or sexual themes. Be sensitive to the Holy Spirit. Ask Him to help you. Remember that Satan uses the gates of your eyes and ears to gain access to your soul as well as your life and home.

OBJECTS

Many people pick up souvenir items that have the potential of providing demons a point of entry to their households and family. At first they may seem harmless, but they carry occult power. When visiting other parts of the world, make sure you hear from the Holy Spirit before you decide to purchase an item. Tribal objects often present problems. Look over items from Native American, African, Mayan, Aztec, Filipino and Haitian cultures. Ethnicity is not necessarily the problem; however, ethnic groups have demonic connections stemming from geographic root spirits.

The issue is with the demonic practices of each culture that will get transferred to the object. This may even include a piece of artwork, mask, jewelry or other objects from these cultures.

Any of the following things do not bring glory to God or may invite a demonic presence: Buddhist or Hindu fertility gods or goddesses, Egyptian images, totem poles, evil depictions of creatures such as lions, dogs, cats or any other creatures with demonic distortions; objects or materials related to religions need to be carefully evaluated as they can bring a mind binding spirit that will blind you from understanding truth.

This would include instruction books Transcendental Meditation using a mantra (the repeating of a word or sound that releases power enabling the mind to settle down.) The danger in this is repeating words and sounds that could activate the kingdom of darkness. Remember what we learned about the power of words. Just because you don't understand the word doesn't mean that it doesn't have power or meaning.

MY EGYPTIAN PICTURES

By the late 1990's I had developed a much better understanding of this spiritual stuff. One year we went to Arizona to visit Mark's parents who were there for the winter. That year Mark was growing tremendously in the Lord. He even brought his Bible with him and was reading it every night!

One day we went to a flea market and I saw these really pretty masks that you would hang on the outside of your garage or patio so I bought them. Then we went to a print shop and I saw the most beautiful artwork of Egyptian faces. There was a handsome man and the other was a beautiful woman. They looked like a king and queen. You would hang them on your wall facing each other. So we bought them, paid to have them beautifully matted and framed and they hung on either side of our bed.

After we'd been home for awhile, I had a prayer meeting at my house and we began praying through the house. When we got to my bedroom my friend Josie and her daughter Lisa both commented on me having those items. They went on and on about the spiritual dangers, the fact that Egypt represented the world, bondage, darkness, etc. But I would not heed their warnings. I told them I already prayed over the objects and I wasn't having any problem with them.

Pat took one look at my masks and said, "What are you doing, you know better." At the time, I was more willing to get rid of the masks than I was the framed artwork. The years went on and I began to develop this class. As I was teaching this class for the first time, I came to the part about Egyptian objects and kept moving. My friend Josie was in the class and called me on it later, saying, I couldn't really do this class justice having those pictures in my house. I was already convicted about having the items even though I didn't see any repercussions from having them in my house.

I began to ask the Lord if there was any damage caused by me having those pictures. It took some time, but He reminded me of how Mark was growing and reading his Bible when we went to Arizona. Then He began to show me that when we came back from our trip Mark slowly began to drift away. It was so slow I didn't realize his heart was hardening again. I didn't know how to address the subject with Mark, since we had spent so much money on them.

Within a few months we were about to move, so I took the pictures down, wrapped them up, prayed over them again and put them in the garage. Now in our new house there was no place to put those pictures, so they stayed in the basement for quite some time.

The time came when I knew I had to destroy and burn the pictures. So on June 28th 2003, I called my friend, Pat and told her I was coming out to the farm; we had Egyptian stuff to burn. As the items were burning, the most hideous smoke began to swirl out of the fire.

I was enjoying the fire and commenting on how wild it was when Pat began yelling, "You get off my property!" Then I chimed in, "Yea, that's right, your power over us is broken and we cast you into outer darkness." This is a perfect example of why we are to go out two by two, so when you're acting like an idiot, your partner has you covered! I didn't even think about what was being released on her property as those items were being burned, but thank God she did. When it was all over I told the Lord, "Ok, I did this completely by faith, now I want to see fruit." Well I saw fruit immediately.

It was less than 2 weeks later on July 4th 2003. It was 90 degrees and I had worked all day. Mark was home waiting for me, he wanted to go to his parents house on the lake for a party. All he wanted to do was to get in the lake on that jet ski. I was starving and asked if we could stop and get something for me to eat on the way. He got so mad at me. It could have ruined our day if I had let it. He was miserable all day long. However, I walked in love, in the spirit, and went out of my way to meet all his needs that day. I crucified *psuche* all day and it was very painful. What I really wanted to do was jerk the slack out of him and tell him to get over himself.

That night we met friends to go see fireworks. My friends noticed his bad behavior and one of them said, "Mark what the ___ is wrong with you?" After the fireworks, on the way home, all I could think about was that I didn't want the sun to set on this wrath. I didn't want to give place to the enemy.

I began to pray in the car and ask the Lord how I should handle it. There was the way I wanted to handle it, by saying what the blank is wrong with you, how could you treat me like this, how could you ruin our day, etc. It would not have been pretty. But I heard the voice of the Lord and He gave me wisdom. He told me to ask Mark what I did to upset him. What! What *I* did to upset *him,* are you kidding me?! But I obeyed and when we got in bed, I asked if we could talk and then asked him what I did that upset him. He began to tell me and I was shocked!

He said that he had waited all day for me to get home so we could go to the lake and then he had to wait for me to change, and then I wanted to eat. He had a plan and I disturbed his plan. Apparently I did this all the time. I never realized he had a plan and that I was a hindrance to his plan. Now I do know how absolutely ridiculous Mark's reason for being upset sounds. But I can also see that for twenty years of our marriage, Mark would get in these miserable places and couldn't get himself out. Then I would be angry with him for his behavior, so this was a huge revelation in our marriage.

Mark and I actually communicated for 3 hours that night about this. He apologized for his behavior and I was able to apologize for thwarting his plans all the time without knowing it. That night I learned how to ask Mark a head of time if he had a plan. Now he tells me his plans and I tell him other things that need to be done and we are able to join both our requirements without getting upset.

That night after we made up, I laid my head on my pillow and I heard the voice of the Lord. He said, "You wanted to see fruit?" He showed me that

Mark's heart was softened. This nasty 'thing' that had silently bothered our marriage was uncovered after twenty years. He showed me Mark's ability to communicate in a way I had not seen before. He also showed me that Mark's heart had become softened toward the Lord again. The time rolled around for me to do the class again and this time Mark was going to take the class for the first time. I knew I better tell him what I did with the pictures before we got to the spiritual house cleaning class. I kept praying for wisdom to approach this subject correctly. The Lord prepared a day when we had a long drive to Canada. He would be trapped, he couldn't walk out, whatever happened it could be resolved before we got back home. This was the day I had to do it.

So that day I began to ask him if he noticed how he had been growing spiritually, reading his Bible and going to church when we went to Arizona. Then I asked him if he noticed how he had stopped reading and stopped going to church after coming home from Arizona. Then I pointed out all the Lord had done recently; he was growing again, going to church and was interested in spiritual things again. I reminded him what happened on July 4th and how his heart was softened and our marriage was changed. Then I told him what the Lord showed me about the Egyptian pictures, the hardening of his heart and how after I had destroyed the pictures, the fruit that came out of it.

After all was said and done, thank God he wasn't mad, he didn't yell, he just asked me not to spend any more money on things we had to destroy, and it was over. All those years went by and I couldn't see the effects those pictures produced in our lives. Even my heart was hardened against getting rid of them. Once I did, the Lord honored my act of obedience. He opened my eyes to see everywhere I was blind and even removed a wrinkle in my marriage.

The reason I shared all this is that we all have things in our house, and we like them, we don't want to get rid of them or think that they could be the cause of any open door or hindrance in our lives. I had a hard head where this was concerned and I am sure I am not alone. So I pray you will be sensitive to allow the Holy Spirit to show you whatever it is you may need to see as well. It is much more important to be obedient than to harbor something that may be harmful to you.

OCCULT OBJECTS

Anything related to the occult must be destroyed completely - any materials, objects or items connected to Satanism, witchcraft, black magic, demon worship, spirit guides (a belief that that the dead survive and can communicate with the living), fortune telling, palmistry or New Age. These would include Ouija boards, good luck charms or amulets (object that is to bring protection or good luck. Can be a gem, stone, statue, coin, drawing, pendant, ring, plant, animal or zodiac sign.)

Astrology items including horoscopes, tarot cards, crystals (allegedly have magical healing and mystical paranormal powers), fetishes (an object believed to have magical powers), water witching sticks, voodoo dolls, pagan symbols, dream catchers (look like a spider's web and their purpose is to catch everything evil including bad dreams), crystal balls or Magic Eight balls are also occult objects.

There is no middle ground on these items. God is clear in Deut. 7:25 where it says, *"you shall burn them with fire"* and Deut. 12:3, where it says, *"lest you be doomed to destruction like it"* as well as in Acts 19:18-20, regarding the destruction of idolatrous, ritual, temple and magical items. We are commanded to break, crush or burn these objects. Do not simply throw them in the trash for someone else to pick up.

Remember that these practices create a spiritual soul tie. Those demons will remain in the family generationally and on the land where they gained entrance as well. We must repent for our involvement, as well as break the curse that follows, in order to stop those demons from traveling down through our generations.

MOM

Years ago my mom had seen a fortune teller and then had forgot about it. In the spring of 1986 I had just recommitted my life to the Lord. Around that time, my youngest sister, Marlo was about fifteen years old and she began to experience such fear and terror that she wouldn't let my mom leave her. Mom used to bring her to me so she could go to work.

At this time, in the City of Rochester, NY we used to host the Full Gospel Business Men's Fellowship at the Holiday Inn downtown. This was my first Christian conference; I went with my future mother-in-law, Patty, my mom and Marlo. Three of us were in the main fellowship room and Marlo was across the hall in a youth room. Benny Hinn was the speaker that night. My mom had to leave early and left my sister with us.

A little while later I see my mom walking up the aisle and she is dragging Marlo with her. I stepped out and stopped her, I said, "What are you doing?" She said she was in the ramp garage walking to her car and she heard the voice of the Lord in her spirit say, "Go get Marlo and bring her to see Benny Hinn." She stopped, looked at her watch and reasoned how late she was and kept walking. It happened three times and the third time the voice yelled so loudly at her, she turned right around and did what the Lord said.

Now, I am stopping her halfway up the aisle and she is telling me that she has to bring Marlo up front to see Benny. Well, you know how sometimes your parents embarrass you? This was one of those times. I thought, 'this man is in the middle of preaching and you're going to do what?' But she just shot right by me and before I knew what was happening, I could hear Benny Hinn yelling, "WOMAN!" And he was pointing his finger at my mother. I was running up right behind her.

He said, "Woman, you have been to see a fortune teller and your daughter has been plagued with a spirit of fear because of it." At this point my mom and Marlo fell flat to the ground. I had never seen anything like this before and didn't know why they were on the ground. Someone got them up and Benny cast the spirit of fear off of Marlo and prayed for both of them. They walked away and he continued preaching. Marlo was never plagued with fear again. Wow!

OBJECTS BELONGING TO SECRET SOCIETIES

Freemasonry, Shriners, Eastern Star, Job's Daughters, Oddfellows, Elks, Amaranth, DeMolay, Rainbow Girls or Daughters of the Nile are all secret societies. Members are often required to take oaths, make inner vows and participate in initiation rituals contrary to God's Word, such as pledging allegiance to ungodly deities. Therefore demons can easily attach themselves to items representing those societies, such as books, rings, aprons, etc. - Josh 6:18; 7:11; Deut 7:25-26. Many of my students have had family members involved in these societies. Upon destroying the items and praying a renunciation prayer found on the internet wonderful praise reports have been reported. If you would like to go through the renunciation prayer do a search on *Unmasking Freemasonry - Removing the Hoodwink*, by Selwyn Stevens.

HEIRLOOMS

Family heirlooms or antique items purchased privately or at an auction may have familiar spirits from dead relatives or past owners. When purchasing an item ask questions and get as much information as you can on the antique.

It is a good idea to know your family history. Ask your relatives about the experiences in your family, understanding the traumas they went through will give you insight into things you may be experiencing. I was seeing symptoms in my life of generational patterns that were a result of issues my ancestors had encountered.

Look for objects that represent other gods, religions, the occult or secret societies. You have the warnings in Scripture that God gave to His people about bringing these things into your camp. Be aware as you look over your heirlooms and antiques. All of these items, as well as those used in temple worship and occult rituals, must be destroyed. Pray over it and allow the Holy Spirit to guide your decision regarding your purchase. When you get it home, anoint it; break any curses and soul ties and loose familiar spirits and possible demonic assignments. Allow God to cleanse and bless it.

GRANDMA

In November of 2003 my grandmother moved to heaven, we all met at the hospital to pick up her things. I had all her clothes in my car. As I was driving home, my car began to be filled with a foul odor. I thought it was the heater so I turned it off. Then I opened my car windows but the smell was so overwhelming I asked the Lord, what is that? Immediately He said to me that it was an unclean spirit. I knew the spirits that plagued my grandmother had lost their house and were clinging to her stuff. I bound them and commanded them to leave her stuff in Jesus' name and the smell left!

Please understand that there wasn't anything demonic about my grandmother. Her childhood was filled with trauma. She was never able to be free emotionally from those traumas and like most of us, was perishing for a lack of knowledge. She carried those things in her soul and they brought her great infirmity to the day of her death. My point in sharing this is to show you how the gift of discernment operates. I could have just ignored the odor, brought the stuff in my house and probably would have started experiencing infirmity somewhere in my life and I never would have known where it originated. This is how familiar spirits operate and travel down through the family lines. This is why we must be sensitive to the Holy Spirit when He is trying to show us something.

GHOST BUSTERS

One Saturday morning while flipping through the channels, something on the *Travel Channel* caught my attention. There were these men that would go into haunted places with their electrical technology and find ghosts. As these men got closer to the spirit, they would describe feelings of having tightness in their chest, finding it hard to breath, being confused, and disoriented. I was amazed because that is exactly how I feel when I am in an unclean environment as well. I saw that this is a common experience whether you are a Christian or not.

On one occasion I went to an estate sale; there were a lot of people milling through the house. As I was walking through the basement, a woman passed me on her way out. She looked right at me and said, "There is a hot spot back there, you'll feel it." I thought to myself wow, she could see that I would know the spot, interesting.

Pastor Jim, his wife Peg, Pat and I went to a minister's conference out of state. We stopped at a Wal-Mart, Jim and Peg went and sat down in the McDonald's while Pat and I wandered around the women's department. After a few minutes I found Pat and told her I didn't feel well. It felt like the room was swirling and I was dizzy. To my surprise she told me she felt the exact same way. We went and sat with Jim and Peg and talked. The Holy Spirit revealed to us that there was someone in the women's department who was a witch and we were picking up on it.

We prayed, broke the power of what we were feeling, hindered any back lash of the enemy, prayed for the woman and then tucked that information away for future reference. That understanding has we helped us a lot. During ministry times when we are praying for others and begin to feel what we now call the "swirly dizzies" we know the person has had occult involvement.

Then one day I was at Home Depot waiting in a long line for paint to be mixed. After some time I began to feel the "swirly dizzies." In the past I would have thought, oh what's wrong with me, I don't feel good. But now I know to pay attention to my environment when that happens. So I began to look around and noticed a girl who went to my high school, standing at the end of the line I was in. I knew she was a witch because she told me so at the class reunion. I began to pray in the spirit quietly and I quickly felt better.

OTHER GODS

Any object in your house that is a representation of a false god, an idol or any demonic figure should be removed. This includes objects that are carved, painted or a stone image: a Buddha, fertility gods and goddesses, Greek and Roman gods, gargoyles, Native American dream catchers, kachinas, (a masked dancer or carved doll in the costume believed to embody a particular spirit, usually presented as a gift to a child) totem poles (a post carved and painted with a series of family or clan crests or with figures representing mythic beings), fetishes (an object believed to have magical powers), and Aztec, Mayan or other idolatrous items from ancient cultures; any distorted representations of lions, dragons or other creatures.

There was a man in one of my classes who travels all over the world and he brings home souvenirs from his travels. The week following the Spiritual House Cleaning class he told me that he had a Buddha and some other pagan god on his mantel for years. He said after my class last Thursday night that he went home and destroyed those objects and threw them in the garbage. Then he said he got very sick. He was sick all Thursday night, all Friday, Saturday, Sunday and most of Monday. His wife pointed out that the garbage was taken away on Monday. So on Monday, when the garbage left, so did his illness. Those spirits were completely removed from the property and he felt better.

My mother-in-law Patty could write a book on all the things she has experienced. One year as I was preparing to teach the Spiritual House Cleaning class, Ma and I began talking about some of her experiences. She shared one of her stories with me. She said that years ago when she was a baby Christian she had a beautiful vase. The vase had a man's face with ram's horns (doesn't sound very beautiful to me). She said one day she was in such mental torment she couldn't think straight. She said throughout the day she kept looking at the vase, but really didn't think much of it. In retrospect the Holy Spirit was trying to show her the cause of her torment, but every time she looked at the vase she would dismiss the thought.

We tend to do this with the objects in our home because we are comfortable and familiar with them. The torment got so bad that she called her friend to come to her house. When her friend got there, she sat on the couch as she had done many times in the past. The friend saw the vase as she has seen it many times over the years, but this time was different. The Holy Spirit was revealing that there was a spirit associated with that vase and it was time to get rid of it. So she called Patty over and asked her to sit on the couch with her.

When Mom sat next to her on the couch and looked at the vase again, she said fear went right through her body. She started screaming, "Get it out of here, destroy it!" Her friend's husband said, "I don't want to destroy it, I have no authority to do that". He didn't want my father-in-law to be upset with him. Patty was so adamant, she forced them to take the object out of her house and said she would talk to her husband about it later. She said at 2 pm that afternoon all the torment lifted and she was in her right mind again. Later she called her friend up and told her she was feeling much better. Her friend told her that her husband felt led to destroy the vase. Patty asked, "What time did he destroy it ?" Her friend said 2 pm, so immediately upon the destruction of that vase Mom's mind cleared.

STEPS TO TAKE

1. **Remove ungodly objects**.

If you or anyone in your family has been involved with false religions, it is wise to get rid of all the material. Destroy all ungodly objects (Deuteronomy 7:25). Burn what can be burned; destroy what can't be burned so that it can't be retrieved, and throw it in the garbage. Do not give it away. Then command any evil spirit associated with that object out of your home.

2. **Cleanse the atmosphere of each room**.

Your identificational repentance for the sins of your ancestors and prior homeowners, positions you to receive the cleansing of unrighteousness - I John 1:9. Go through your house and repent for any known sin that has been committed in each room, even before you lived there. If someone else occupied your home before you, ask the Lord to show you what needs to be prayed in each room.

Trust the impressions you get from the Holy Spirit during this process and repent for these sins also. Use the Keys of the Kingdom in Matthew 16:18,19 which says that "Whatsoever you bind and loose on earth will be bound and loosed in heaven so that the gates of hell will not prevail against you." Break the power of wrong words, agreements, acts of sin and demonic assignments. Bind up evil spirits you may think have had a place of rule there and command them to be loosed.

Use scriptures pertaining to your area of need and read them aloud as you go through each room. Speak specific blessings that would pertain to each room and plead the Blood.

Think of why each room was designed and bless that purpose. You may use oil to anoint the doors, windows and objects as a symbol of Jesus' blood; and commission the angels to be released in that place to enforce

239

your covenant of peace that nothing should be missing or broken and all should be restored.

3. Consecrate your property.

Walk the perimeters of your property and repent just as you did in the house. Be sure to break the power of wrong agreements, wrong words and all ungodly covenants that may have taken place there. Then declare that the land is consecrated or set apart for the Lord.

This physical act helps to establish spiritual perimeters. Begin to ask the Holy Spirit to reveal to you the sins committed in that place and if there is any blood that cries out from the sins of your ancestors and from the previous tenants of that land. Blood cries out for justice down through the generations. The blood of Jesus is the perfect sacrifice. Pleading His blood over the ground will cleanse the stained ground that has come down from generation to generation.

You can get wooden stakes long enough to drive completely into the ground. You can write scriptures on the stakes, anoint them with oil and post them on the north, south, east and west corners of the property. You may also want to take communion on the land and bury the communion in the land as you consecrate it back to the Lord.

4. Ask the Lord to fill your home with His presence

Take communion with your family. Sing and pray as a family and speak the Word in your house.

Periodically go through your home and check for any new objects that should not be in your home or pray through any new sin issues that have come up. Stand in the gap and repent for others in your home daily and take communion often. This should prevent the enemy from infiltrating your home again with spiritual darkness.

To read about what curses on our body or land look like, read Deuteronomy 28:15-65.

I want you to know that there are many wonderful books thoroughly devoted to just this subject if you would like to investigate further. Two books I suggest are: *Protecting Your Home from Spiritual Darkness* by

Chuck D. Pierce and the other is *Portals to Cleansing* by Dr. Henry Malone.

ENCOUNTERS OF THE GOD KIND

Over the years I have had numerous experiences with the kingdom of darkness. I don't want to leave this chapter without bringing Glory to God. I also have had several encounters with the Kingdom of God. Some of which I have already shared in previous chapters. The vision and preparation for this book has been a God-given assignment on my life. Right after we were married, I tried for nine years to conceive a second child. Every time I prayed and asked the Lord if I would become pregnant or not, but I never got a definitive answer. What I did get was that water running in my heart. At the time I took it to mean yes, I was going to conceive. I had repeated dreams of me being pregnant; all the while thinking it meant I would become pregnant naturally.

In retrospect God was showing me I had conceived, I was pregnant with this book. In 2002 I began teaching this class using handouts. Then I got the vision to create a workbook and have a corresponding DVD Set to go with it, so it could be used by other churches and small groups. One night after years of dreaming I was pregnant, I had a dream that I gave birth! I came home one night after teaching and my heart began to pour water again. It had been years since that had happened to me. But every time it happened it was centered around my conceiving or being pregnant.

In October of 2005, I stepped out into the next stage in my ministry, by teaching this class in another church. Then four weeks into the class on October 28, 2005, I found myself wide awake at 6:35 am. This was very unusual for me. I opened my eyes and saw what looked like a glistening dome over my entire bed. It almost looked like the reflections you see when oil and water mix.

As I looked around my bed I could see what looked like glittering specks of light. It seemed as though there were four angels posted at the four corners of my bed with their wings spread and all touching. It was so intense to see. I checked my feelings because I couldn't say that I "felt" the presence of God at all. I watched this for 20 minutes.

Towards the end I could still see them in the room but not right up next to the bed anymore. Then at 7:00 am Mark got up and turned on the light and I couldn't see them anymore. I told him what happened and he was upset that I didn't wake him up to see it too. I apologized and said, "I don't know why I didn't wake you up either." He said, "Well, if it ever happens again you better wake me up."

So the very next night I was awakened in the same way and there it was again. I woke him immediately. I said, "Mark open your eyes." We both laid there looking and talking about what we were seeing. It looked like a canopy yet it was see-through. There were small light green orbs of light flickering all over the room. Mark got up and covered the little red light coming from the cable box. He closed the curtains. He tried to find any natural reason for what we were seeing. Yet there they were, all over the room. We began to pray and the Holy Spirit revealed to me that I had given birth and stepped into the call of God on my life and these were the angels assigned over my ministry!

On February 27, 2007, I was suddenly wide awake. I looked at the clock and it was 4:45 am, Mark had already left for work. I was laying there a few minutes when the doorbell rang. My doorbell is one that gives a long beautiful song-like chime. I laid there in shock that someone was actually ringing my bell at this hour. I snuck out to the hall and looked down to the driveway. There was no car and no footprints in the snow.

I was not gripped with fear, but I was wondering what was happening. I thought if it was my family, if something was wrong, they would be calling my phone as well. I decided not to go to the door and went back to sleep. In the morning I went to the front door where the chime rings. We don't shovel that sidewalk because everyone uses the side door. There were no footprints in the snow, to either door! At that moment I realized it was the Lord, He was at my door! 2007 was prophesied to be the year of the open door. I believe He was showing me it's time, He's at the door. There was a door the Lord was about to open on my behalf and there were doors I needed to open and walk through.

Two weeks later on March 11, 2007 at 8:20 am the doorbell rang again. This time Mark was home and heard it as well. Again no footprints. I believe both these encounters of the God Kind happened twice; once for me, the second time for Mark as a confirmation and to show us this was for both of us. We remain sensitive to the things of the spirit and are enjoying the encounters of the God kind much more than the encounters of the demon kind.

PRAYER

Father, I have learned in this chapter that through the open door of sin the enemy is able to stake a claim to particular areas of my life. Not only has he gained access because I have been one whom he may devour, but in my ignorance I have delivered to him my God given authority over this earth so he has had legal right to my possessions, my home and the land on which I live.

I stand on II Chronicles 7:14, as I humble myself and pray and seek Your face. Father, I now turn from my wicked ways so You will hear from heaven, forgive my sins and heal my land.

Holy Spirit, I ask You to quicken me and make me aware of when I am missing the mark and opening the door to the kingdom of darkness through ignorance. Reveal to me every place where I am perishing for lack of knowledge. Help me to recognize every place where the enemy has a foothold in my life so I can drive him out.

I choose not to let the sun set on my wrath. I choose to walk in love so my faith will operate effectively. I choose to resist fear and walk in my God given authority. I make a conscious decision not to accept as normal the manifestations of the kingdom of darkness and the curse anywhere in my life.

I choose to take the Kingdom of God by faith and by force. I choose to possess my promised land of more than enough and drive out every spirit that has defiled me. I choose to rebuild the hedge of protection around me and enforce my covenant of peace so there will be nothing missing and nothing broken anywhere in my life.

I declare that blessings track me down because I possess my promised land and have driven off the previous tenants. I stand on Joshua 21:44 and

I am grateful that You, Lord, have given me rest round about, according to all that You swore unto our fathers; that You have delivered every enemy into my hand; that there has not failed of any good thing which You have spoken; all has come to pass. I love you, Lord, and I am so grateful for Your provisions!

PRAYER FOR YOUR HOME

Lord Jesus, I stand in the gap and repent for any sins that have brought an iniquity in this home, whether by my family, any previous tenants or me. I break the power of every wrong word ever spoken and every wrong agreement with the kingdom of darkness and declare that no weapon formed against us shall prosper; and every tongue that has risen against us in judgment, I condemn right now.

I confess our sins before You and ask You to forgive us and to cleanse us and our home from all unrighteousness. I break the power and legal right of any curse and all demonic assignments over us and our home as a result of any open door of sin.

I declare that Christ has redeemed us from the curse of the law, being made a curse for us. I cancel all spells, psychic powers, witchcraft, sorcery, incantations, impartations or assignments over us. I bind every spirit of infirmity, fear, spiritual blindness, poverty, lack, bondage, stupor, divination, strife, anger, bitterness, division, lying, heaviness and jealousy.

I speak to every evil spirit in operation against us and I tear down and distort all communication between you. I speak division and confusion to your plots, plans and schemes and dissension among your ranks. I declare that you are a kingdom divided against itself and are being brought to utter desolation, in Jesus' name - Matthew 12:26.

I tell you that you are loosed from your assignment in this place and over us, in Jesus' name. I plead the blood of Jesus for protection. I forbid you to cross this bloodline. I also sever any and all soul ties from previous tenants to this home and loose all familiar spirits from here, in Jesus' name. I thank You, Lord, that You have given Your angels charge over us to protect us and keep us in all our ways.

PRAYER FOR YOUR LAND

Lord Jesus, I stand in the gap and repent for any bloodshed, immorality, idolatry, stealing and broken covenants that may have taken place on my land. I break the power of every wrong word ever spoken and every wrong agreement with the kingdom of darkness and declare that no weapon formed against us shall prosper; and every tongue that has risen against us in judgment, I condemn right now.

I confess these sins before You and ask You to forgive them and to cleanse this land from all unrighteousness. I break the power and legal right of any curse and all demonic assignments over this land and our home as a result of any of these open doors. I declare that Christ has redeemed us from the curse of the law, being made a curse for us.

I cancel all spells, psychic powers, witchcraft, sorcery, incantations, impartations or assignments over this land. I bind every spirit of lying, stealing, infirmity, fear, spiritual blindness, poverty, lack, bondage, stupor, divination, strife, anger, bitterness, division, heaviness and jealousy. I speak to every evil spirit in operation against us and I tear down and distort all communication between you. I speak division and confusion to your plots, plans and schemes and dissension among your ranks. I declare that you are a kingdom divided against itself and are being brought to utter desolation, in Jesus' name - Matthew 12:26. I tell you that you are loosed from your assignment on this land, in Jesus' name.

I plead the blood of Jesus for protection and I forbid you to cross this bloodline. I also sever any and all soul ties from previous sinners or owners on this land and loose all familiar spirits from here, in Jesus' name. I thank You, Lord, that You have given Your angels charge over us to protect us and keep us in all our ways.

Emotional Healing

Too often we put a band-aid on a wound, but what we bury alive, stays alive. See how to receive inner healing and have the sting removed from wounds, traumas and memories.

Chapter Eight

The kingdom of darkness and the influence of the enemy in the life of a believer have been discussed at length throughout these chapters. In the first chapter we learned that Adam handed over his authority and all the kingdoms of the world were delivered unto Satan, establishing the law of sin and death - Luke 4:5-6. At that moment Adam was born again from spiritual life to spiritual death. Man's soul; his mind, will and emotions became the dominant force of his being, and his logic, reason and intelligence was now being influenced by the kingdom of darkness. The sin of Lucifer was passed on through the sin of Adam and has infected all of mankind.

Throughout these chapters we have learned how the Kingdom of God and the kingdom of darkness operate in our life. We have been taking an x-ray of the inner workings of our soul and we have seen that our soul houses everything that has ever happened to us. It is where all of our memories, pain from trauma, unmet needs, unhealed hurts and unresolved issues have been stored.

As life happens and information comes in to us, we create memory that forms a branch / dendrite on a nerve cell in our brain that looks like a tree. If a thought is negative or fear based, a thorn will develop on the dendrite branch.

These thorn trees of our mind have formed the deception in our perception and have become our triggers and areas of weakness. The network of branches are where strongholds, soul ties, unforgiveness, word curses and generational issues have taken root and are producing fruit in our lives.

As a thought is developed it activates the hypothalamus, which is the heart of our endocrine system, and responds to our thought life to release the chemical emotion related to the thought.

This explains why we have the 'feelings' that keep us making the same mistakes. They keep us in bondage, in the whirlpool flow of the kingdom of darkness. These have become our internal blueprint and the filters through which we make the decisions that affect our lives.

An x-ray of our soul would show the trees in the cortex of our mind, our experiences in life, the good times and the bad. We all have images that have made impressions deep into our being, especially concerning our longing for love and value, which have become fixed beliefs / dendrite branches. As soon as a familiar situation triggers a memory and emotions arise, our reactions respond. These places have left us with scars, but Jesus knows how to heal every place we hurt. In this chapter I will share with you just how the Lord healed me and how I pruned the trees of my mind. I am confident that you will experience Jesus healing your broken heart and binding up every wound as well.

These places within us are open doors for evil spirits in our soul / life. Every place our soul is yet unsurrendered to the lordship of Jesus Christ, or has not yet received inner healing, has left us open for demonic influence and oppression.

Ephesians 4:27 tells us we are not to, *"...give place to the devil."* This verse is saying for us not to give, offer, yield to or deliver up any foothold to the enemy of our soul. Don't let him secure a position or place in our lives where he can steal, kill and destroy.

Proverbs 23:7 says, *"...for as a man thinks in his heart so is he:"* As we open the gate of our soul / mind, to the enemy's negative thoughts, it will give him place to create our future. The ability to live successfully will come as we learn to continually take every thought captive to the obedience of Christ - II Corinthians 10:5.

Proverbs 25:28 says, *"He that hath no rule (self-control or restrain) over his own spirit is like a city that is broken down, and without walls."* The Old Testament is describing our spirit here as the entirety of our being. Remember that our spirit has a soul, and together they live in our body. Our life has been like a city whose walls have been broken down, so we are being destroyed because we have had no control of *psuche*. We have been failing in our relationships, our health and many areas of life because we haven't recognized or received instruction on these things.

We know that our soul, when not governed by our spirit, will naturally generate wrong desires (like a whirlpool), even though we may have had some success at harnessing our external behavior and crucifying our soul, which is a necessary part of our spiritual growth and development. We will have to closely x-ray our soul to know if these issues we continually harness and crucify are coming merely from an unsurrendered soul or from a demonic source that needs eviction.

We have been learning that when we sin we open ourselves to the influence and possible control of evil spirits. We must understand that these spirits cannot "possess" or own a Christian. Demons dwelling in Christians are trespassing. They do not have ownership rights; therefore they are subject to eviction in the authority of the name of Jesus.

Matthew 15:22-28 is a great example of this; it says, *"And, behold, a woman of Canaan came out of the same coasts, and cried unto Him (Jesus), saying, 'Have mercy on me, O Lord, thou son of David; my daughter is grievously vexed with a devil.' But He answered her not a word. And His disciples came and besought Him, saying, 'Send her away; for she crieth after us.' But He answered and said, 'I am not sent but unto the lost sheep of the house of Israel.' Then came she and worshiped Him, saying, 'Lord, help me.'*

But He answered and said, 'It is not meet (good) to take the children's bread (healing and deliverance is the children's bread), and cast it to dogs.' And she said, 'Truth, Lord: yet the dogs eat of the crumbs, which fall from their masters' table. Then Jesus answered and said unto her, 'O woman, great (strong) is thy faith: be it unto thee even as thou wilt.' And her daughter was made whole from that very hour."

These verses show us that everyone is subject to the kingdom of darkness and demonic oppression; it is natural under the flow of the kingdom of darkness. Jesus called deliverance the children's bread. Jesus was sent to the lost sheep of the House of Israel, and that's us. In other words, those who had a covenant relationship with God (His children) were positioned to receive healing and deliverance from demonic oppression.

CAN A SPIRIT-FILLED CHRISTIAN HAVE A DEMON?

The answer is made clear by remembering that our body is the temple of the Holy Spirit. Paul was using a prophetic picture comparing our body to the temple - I Corinthians 6:19.

The temple in Jerusalem had three parts:

- The Outer Court – representing our physical body.

- The Holy Place – representing our soul.

- The Holy of Holies – representing our spirit.

The three compartments in the temple correspond to man's triune being – man is a spirit, his spirit has a soul and his spirit and soul together live in this earth suit called a body. The presence of God dwelt solely in the Holy of Holies which would be our born again spirit. The Holy Spirit desires us to submit every area of our "temple" to His control. From our spirit, under the leadership of the Holy Spirit, we are to govern our soul / thoughts, will, emotions and then direct our bodies accordingly.

Jesus found defilement in the Jerusalem temple; however, the defilement of the moneychangers and the merchants with doves and cattle were not in the Holy of Holies (where the Spirit of God dwelt). They were in the outer courts of the temple. Ephesians 4:30 tells us our spirit (the Holy of Holies) is sealed until the day of redemption. So there can not be any evil spirits dwelling in our spirit.

Jesus proceeded to "cast out" all who defiled the outer courts - Matt 21:12. The whole account is a prophetic picture of deliverance and what Jesus wants to do in our "temple." Defilement is not in the spirit of a Christian but in the "outer areas" of his soul / mind, will, emotions and body.

So then, there can be defilement in the outer areas of our soul and body, while the presence of the Lord remains in the Holy of Holies, which would be our spirit. For example, do you know of any Christians that still struggle with areas such as various bondages, addictions, fear, depression, suicidal thoughts, rejection, anger, etc? It grieves the heart of the Holy Spirit for us to be in this condition. He wants His entire temple cleansed and every defiling demon cast out. Christians can be demonized, controlled, manipulated, oppressed and opposed by evil spirits. However, an evil spirit cannot own or possess a born again child of God because the Holy Spirit of God now dwells in our spirit man.

We have been learning that even though we have been translated into the Kingdom of God spiritually, we can still allow the kingdom of darkness to rule in our soul and body. Every area in our life where our soul is in charge and unsurrendered to the lordship of Jesus creates a struggle for us.

Growing up as a baby Christian in the late 1980's, a common belief was that any problem you had was a spirit that needed to be cast out and you would be better. Over time I noticed the wound or trauma the spirit had occupied, the mental agreement you gave it, etc; kept the door open for the spirit's return. In our church we have people take this class before we will minister deliverance to them. This approach closes all the doors first then the spirit cannot return.

We have learned that there is a war within our members - the Kingdom of God in our spirit and the kingdom of darkness in areas of our unsurrendered soul. The choice is ours as to which kingdom or source of influence we will obey. Our objective is to walk in the spirit and make our soul and body come into alignment.

If you feel helpless or powerless over something, or if you feel out of control, that could be an indication. Normal temptation comes from the outside and you are able to resist it. If you feel the resistance from the inside and can't say no, if you are unable to fully surrender to the will of God in any area of life, if there are areas of your soul that are a source of constant harassment or weakness, you are probably being influenced by an evil spirit.

I first started attending New Testament Christian Church in 1987; shortly thereafter the elders came and prayed through my house in Hilton and the demonic manifestations stopped. After that, they began praying for me because I was being tormented with fear; fear of the dark, fear of the dead, fear of being alone. As a teenager I had watched occult themed movies like *The Exorcist* and *The Omen*. Watching these movies was an open door for a spirit of fear.

One of my areas of torment came from the movie *Nightmare on Elm Street*. Every time I closed my eyes I saw the face of Freddy Kruger. During one of my many prayer sessions, after dealing with all the occult themed open doors, the person praying over me literally called out the spirit behind Freddy Kruger and commanded it to leave me. It left immediately and has never returned.

I never felt anything dramatic when spirits left me, I usually yawned a lot. When you yawn you release breath. The word for breath is spirit / *pneuma*. It is the origin of the word pneumonia. So for me, yawning was always the way a spirit left me during times of prayer. Many have experienced coughing, a deep sigh, crying or screaming, anything that releases breath.

After prayer, fear was not coming from within me anymore, but it was coming at me from the outside. I remember driving home on a long, dark, country road, by myself and suddenly being gripped with fear. I had learned how to submit to God, resist the devil and make him flee. I began saying, out loud, "Fear, I bind you in the name of Jesus and I command you to get away from me. The Lord has not given me a spirit of fear but of power and of love and of a sound mind." I would literally have to repeat that scripture over and over until I could feel fear lifting. That was the "heat of the battle" as they say, when you have to 'man up' and do your own warfare, because no one else can do this for you. The more I resisted, the less the enemy came at me with fear; he knew he didn't have that place in me anymore.

That didn't mean I was completely free of him. The enemy of our soul turns his knowledge of every fear, trauma, all our emotional needs, painful memories, every trigger and any open door of generational curses, that we have into an arsenal of weapons against us. The first big one I got rid of was fear. There were still a lot more in hiding.

One weekend we had a girlfriend's retreat up at the cottage in the Thousand Islands in upstate NY. My friend Pat and I were on the jet-ski and slowly going out of the docks into open water. I was driving and she was behind me with her arms around my waist. She was leaning over watching, as we pulled out of the docks, I opened up and started to go fast. As I did, she squeezed me and yelled for me to stop. Now sitting out in the middle of the water, I asked her what was wrong. She told me she felt like she got slammed with fear, and she knew the root. It was coming from a trauma she experienced many years ago.

When we experience trauma it is like a laceration to our soul. In that wound is where spirits can dwell, filtering our perceptions of future experiences. In Pat's case her husband had been in a snowmobile accident several years earlier, at that time it was critical.

Her son-in-law came to get her and put her on the back of his snowmobile and was taking her out to the accident site. When she got to her husband his skull was open and bleeding. She experienced a rush of fear. However, when she got on her knees next to him, the spirit of faith took over and she began to prophesy that he would live and not die. She kept speaking life over him throughout his whole recovery. Long story short, by the time Mercy Flight got him to the hospital his skull was miraculously closed and the healing process had begun. He did sustain some brain damage and she did have to use her faith and press against the pressure of what the doctors were saying. In the end he was completely made whole, praise God!

So sitting behind me on the jet ski that day, with her arms around my waist, leaning over watching, as we started to go fast, triggered that experience and the emotion of fear. Pat is a strong woman of God who doesn't normally struggle with fear, so this kind of attack was highly unusual for her. We knew exactly what was happening, the enemy knew of the trauma and used it as a weapon, but it did not prosper because we knew exactly what to do about it. We addressed the fear, prayer broke its power and we were able to play on the water all day. Had we not understood spiritual laws and known what to do, this day could have gone very differently. We would have had to go back to the house and she may have been sick to her stomach and upset for the whole weekend.

This very thing can happen to any one of us, we can be in an environment that triggers a negative emotion. We don't know why we "feel" the way we do and it ruins our day. It is my heart's desire that as you are going through this book you will begin to identify your thorny triggers and neutralize them so they no longer have power over you.

So many of us, even as Christians, are still bound by issues like rejection, fear, insecurity, wounds, anxiety, lust, anger, suicidal thoughts and many other emotional disorders. These issues make us feel like we are bleeding emotionally, which is the chemical reaction from the thorn trees and our amygdale (the part of your brain where these memories are stored). As we have seen, these emotional disorders can then effect the health of our body.

However, the enemy is not the root of our problem. He only triggers and accesses what already exists within us. The root of the problem is a damaged and wounded soul.

The adversary knows exactly what kind of stronghold / belief system has been developed within us to protect where a trauma occurred, that void where needs were never met, the place where our emotions are still bleeding from an unhealed hurt. He knows whether these places of access stem from unhealthy soul ties, areas of unforgiveness, a lack of releasing others, word curses or generational issues. Evil spirits access these places much like an infection is able to access a wound. Then they hinder our relationships and torment our soul, affecting the prosperity of our entire life.

We cannot find real freedom by a strong will to survive or by working a program. Many times this can be the equivalent to putting a leash on a demon. Eventually they pull and pull on that leash until we have released more and more of our freedom.

The only way to be free from the inside out is to strip our infected soul nature of the kingdom of darkness and everything it derives power from (that's *The Answer* in a nutshell!) Be willing to come out of agreement with every damaging belief system we have clung to and the walls and strongholds we have built to protect ourselves.

Break unhealthy soul ties, wrong words, generational curses and walk in repentance, forgiveness and release daily. By living in this level of spiritual maturity, we will posture ourselves in the Kingdom of God and spiritually realign our life. The proper alignment for the life of a believer is when our spirit is being influenced by God, filtering it through our soul / mind, will and emotions, and then living it out through our body.

When we do this, we have submitted ourselves to God and are then able to resist the devil, so he will flee from us - James 4:7. The DNA of God is already deposited within our born again spirit and it needs to be released through our soul / mind, will and emotions and expressed out through our life. The problem has been that when the God DNA tries to exert influence, it hits our thoughts that are programmed contrary to God's word and our soul begins shutting it down. Our life expressions have been ones of dishonor, anger, acting out pain, fear, etc. This doesn't mean that the fruit of God isn't with in us. It means it is being suffocated by our soul issues.

Believers immediately blame whatever appears to be wrong on evil spirits. It's always the enemy that's attacking us. This maintains the victim mentality. When we do this, we are denying our own responsibility in a situation.

In reality, it is the ugliness from our unsurrendered and unrepentant soul that has given the kingdom of darkness that seat of influence within us. So we have to stop this mentality of being a victim, blaming our parents, childhood or friends. We all have junk in our trunk.

I encourage you to stop sitting back and saying, I can't do this, it's too hard. No, we all have a responsibility here to stop behaving badly. We have to stop believing that, "This is just the way I am," as if there was no way to change it. The truth is that we can do all things through Christ who is within us strengthening us - Phil. 4:13. We do have the ability to do what's right. It isn't easy but it can be done and the Holy Spirit is here to help us all along the way!

> Jesus taught us that upon the solid rock of the revelation that He is anointed with burden-removing, yoke-destroying power; that He would build His Church (that's us), and the gates of hell would not prevail against it (us). He gave us the *"keys to the kingdom of heaven: and whatsoever you bind and loose on earth shall be bound and loosed in heaven."* - Matt 16:17-19.

Too often we do not use these keys effectively. We have done spiritual warfare by binding evil spirits in the name of Jesus. When we do, we have deactivated their power temporarily. However, if the damage within our soul is not healed, another like-spirit will access that "place" and we will be in the same situation as before, never finding any real freedom.

For example, a person who has been rejected and abused may be tormented by a spirit of rejection, causing them to feel overly sensitive. These people have real trouble seeing themselves as who they are in Christ. They will stay away from others and even appear to not like anyone because they are afraid of being hurt and rejected again.

People who have been taught to believe they are sickly and weak will secrete chemicals from that belief system that will make them sick and weak. They can also attract a spirit of infirmity which finds easy access because of the place of mental agreement reinforcing their wrong belief systems. It is a vicious cycle.

There is no real deliverance in only binding and loosing a spirit from you if you don't close all these possible doors, and prune your thorns by changing your mental agreements. If this has not been accomplished, a like-spirit will immediately re-establish access and intensify its attack on us. The door of access must be closed.

We remove thorns and keep doors closed by:

- Maintaining our love walk in the spirit and do not let *psuche* / our soul be in control.

- Coming out of agreement with the enemy and his deceptions.

- Going through personal repentance for our actions.

- Forgiving and releasing ourselves, God and others as necessary.

- Destroying unhealthy soul ties.

- Breaking the power of wrong words.

- Dealing with generational issues.

Like I said, the enemy knows every painful thing that ever happened to us and is always ready to touch us in that place when he gets a chance.

MY DELIVERANCE

After coming to my church in 1987, I was still a baby Christian, struggling with fear and anger especially toward men who behaved badly. I was very negative, I felt weak and sickly. The people who prayed with me led me through prayers of repentance for the lifestyle I had lived, in the bars, with men, doing drugs, my participation in the occult and demonic movies, as these were all open doors.

After my confession and repentance of these things I did begin to feel "flu like symptoms." I remember saying, "I don't feel well, I feel like I'm getting sick." Pastor said to me, "That's ok, they're just manifesting, they know they are on their way out!" As he commanded them to leave, all I wanted to do was cry.

When it was over I didn't feel sick anymore, I felt so clean inside and my life really began to change. I started growing strong in the Lord, I became a mighty warrior and intercessor and the gift to study the Word of God and teach manifested itself in my life in a great way. I began to have small groups in my home and teach bible studies in church. I was learning so much and had such a passion to teach others how to live a victorious Christian life.

I was amazed at my transformation because growing up I didn't want to go to college, all I wanted was to be married, stay home and have babies. Now I understand that was because of what I lost at my parent's divorce. I had a mental agreement within me that I had to replace what I had lost to feel whole. So I was shut down to any other direction for my life. All of these giftings had been deposited within me, but were being suffocated by all the junk in my trunk.

RAGE

Although I used this testimony in the chapter on Strongholds, I feel it is relevant to this chapter also.

Fast forward fifteen years, I had grown in my Christian walk and thought I was doing just fine. Then someone I love very much was in an abusive marriage. While trying to show her that the behavior she was experiencing was abuse and trying to counsel her through her difficult situation, I began experiencing tremendous deep emotional pain, anger and depression that seemed to paralyze me. I really didn't understand what was happening to me and I couldn't get out of this horrible place. One day while on the phone speaking with an abuse counselor about my loved one, I couldn't stop crying. I mentioned that I had experienced that same treatment over 20 years ago. I have since come to marry a wonderful man who never abused me, and I couldn't understand why I was feeling such deep emotional pain when the abuse was not happening to me.

What that counselor said to me that day started me on a journey to my own inner healing and freedom that has resulted in the development of this book. She said I was being re-traumatized. Re-traumatized! I had never heard of such a thing, but it made perfect sense.

My Pastor taught me, "What you bury alive stays alive." What I never realized is that I was never emotionally healed in those deep places. And while I was trying to help my loved one, it was her situation that acted like a trigger, setting off emotions that ripped the scab off an old wound in my soul. The Lord reminded me that over the years whenever I would see or even hear of abuse of any kind, it would have this kind of effect on me. Suddenly it all made sense. Why I couldn't watch the tv show Cops, why I had a short temper, why men behaving badly made me so angry. There were still thorns on my dendrites where those events were stored.

I knew I had a problem with men; and trying to be a good Christian I put forth my effort to walk in love. However, that didn't change the fact that not only a man, but anyone I saw behaving badly made me burn with rage. That rage came out in many different areas in my life. I had ungodly beliefs, attitudes and judgments that affected my emotions and decisions, holding me a prisoner within myself.

Although I purposed in my heart to continually forgive and walk in love, I never understood that a part of forgiveness was to release others from every expectation I had in them to behave differently and to choose to see them through the Father's eyes. I came to understand that hurting people hurt people. At the time I was still ignorant of how to release others, and my inability to see through the Father's eyes caused me to view people through my thorny judgments and filters holding me in bondage.

When I started putting this material together, I was able to prune those thorns by repenting and changing my mind. The Lord delivered me completely from this wound and all the rage and strongholds that surrounded it. I was able to not only forgive but also completely release everyone from every expectation and disappointment I had in them.

I was so grateful to have cut this thing off at the root, to have found inner healing and to have all that deep emotional pain come to an end. The fruit of that healing has been long lasting. My true test came as I encountered a man who was not only behaving badly, but was also causing someone I love very much a significant amount of deep emotional pain. In the past this would have put me over the edge.

This time I did not experience that rage; and instead of just responding in love, as an act of obedience, I could actually see this man through the Father's eyes, free of my thorny expectations and judgments of him, and love him with the love of God.

I thought, "Well, that's it, I am all better now!" I could not have been happier. Certainly there was nothing else at work within me that was still affecting my life. That was the big one that I always had to crucify.

Yet over the years as I have continued to teach this class, every time through, something else that I had buried alive began to surface. No one was more shocked than I was when the Lord put His finger on yet another place within me that He desired to heal.

ABANDONMENT

After Mark and I were married he would want to go play cards with his friends on Friday nights. I absolutely hated that he would do that. He used to say to me, "I am not in a bar, I am not out drinking, I am home every other night, I work hard, I pay the bills." In other words I am not like all these other guys, what is your problem? He was right, what was my problem? I didn't know why I had that problem. On card night, knowing he was about to leave, I would order myself a pizza as a reward for having to sit home alone on a Friday night. Then I would end up eating the whole thing and feeling sick about it.

I now understand that eating the whole pizza was me trying to medicate an emotional pain with food, although at the time I had no idea that was what I was doing. I never found any real freedom in eating that pizza, it only made me feel worse, yet I did it repeatedly. What I have come to learn is that I was medicating the 'feeling', which I now know was abandonment, with food.

When I had this revelation, I had taught *The Answer* class many times so I had learned some things. Then one Friday night Mark was getting ready to go play cards. This night, I actually stopped myself and asked the Lord, "So why do I feel sick every time Mark wants to leave?" As soon as I uttered those words, the Lord spoke inside of me and said the word "abandonment."

Abandonment? I was shocked! I was never abandoned (or so I thought). I was learning a lot about myself by teaching this class. Yet I really didn't know what to do with the information of that word "abandonment" so I just left it there and kept it in prayer.

Mark came downstairs ready to leave and I was standing in the kitchen. I told him what I just asked the Lord and the word the Lord said to me. I was kind of in shock. Mark said, "Come with me, let's take a ride." We pulled into Blockbuster, I said "What are we doing?" He said, "I am going to stay home with you, let's pick out a movie." At which point a flood of tears welled up inside of me, but I just had to shove them back down because this wasn't the time or place to fall apart. I wasn't even sure why I was falling apart.

Every time I have taught this class, the Lord has healed me in yet another area I didn't know I needed healing. It has been like peeling layers of an onion in my soul. Every year I would be teaching and the Holy Spirit would put his finger on yet another spot.

A few months later in 2003 my grandmother graduated to heaven. I was so happy for her because she really had no quality of life her last several years on earth. A few days after her passing while driving home from work, I had what I now call a "soul-ar eruption." It was a memory of the day when my father left home twenty-seven years ago. It came up out of my soul / amygdale with all the emotional pain that went with it. It seemed to just jump up, flash before me then, as quickly as it appeared; it disappeared along with the pain.

260

I literally gasped when it happened. I said, "Lord, what was that?" I didn't hear an answer. That day my friend, Pat was coming over for lunch. I told her what happened and how fast and intense the pain was and then in a moment it was gone. She said, "Really? I bet I can touch it." I said, "How?" She said, "So, tell me about that day your dad left." Well, when she said those words, the emotion began coming up again. I quickly stuffed it back down inside of me. I said, "Wow, I can't believe that emotional pain is within me, especially since I never even experienced that pain when my father actually left."

My father and mother divorced when I was sixteen years old. For many years they were not friendly with each other. Years after my mom, my sisters and I found Jesus, mom and dad's relationship began to heal. In the early 1990's we began having the family all together again for holidays, birthdays, and my mom, dad and his wife all became great friends. My family has been completely restored for many years! So how is it possible, that after all these years of family wholeness, I could have that kind of emotional pain, and why now?

Pat pointed out that my grandmother had just moved to heaven. And even though I was happy for her to be released from her body, it was still a great loss. That great loss was actually a trigger bringing back another great loss in my life; the loss of my father, my home, my security and life the way I knew it when I was sixteen. This event at the age of sixteen years old sent me on a spiral of bad behavior and ungodly living for ten years until I got saved at the age of twenty-six.

What I came to learn through this conversation with Pat that day is that I had subconsciously buried the pain as a coping mechanism, and then medicated it with drugs, men and bad behavior. I never did grieve the loss and as a result that pain was still buried alive within me.

In life, situations and circumstances have an ability to trigger something inside our soul that causes us to react in a way we wish we didn't. Like the rage I felt watching the dysfunctional behavior on the television show Cops, just watching that show made me burn inside. Or like me feeling sick when Mark wanted to go out on Friday nights. I had never bothered to ask the Lord why I felt or responded to things the way I did. I just accepted certain feelings, behaviors, attitudes and beliefs as a part of who I was. Then, trying to be a good Christian, I worked on stuffing them and behaving in a godlier manner. I now realize that when we stuff our emotions, what we bury alive stays alive. Unfortunately they are still at work within us filtering our perceptions and then manifesting out in many other areas of our life. These things truly have the ability to affect our health, family and relationships with others, as well as with the Lord.

Jesus said it is the truth you know that makes you free. Even though I was leading small groups, bible studies and was a strong mature Christian, the lack of truth in this area kept me in an emotional cycle that still had affects on my marriage, my parenting skills and my relationships.

So the loss of my grandmother triggered other great losses in my life. First Mark going to play cards and the Lord showing me I had abandonment issues. Then the soul-ar eruption of the day my father left, then thoughts of the first five years of my daughter's life began to surface. By the time my daughter was two I was divorced, lost, working at the bar and behaving badly. I found my husband Mark and came to the Lord by the time she was six years old. But for those four years in-between I carried a lot of shame and guilt for the type of mom I was when she was so young. I had an expectation in me to be better, to have known better and I kept myself on the hook for many things. Thoughts of these empty years began to torment me until I realized I had to forgive myself. I shared my healing process of forgiving and releasing myself for those years in the chapter on Forgiveness Therapy.

This soul-ar eruption brought up many issues in one week. My soul was bleeding badly, I was amazed at all the Lord was pulling out of me. I knew when my healing came it would be great. But for right now it really hurt. My daughter came over on one of the many days when all I could do was cry and apologize for my lifestyle when she was little. She had no memory of anything, it hurt me more than it hurt her.

I was unable to get through this emotional bleed alone so I called Pat and asked if we could get together. As I already shared in the chapter on Forgiveness Therapy, I was able to forgive and release myself for the first five years of Jenelle's life. As the counseling session continued, Pat touched that place in me again. She asked me to tell her about when my father left. I told her that he took me for a walk around the block, explained that he and mom weren't getting along and that they were going to live apart. I am sure that he said a lot more to me than that, but that was all I could remember. She asked me if I cried. I said, "I don't remember crying." She asked me if I asked him not to leave, I don't remember saying anything at all. She said, "Well what did you do?" I said, "I started smoking pot, and being bad." Pat said, "Oh so you medicated with drugs?" Wow, I guess I didn't realize that's what I was doing.

Pat made me see that I had never grieved. What was happening to me was suppressed grief for so many losses that needed to be released. It made perfect sense. I knew I had been crying for a week but those tears were just pain from an emotional bleed, that was not a grieving process. Pat counseled me to give myself permission to grieve, to say things I should have or would have said but didn't. It was time for me to get alone with God.

I left that session with Pat and I couldn't cry anymore. I felt emotionally constipated (sorry for that one). That whole weekend I suppressed the grief and I remained bound.

Then Sunday afternoon on the way home from the grocery store, here it comes! Oh no, now's not a good time Lord, there's food in the car, I have things to do. There was no stopping it and really, I didn't want to be bound anymore. It was like going into labor, you have to go with it. So I drove to a nearby school and parked behind it. The Holy Spirit Himself was taking me to a place of emotional healing that only He could.

I let myself cry but this time I cried with purpose. On purpose I pushed from the heart of my being and cried about my father leaving. I said out loud, "Dad don't go," words I should have expressed at the time. I had to say, "I forgive you, I release you." Then I pushed like I was giving birth, I pushed sound up and out of my mouth, I pushed out abandonment. I said, "Abandonment, get out of me." I screamed and pushed and cried the pain out. Then it all stopped. I thought, "Oh good, it's over." I sat there a few minutes and then much to my surprise another wave came.

I had never done this before and I really didn't know what to expect. Then another wave and another wave, I began taking an x-ray of my soul and identifying what I was grieving. I grieved the road my life took as a result of losing my home, my family unit, my security. I pushed, screamed, cried and said, "Fear of being alone, get out of me, fear of men, get out of me, hatred of men, get out of me, rage and anger, get out of me, insecurity, get out of me." With each of these I pushed on purpose like I was pushing a spirit out of a wound in my soul.

Then I prayed for myself in each place. On purpose I developed a constructive imagination. I applied the blood of Jesus over my soul. I got an inner-image of the blood going into every crack, crevice, place of hurt and healing my broken heart and binding up my wound. I began to bless myself and say what the Word of God says about me. So I literally pushed out all the junk and then received the washing of the water of the Word from all unrighteousness. I got an inner-image of myself getting up whole. That day I was pruning my mind and changing the structure of my brain. With all the righteous thoughts I was choosing to agree with I was creating a new nerve pathway and a new blueprint for my life. The Holy Spirit and I were doing self deliverance and I highly recommend it. It was the most fruitful prayer, inner healing and deliverance session I have ever had!

When this was over I was exhausted but I felt so very free. For all these years I never knew those "things" were inside of me. I knew I had buttons, I knew if you touched me in a "place" you could bring up pain, but who doesn't have those spots? We all have junk in our trunk. Developing *The Answer* has healed me in places I didn't know I needed healing.

I understand that people don't want to do what I did, because it hurts. We are so practiced at stuffing it, medicating it, and putting a leash on it, that it becomes our lifestyle. That practiced lifestyle is also why we are sick, and not prospering in our lives. This is why the Apostle John wrote in 3 John 2 - *"Beloved, I wish above all things that thou mayest prosper and be in health, even as thy soul prospereth."* We prosper in every area of life with the same measure that we will prosper in our soul. What was happening to me in the car that day was some deep soul cleansing and I was receiving the prosperity of my soul to wholeness.

You can't make yourself go to this place. The Holy Spirit has to lead you there. You will know when He is leading you there because it will be at the surface and you will have a choice whether to; stuff it, medicate it, or deal with it. I pray that when the Holy Spirit is leading you to deal with it, that you will trust Him and go with the flow. Remember He knows how to heal you everywhere you hurt.

WORTHLESS

As I continued to teach this class people would constantly tell me that I needed to get this material out to the body of Christ. I agreed completely, I think every new believer should be immediately taken through this material so they can learn how to walk. Far too many Christians still have pampers on twenty years later. I believed in this class completely, after all it healed me and a church full of people around me.

As time went on God started giving me vision. I could see this as a workbook, I knew I had to have the class recorded. I knew eventually I would have to take it from workbook form to readable book form. However, the thought of trying to market this material, make a phone call, or write a letter made me feel physically sick, so I would stop.

One day at staff prayer, Pastor Jim and Pat were praying for me and my ministry. I was praying in the spirit in agreement with them, when this feeling of being overwhelmed at what all this really meant came over me. I felt that I was not able to do this, fear was rising up within me. I said silently to the Lord, "You don't know who I am." Immediately I heard the Lord, very loudly say back to me, "NO! You don't know who you are!" I agreed quickly with the Lord, as that was correct. I didn't know who I was, who He called me to be, what He called me to do. I am still working on seeing myself through His eyes.

One day I was talking with Pastor about this, he said, "Donna, you are not promoting yourself, you are promoting the material." I can agree with that mentally but it didn't make me feel better. I have had so many prophesies over the years saying that I would be doing exactly what I am doing. That I would be a teacher in the body of Christ, that the assignment the Lord gave me would be nationally known with international influence.

265

Big things were spoken and they bore witness in my spirit. God had given me vision for all of this. I was still pregnant for most of it. Yet for right now, I was stuck again.

So I began examining my life for value and a sense of self-worth. Growing up I was surrounded by love and acceptance from my family and friends. However, as young adults, so much of who we are is being developed in our high school experience. For me, they were the worst years of my life. My father had just left, I got in with the wrong crowd. Someone told a lie about me and stirred up the tough girls in school so they would want to beat me up. I was in fear every day, I got high every morning before school just to cope. I don't know how I passed any classes, much less graduated. After graduating, I was in an abusive relationship and I think being verbally, emotionally or physically abused reinforces a feeling of worthlessness and not having any value.

Even after being a Christian for twenty years, my self-worth had not changed. I could still feel at the core of my being worthlessness, I was insecure within myself. As you know, I was in search of my own freedom when I gathered this material. Now here is this "worthless" thing, it's just there, being exposed as something new I had to face. I was meditating on who I am in Christ, doing my "I AM" list, everything I teach others to do. I knew my authority as a believer, for me that wasn't a problem. It was my ability to go out of my comfort zone and take *The Answer* to the body of Christ, yup that was a problem. I had said many times, Lord if all this was just for me and the people around me to get free, I am fine with that. However, deep inside I knew He wanted more from me.

One day my dad and I were having a conversation on the phone. We were talking about how hard I work and how I feel tired when I get home. He began telling me what he does in a day and he's in his seventies and I was only forty-seven. He encouraged me to see a doctor or increase my vitamins. It was typical parent-child conversation, he didn't say anything that should have made me feel bad. I have done the same thing with my child and tried to encourage her and give her different suggestions. However, as soon as I hung up the phone this emotion of being worthless, not measuring up, that nothing I do is ever good enough, came flooding up out of me. I was crying and crying. Oh boy, here I go again. Now I know enough that when I am experiencing a negative emotion like that, I need to seek after the root.

I was already feeling like nothing I ever do is good enough. I perceived what my father was saying to me that day through the filter that was reinforcing my wrong belief system. I started thinking about how my dad has always encouraged me to go the extra mile; I have always had his love and support my entire life. However, the internal response in me said, I'm not good enough. I could see that the enemy planted that thought in me as a child and I had unknowingly agreed with it. I was clearly learning how important it is to identify what our children are really thinking, because they internalize, have wrong agreements, and build filters that affect their entire life and we never realize it.

So I called Pat, as I usually would in these situations and said, "I have one at the surface," and asked her to talk me through this. After talking for a while she said, "Well you already know the answer." I said, "Of course I know, I do my "I AM" list, blah blah blah." After we hung up I said, "Okay Lord, I don't think I need deliverance, or healing of a traumatic memory, so how are you going to heal this one?" I cried, pushed out the pain, did what I know to do. I came out of agreement with thoughts of being worthless. This class, this book, this information is not worthless. I am behind this material 100% because of all the fruit it has born not only in me, but the people around me. I believed in the material, but I didn't really believe in my ability to deliver the material.

I kept this "issue" on the front burners in my prayer life and was asking the Lord how He was going to heal this one. The Lord has healed me in so many different ways. I am not telling you that this is how you are going to be healed or even laying out a pattern of how to receive healing. But I am saying that the Lord knows how to heal everyplace we hurt if we will let him.

Here is how my healing began. One day I was driving home - you always remember where you were when God speaks to you. I was praying and saying, "Lord, how are you going to heal me of this, I don't read enough, I don't pray enough, I don't feel that anything I do for you is good enough. I constantly measured myself against people like Joyce Meyer, Paula

White and Gloria Copeland, who are three of my mentors. I said to the Lord, "I don't talk eloquently like they do; I just don't measure up as someone I think you would want to use." Then I said, "Lord, this is me, this is all I've got, if you can use me great, if not, I am satisfied just staying home and being a wife and mother, but I don't want to feel any more internal pressure to be something I am not."

That day after all my ranting and raving in the car, He reminded me of an experience I had about twelve or thirteen years earlier. A group of us from church went to a tent revival to hear Christian and Robin Harfouche in Batavia, New York. I had never heard of them before but I went expecting. During the meeting Christian asked for ministers to come forward, he wanted to pray for them. Inside of my heart I felt I wanted to go forward, but I was not a minister. I did host a home group, but that was it. Mickey, an elder in my church called down the aisle to me and said, "Donna, get up there in that altar call, that's for you!" I said, "But I'm not a minister." He said, "Get up there!" So I did. Now I was standing at the end of a long line in the front of the tent. I was positioned in such a way that the lights behind me were casting my shadow on the tent wall in front of me. I could see what Christian was doing, he was coming down the line and praying for people. They would lay down and soak in the presence of God and while they were laying there, Christian's wife Robin would lay hands on them and bless them and pray for them further.

I saw what was happening so I put my head down, began to pray and wait on the Lord. While standing there, I felt a man come behind me and press his body against mine. He was really tall, I could feel his chest against the back of my head. Now here I am, standing at an altar call, trying to be in the spirit, while feeling this man standing right up against me. I was thinking it can't be that crowded up here, so naturally it bothered me. I started pressing backwards against him so he'd get the message to back away from me a bit, but he wouldn't move.

Then I opened my eyes and looked at my shadow in front of me on the tent wall and no one was behind me. Shocked, I put my head back down, still feeling this person behind me I began saying, "Lord, is that you?" By this time Christian had arrived to pray for me. I have no recollection of what he said, I had purposed to just relax, and allow myself to lay down in the presence of the Lord and just remain there because I felt He was doing something with me.

While laying there, I could feel hands all over me. There was a hand on my head, my chest, my arms, my stomach and my legs. At the time I was not in the spirit at all, I was reasoning in my mind thinking wow, how many people are praying for me? It was only his wife Robin who I saw praying for people. The funny thing is I couldn't hear the sound of anyone's voice praying. I was the last person Christian had prayed for and then he was preaching again. I was still laying there. Some time had gone by and all these hands were still all over me. So then I was thinking, I am ready to get up but there are people all over me touching me. So I opened my eyes as if to say okay I want to get up now. When I opened my eyes no one was there. I was all alone. I quickly closed my eyes again in utter shock and I could still feel hands all over me. So I continued to lay there even longer saying to myself, wow there are really hands all over me. I was trying to press against the hands because I felt them so strongly all over me. After quite a while I really felt like I needed to get back to my seat. When I got back to my seat, I asked the people I was with if anyone ever came and stood behind me or was there anyone laying their hands on me while I was on the ground. They told me I was alone the whole time. I went home that night not fully understanding what happened, but I did understand that the Lord wanted me to know He was with me, so I wrote it all down.

So back to the present day, I am driving home in the car asking the Lord how He was going to heal me in this place of feeling worthless. The Lord reminds me of the tent meeting and my first altar call as a minister. He tells me, "Donna that was the day I ordained you into ministry. That was Me standing behind you, I made sure you knew I was there. That was the ministry of angels surrounding you on the ground, they are assigned to you and your ministry." Jesus, Himself was and is standing behind me - Selah.

God had healed me close to thirteen years ago and I just received it that day in the car. Sometimes the Lord will bring you back to an event to open the eyes of your understanding so you are enlightened, and that revelation can change your mind, remove a thorn and heal your broken heart.

I urge you not to measure your pain against someone else's. I thought going through the trauma of my parents' divorce was nothing compared to the horrific abuse and trauma that other people go through when they've suffered great losses in their lives. I condemned myself for feeling so bad compared to what other people go through. After all, who doesn't get divorced today? What I have come to understand is that pain is pain. No matter what caused it, how big or how small we feel the trauma is, it still hurts and needs healing.

TRAUMA

I would not have viewed my parent's divorce as a trauma. In reality it was, because it traumatized my life the way I knew it. My home was gone, my security, the family unit wasn't whole anymore.

Trauma can be an open door in our lives for the entrance of a spirit. In order to receive the restoration of our soul and for a trauma to be healed, just binding and casting out a demon won't get us very far. It is the memory of that trauma that needs healing. Exposing wounds or painful memories to God's truth removes the thorn, brings healing and closes the door on their power to afflict us.

What we bury alive stays alive. Unfortunately, we have buried alive or "stuffed" many experiences that are the traumas, unhealed hurts, unmet needs and unresolved issues of our lives.

II Corinthians 10:5 says we should be, *"Casting down imaginations, and every high thing that exalteth itself against the knowledge of God, and bringing into captivity every thought to the obedience of Christ."* We discussed this scripture and how to do this at great length in the chapter on Strongholds.

There are destructive imaginations, considerations and intentions that have held us in bondage. For instance, if we consider a memory that brings us to a place where we are hostile and angry with God, questioning Him and saying "Where were You?" that imagination needs to be cast down. It is being exalted above the knowledge of God.

270

By virtue of the law of reciprocals, there are also constructive imaginations, considerations and intentions. The truth is that Jesus was and is with us at all times.

He has cried over every hurt we have ever endured. It is also a truth that He cannot violate man's free will. Even though He was right there and saw it all, there was nothing He could have done to change or stop some of the things that have happened to us.

GOD, WHERE WERE YOU?

Far too often in ministering to people I have encountered a belief system that has been a hindrance in their ability to receive from God. I used to share in this mindset so I understand where they are coming from. I want to take some time to correct this wrong thinking. The Bible tells us in Mark 4: 18, 19, that a seed sown among the cares of this world (thoughts, belief systems) will be unfruitful. Because of our ingrained belief systems, it is sometimes hard to receive truth when it is presented. My belief systems changed when I realized what I heard other Christians say about God was their interpretion of God in light of their circumstances and not in light of His Word. So I went in search for these answers for myself.

In the world today we see and hear of many tragedies. We hear people say things like: "God is in control of everything that happens", or they say, "God, why did you allow that?" Or, "God allowed it for a reason to teach you something." Or, "If there is a God, why is there so much suffering in the world?" The most popular being, " Everything happens for a reason."

Through these commonly used phrases we have developed a belief system that whatever happens *"God allowed it"* because *"He is in control."* I think we have mistakenly mis-used the word *"allow"* implying that what ever happens it was authorized by God.

I have found this belief system to be a deception in our perception. The truth is, God has to *"allow"* everything because He will not violate man's free will, He will not trespass against us. That does not mean everything that happens was authorized by God. I respectfully want to clarify this line of thinking so that you can receive your healing.

271

In Genesis 1:26 God said, *"Let us make man in our image, and after our likeness: and let them have dominion...over all the earth."* We have been given dominion by the Godhead over all the earth. He didn't say let man have dominion with us. God excluded Himself from having dominion over the earth.

The word *dominion* means – supreme authority, sovereignty to rule, absolute ownership, the power of governing and controlling, power to direct, use and dispose of at your pleasure, over all the earth. Legal authority to dominate the earth has been given to mankind only, not angels or demons, and we are to do just that!

Man is a spirit with a physical body. Only spirits with physical bodies can legally function in the earth realm. This explains why Satan needed Adam's agreement, it gave him access to his body, his words and the earth. This also explains why demons need our bodies to bring about stealing, killing and destruction; and why Jesus needed a physical body to redeem us from the curse of the fall. God Himself will not trespass against these laws.

Then God put man in the garden to dress and to keep it (protect as a bodyguard or gate keeper.) And the Lord God commanded him, saying, *"Of every tree of the garden thou mayest freely eat; But of the tree of the knowledge of good and evil, thou shalt not eat of it; for in the day that thou eatest thereof thou shalt surely die."* - Genesis 2:15-17. The extent of God's ability to "control" what Adam did was when He said, "don't eat it."

If God were "in control" like we hear so many say, that day in the garden would have been the time to display His control. He could have slapped the fruit right out of Adam's hand and saved the entire human race. If God could have stopped anything, He would have stopped Adam from switching lords in the garden, thereby giving his dominion over the earth to Satan, establishing the law of sin and death.

Think about it for just a minute, if God were in control of everything happening on planet earth today, wouldn't earth look like heaven? Man was given a season of time, an earth lease so to speak, when that lease is up, you can bet, God Almighty will show up and there will be a whole lot of shakin' going on!

Until that time, there are spiritual laws in place. God gave the earth to Adam, and Adam gave his lordship to Satan. The whirlpool was set in motion for the kingdom of darkness on this earth. We have identified spiritual laws in every chapter. There are laws that govern thoughts, words and actions that produce generational curses or blessings. We saw every step Jesus had to take as a man to reverse the curse of Adam's disobedience. If laws were not in place, Jesus could have just wiped the whole mess out and taken dominion. But that would have been against the law.

According to the laws in place, Jesus needed a physical body to redeem us from the curse of the fall. He had to come to earth as a man and follow all the laws, fulfill all the prophesy of words spoken, and destroy the power of sin and death with His Body in order to grant us access to the Kingdom of God. God Himself must work with in the boundaries of these laws.

This is why there is so much power in prayer. We are yielding our agreement in prayer with God and His Word giving Him access to move through our obedience, bringing His Kingdom on earth as it is in heaven.

So now you can see that telling Adam not to eat the fruit was all the "*control*" the Lord had. This is still how He works with us today. When we are about to sin or do something we know we shouldn't, a still small voice is telling us not to do it. Whether we hear the voice or not, He is still here and He is still speaking. We have ignorantly called the voice of the Holy Spirit an unction, a feeling, or we say things like, "Something told me I should have done this instead of that."

We usually push right past that voice and then go do what we want anyway. God has never bound my hands and feet, thrown me to the ground and prevented me from doing what I wanted. However, that still small voice of the Holy Spirit has been a constant; He is faithfully trying to get me to go in another direction without violating my free will.

As a young Christian I heard things like, "God allowed that for a reason to teach you something, and nothing happens unless God allows it." I could see that this belief system brought comfort to those who believe it. However, it also postured them to receive anything the enemy wanted to do to them. They received stealing, killing and destroying as "God allowing it." I watched many believers lay down under the kingdom of darkness, thinking it was the hand of God and there was something they had to learn, instead of fighting the good fight of faith.

Over the years I have heard others say things like; God allowed me to have this sickness, get in that car accident, be abused, go through divorce, have my child die, etc. in order to teach me something or bring them to salvation. Hearing other Christians describe God in this way never brought me any comfort. It made me think that God caused my parents to divorce, had my father leave, so that I would get on drugs, go from man to man looking to have my needs met to teach me something and bring me to salvation.

This thinking made me depressed and completely hindered me from trusting God or placing my faith in Him. After all, you never know what God will do to you next. If I was sick I couldn't pray in faith for healing because maybe God wanted me to be sick to teach me something. So naturally I laid down under sickness and all manner of stealing, killing and destroying that the enemy brought my way waiting for what other lessons I needed to learn. Instead, I should have been resisting the enemy. Hopefully, when we go through a hard time we will come out the other end having learned something. I have watched many people who have this belief system go through hard times and never learn a single lesson. It is important for you to understand that these situations are not designed by God to teach us or bring us faith. If that was a truth we should all be faith giants. Faith comes by hearing, and hearing the Word of God - Romans 10:17.

You can't stand in faith if you don't know the will of God. Be assured right now that healing is always the will of God. What if we are praying for someone to be healed and they die anyway? Scripture tells us we perish for lack of knowledge - Hosea 4:6. Many times we have no idea of the spiritual laws that were set in motion long ago. There are many factors involved in healing, what we do know is that the Scripture shows us that Jesus never put sickness on anyone, He paid a great price for sickness to be removed. He never told anyone that they had to suffer a little while longer because they hadn't learned their lesson yet. He came revealing the heart of the Father to heal and deliver. So even if someone fails to receive their healing and passes over to the other side, death is not defeat, it is still a victory for the believer.

Galatians 6:7 says, *"Be not deceived; God is not mocked: For whatsoever a man soweth, that shall he also reap."* When things happen, instead of thinking, everything happens for a reason or God, did you allow this to teach me something? You need to understand that in the earth realm "stuff happens" because there is a whirlpool cycle of pressure from the kingdom of darkness. We can not live here and expect that nothing will ever go wrong. So begin searching by asking, what was sown that this harvest is coming in? Not being able to discern the hand of God from a weapon of the enemy or the reaping of a harvest, has left believers double minded, unstable in their ways and unable to receive from God. If you can't identify the cause that is leading to an effect, then perhaps it was just a weapon formed. In that case, know that weapons will be formed but they don't have to prosper! Then begin doing the warfare that is needed. It wasn't until I started identifying spiritual laws that everything fell into place for me.

So many times when things happen in our lives we are reaping what we have sown. Or sometimes we may unfortunately be involved in the reaping process on someone else's harvest. When I found myself reaping, I was ignorantly crying out to God saying, "Why did you allow this?" After understanding the laws of the spirit I could see the deception in my perception. Once I understood, I could see that when my parents got divorced, I was reaping what they had sown. They were reaping what generations before them had sown. They were perishing in their marriage relationship for lack of knowledge.

As the Holy Spirit was correcting all my wrong thinking He began showing me things like: would you put your daughter's hand on the hot stove and burn her fingers in an effort to teach her not to touch a hot stove? Of course not, that would be child abuse. Yet we accuse God our Heavenly Father of acts just like that. We think 'He allowed' our hurts, traumas and pains, that they were designed to teach us something and bring us to maturity. We ignorantly think that bad things couldn't have happened to us at all if '*He didn't allow it, after all He is in control.*' Our perceptions of God have been perverted by the prince of darkness. They do not line up with the truth of the Word of God. God does not hurt us so that He could heal us and get the glory.

The problem in the body of Christ has been that Christians have been interpreting God in light of their circumstances. We look at our circumstances and then we rationalize; God where were you? How could you allow that? Maybe you were trying to teach me something. Maybe you will use this to bring you more Glory. Then what we come up with is not truth at all, but it becomes our doctrine. In error we have created God in our image. We think He acts like us.

One woman said when she was a child her father passed away. A well meaning Christian said to her, "God needed your daddy as an angel in heaven." The little girl thought, God, I needed my daddy too. That day a destructive belief system about God as a Father was formed in that little girl's mind. That belief system hindered her from having a right relationship with God for decades.

Instead of this line of thinking we should be interpreting our circumstances in light of the Word of God and the function of spiritual laws. When you find yourself in a predicament, the questions you should be asking are; what did I sow? What words did I say? What actions did I do? Is there a curse in operation, is there a thorn producing this fruit? If you find your heart clean, then unfortunately, you're possibly being affected by someone else's harvest coming in or by a weapon formed by the enemy to get you off your destiny. While you are in this process, the still small voice of the Holy Spirit will be trying to instruct you. He was trying to instruct you before you got there. I have experienced the Lord giving me warning dreams before an event occurred so I wouldn't be caught off guard.

This belief system I have been carefully trying to dismantle is one of the biggest stronghold belief systems, one of the greatest areas of deception in our perception that the enemy has sown into our minds. In ministering to people, I have had to correct this wrong thinking again and again before they were able to receive their healing.

As we have seen, manifestations of the curse come naturally through the open door of sin and giving place to the enemy. Ecclesiastes10:8 says to us, *"He that diggeth a pit shall fall into it; and whoso breaketh an hedge (enclosure, fence, wall), a serpent shall bite (strike, sting, oppress) him."*

The hedge was put in place by God. It is activated through our obedience and deactivated through our disobedience. Our disobedience causes us to "give-place" to the enemy. Agreeing with wrong thoughts is an act of disobedience and the wages of wrong thinking produce thorns and then our chemical factory will translate our thought life into a physical state that will produce death - Romans 6:23. In all these examples, the enemy can secure his position in our lives, homes and families for generations.

So when can we rightly say God is in control? In Scriptures when the children of Israel were walking in obedience, God was referred to as the God of Heaven and earth. When the children of Israel were walking in disobedience God was referred to only as the God of Heaven. So when we are walking in obedience and the hedge is up, we have positioned ourselves under the Authority of the Father, then we allow Him to have control in our lives. The Holy Spirit is here to lead us and guide us, He will order our steps in a prosperous way. If we are submitted to Him then we can rightly say, we are allowing God to be in control. Remember we are the ones in authority here so we either 'allow' God or we 'allow' the enemy by way of our mental agreements, words and actions.

Now in the case of child abuse, no child has done anything to warrant abuse of any kind. Then why does it happen? Perhaps there has been incest in the family line like in my family, there was a generational curse in operation, there was a bend in the DNA on one branch of my family line that allowed a spirit of perversion to effect several family members. Did God authorize that to happen in my family? No. Did he allow it? Only in the sense that it would have been illegal for him to step in and stop it. He has to allow everything that happens in the earth under the whirlpool cycle of the kingdom of darkness, because He gave man dominion over all the earth. He functions within the laws, that is the Sovereignty of God.

We have mistakenly thought that God allowed / authorized us to be sexually abused so that someday we can minister to other abuse victims.

NO! If you were abused and then healed and set free, of course God wants to use you to help others. That is the redemptive power of God in operation. But your abuse was not ordained by God just so you can help someone else. What we know for sure is that seeds were sown, spiritual laws were set in motion, weapons were formed and a child was hurt.

For any tragedy you have ever experienced in your life, you may be asking why did this or that happen? I am not saying I have all the answers as to who did what and why things have happened. But one thing I do know is that God does not author bad things to teach you a lesson and bring you to maturity!

Hebrews 12:7-11 says our earthly fathers chastise (or train) us according to the flesh, but our heavenly Father chastises us in our spirit because He is the Father of our spirit.

II Timothy 3:16-17 explains that He delivers that spiritual chastisement through His Word, *"All scripture is given by inspiration of God, and is profitable for doctrine, for reproof, for correction, for instruction in righteousness: That the man of God may be perfect, thoroughly furnished unto all good works."* The Word! That is what God uses to train us - not trials and destructive circumstances.

That's why James 1:13 says, *"Let no man say when he is tempted (tested or tried,) I am tempted of God, for God cannot be tempted with evil, neither tempteth He any man (with evil).* James said, don't even say that God was behind evil. Jesus made it clear who is behind all evil when he said, *"The thief comes to steal, kill and destroy. I am come that they might have life, and that they might have it more abundantly."* - John 10:10

With all this being said, the truth is that Jesus was and is with us at all times. He has cried over every hurt we have ever endured. It is also a truth that He will not violate man's free will. Even though He was right there and saw it all, there was nothing He could have done to change or stop some of the things that have happened to us. However he can heal us everywhere we hurt.

HEALING OF A MEMORY

So, where was God in our trauma? In John 14:26 Jesus says, *"But the Comforter, which is the Holy Ghost, whom the Father will send in my name, he shall teach you all things, and bring all things to your remembrance (leads us backwards), whatsoever I have said unto you."* Even though something may have happened years ago, there is no time or distance in the spiritual realm. We have learned in the healing of a traumatic memory, such as an abuse of some kind, that we can ask the Holy Spirit to walk back into the dark places of our life and heal us from the inside out.

The Holy Spirit is able go back into a memory with us and show us exactly where He was and what He was doing. This, then, replaces the image of our perception of what happened to us. This knowledge removes the thorn and takes the sting of the event away. It also renews our perception with the truth of what was really happening at that moment. The Holy Spirit overwrites our perception with the truth so that we can move forward!

When we have experienced something traumatic we tend to see that situation with blinders on. We are only able to see from our perspective. The Holy Spirit is able to remove our blinders and show us the truth of the whole picture of what was happening at that time. We have found that healing of a memory is needed before we can command a spirit to leave that wound and have it remain gone. It's much like removing the sting of the infection before the wound can fully heal.

This was the case for me. I felt free for years until something happened that triggered an old wound. It was my response to the trigger that showed me I was not healed in that place.

Healing of the memory allows the sting to be removed by creating a new memory, a constructive image that replaces a destructive image for us in that place. When this happens we are literally changing the structure of our brain. The blueprint of our nerve cells and dendrites are changing and we are creating a new and healthy nerve pathway.

The healing of that wound closes the door of access, making the eviction of an evil spirit permanent.

279

In Luke 4:18 Jesus said, *"The Spirit of the Lord is upon me, because he hath anointed me to preach the gospel to the poor; he hath sent me to heal the brokenhearted (those who have been; shattered, broken in pieces, maimed, crippled, crushed, violently ruptured), to preach deliverance to the captives, and recovering of sight to the blind, to set at liberty them that are bruised,"*

The Holy Spirit of Truth will bring to your remembrance where you are brokenhearted, fragmented, and shattered in your soul. He will bring recovering of sight where you were blind to His presence in that memory. Once you are in a memory, ask the Holy Spirit to show you the true picture of what was happening during the trauma. Understand that your emotions were not being influenced by the whole truth. Once the Holy Spirit shows you the whole truth, your emotions will not be able to lie to you anymore. This then brings deliverance to the captives and sets at liberty them that are bruised.

I encourage you not to dig up memories on purpose. Instead, pray and tell the Holy Spirit to get you ready to be healed. It is a good idea to keep a journal of triggers, soul-ar eruptions and dreams. Be sensitive to the Holy Spirit as He will lead you to a place that needs healing. Do not try to manipulate this process yourself.

The Lord healed me of the first five years of my daughter's life in a very unusual way. On weekends during those years, I would put her to bed, get a sitter and go out. I felt guilty for not being home every night with her.

My healing came in a dream. In the dream I was in a room and I was holding my baby. The room was sealed shut from the inside. He showed me that the room was a place in my heart that was painful for me and I had shut it off.

I now know that this place is a literal structure called amygdale in our brain. In your amygdale is where all your memories and the events of your life are stored. It is the library about you.

While in the room holding my baby, the Holy Spirit was leading me backwards. I felt like she was sleeping and I wanted to put her to bed so I could go out. In the room, in the dream, in the spirit, while feeling like I needed to leave, it was as if the Lord said to me, "No, just hold her." So I just sat there and held her.

What I encountered then was that void in my life where I felt I had lost that time, but now I was able to sit there and just hold my child. I held her all night long. When I woke up, I realized that I had been taken back in the spirit to that time and allowed to overwrite my emotions. I didn't feel that longing and ache anymore. There are no set rules for healing, just know that we serve a very personal Lord and He knows the best way to heal you.

Luke 10:30,33,34 - *"And Jesus answering said, A certain man went down from Jerusalem to Jericho, and fell among thieves, which stripped him of his raiment, and wounded him, and departed, leaving him half dead ... But a certain Samaritan, as he journeyed, came where he was: and when he saw him, he had compassion on him, And went to him, and bound up his wounds, (trauma) pouring in oil and wine, and set him on his own beast, and brought him to an inn, and took care of him."*

I was so happy to see that the Bible does talk about being traumatized. People have said to me that the Bible doesn't talk about what they have experienced. This man experienced being stolen from, beaten and abused. He experienced the same emotional pains that contemporary people do.

The oil represents the presence of the Holy Spirit and the wine represents the Word of God, the blood of Jesus and forgiveness of sins. We can see then that the Holy Spirit, through the ministry of Jesus Christ, has been sent to deliver those who have been shattered by trauma. A way has been made for our broken, shattered hearts to be healed.

When our bodies become wounded, our skin lacerates. When our souls have been wounded, it feels as if they fragment or shatter. The healing process is the same for both. Just as it hurts to clean out a physical wound before healing can begin, the soul must be cleaned out as well by removing the sting of the trauma. Healing of the memories allows the Lord to deal with the root of many of our problems. Too often we are just trying to cut off the fruit instead of destroying the root. Allowing the Holy Spirit to overwrite our traumas replaces our painful memories by instilling the truth from God. It brings the restoration and deliverance of our shattered souls.

Remember that Jesus was anointed with burden-removing, yoke-destroying power so that the gates of hell would not prevail against us. When Jesus walks us back through a memory, He removes the burden and destroys the yoke that memory has had on us. Then we can effectively use the keys of the kingdom to bind, loose and evict the enemy. Once we have been made free, maintaining deliverance is our responsibility. We have a free will; and if we choose to come back into agreement with destructive imaginations and suggestions, the result will be that the thorns will grow back and we will begin to think the thoughts and feel all the emotions again. They will determine our behavior, and we will be re-opening the doors that were shut and thereby giving access to our souls back to the enemy.

Many times people have come in for counsel because of a haunting memory. We will say okay, lets visit that memory and look for the Lord in that place. There was one woman whose son was killed in a car accident. She was crying out, "Lord, where were you?" Then she saw her child at the moment of the impact being ushered into eternity. The Lord knows our departure date and is ready to instantly move that person out of this kingdom and into His.

One woman was tied up, crying out, "Lord, where were you?" She said in a constructive image she saw the Lord walk into the room and untie her, he unlocked her door and carried her outside to freedom. That was the heart of the Father for her at the time of her trauma. She was able to experience His will in the spirit. Anytime she has ever thought of that day again, she sees her encounter with the Lord and not the trauma.

Another woman was being abused repeatedly by her stepfather in the bathroom and crying out, "Lord, where were you?" Then she said, I see Him, He is sitting there and he is crying over what is happening to me. For years she would feel sick being in a bathroom. After the Lord overwrote her trauma all negative emotions associated with the bathroom were gone.

One woman had a memory of being a little girl and her parents left her at her grandmother's house. She was standing on the back of the couch watching out the window as they pulled away. It was at that moment that rejection found a place within her. When she revisited that memory she saw the Lord grab her up off the couch and hold her in His arms. This healed her broken heart and bound up the wound. Now rejection was able to leave her soul. It had no more place to reside.

After being with many women as they experienced the Holy Spirit re-writing a trauma, I had a particular moment in my life where I was not where I should have been. It made me feel shame. When I visited this memory I asked the Lord to show me where He was. Within a few moments I saw him in the corner of the room sitting down with His head between his knees sobbing for me. The sting from the thorn in that memory holds no more shame for me.

The truth is that He was there, He was with us through every event of our lives. It is also true that He couldn't do anything to stop what has happened to us, but if we ask Him, He will show us exactly where He was. Once we go from having partial vision to having complete vision of a situation, it re-frames that experience for us removing the thorn and over writing the trauma. It helps us to see from God's perspective, creating a new blueprint and nerve pathway.

It is a powerful ministry of the Holy Spirit to be able to, "bring all things to our remembrance by leading us backward" thereby overwriting a trauma with truth. He heals the brokenhearted, brings deliverance to the captive, and recovering of sight to where we were blind to His Presence, so He can set at liberty every place we are bruised.

POSTURE FOR DELIVERANCE

1. Repent of all sin, including being a soulish Christian. Destroy unhealthy strongholds and soul ties, and break the power of all wrong words working against your prosperous life. Choose to walk in the ways of God. Ongoing sin in your life is an open invitation to demons and brings a snare to your soul. Genesis 4:7 says, *"If thou doest not well, sin lieth at the door and shall rule over you."* Yielding to sin is yielding to the devil. Romans 6:16 says, *"Do you not know that to whom you present yourselves slaves to obey, you are the one's slaves whom you obey, whether of sin to death, or of obedience to righteousness?"* Our thoughts, emotions, memories, bodies, relationships, even our abilities

have become enslaved as a result of the events in our lives. It is time to become enslaved to righteousness.

2. There must be unqualified forgiveness toward all others, no matter what they have done, how many times they have done it, or whether they continue to offend. Forgiving yourself is also mandatory. Remember forgiveness has nothing to do with your feelings but everything to do with your obedience. By harboring unforgiveness and not releasing it, you have turned yourself over to demons for torment - Matthew 18:21-35. Maintaining unforgiveness in our hearts is like drinking poison and hoping the other person dies. Unforgiveness is only hurting us because our chemical factory will translate our thought life into a physical state, poisoning our life. Forgiving and releasing others does not make what they did okay. It is the process of taking the torment out of our soul.

3. There must be a complete separation from every association, no matter how casual, with the occult, cults, and Eastern Religions. This separation includes the destruction of all books and paraphernalia associated therewith. You must renounce all involvement you have ever had with them - Deuteronomy 7:25-26, 18:9-13; Acts 19:19-21.

NOW WE ARE READY TO HEAL A MEMORY

4. If there is a memory that is holding you captive, then quiet yourself before the Lord and ask the Holy Spirit to take you back into that memory. The temptation will be to resist this process because it hurts. Blame is put on the enemy for bringing up something that is under the Blood. If a memory keeps coming up, consider that it might not be the enemy bringing it up, but the Holy Spirit trying to heal your broken heart and bind up your wounds.

5. When you get into the memory, it will look the same to you. Pray and ask for the eyes of your understanding to be enlightened, so that you can see the spiritual realm and what was going on there during the time of trauma. Ask the Lord to show you where He was. Look around and be open to see something new. You may perceive His presence or become aware of something He wants you to know. You can expect the Holy Spirit to be your Guide and Comforter revealing all truth to you.

Remember we want to see the whole picture and all the players from the Father's perspective, not what we have believed through deception in our perception and the filters on our soul. We see in part, God sees the whole picture. He knows exactly what spiritual laws were set in motion leading up to the event. Allow the Holy Spirit to develop a constructive imagination that will make you free from the destructive imagination that has held you in bondage - II Corinthians10:5 and John 8:32.

6. You will probably experience familiar emotions that were present at the time of the trauma. Do not be afraid. The Holy Spirit is there to reveal Himself to you and bring healing to that memory. These emotions indicate where you were traumatized and will also be the indication of when you are healed as your chemical factory will stop secreting those emotions.

7. Be especially aware of any other feelings, such as fear, rejection, anger, bitterness, shame or abandonment. These emotions will show you where you have toxic, thorny thoughts, where demons may be hiding and who they may be. It is possible for your emotions to have been so damaged by the trauma that it left an open door for demonic entry. In that place is probably a lie you have believed and a door that must be closed. Remember that every place we agree with the enemy gives him power to bring destruction to that place in our lives. Please don't let this information frighten you, but understand that Jesus made a way for our souls to be healed.

So if you are in the memory and feeling the pain, allow yourself to cry, scream and push the pain out on purpose. This is more than just crying, I call it crying with purpose because you are purposefully pushing it out. Be sensitive to what the Holy Spirit is showing you. You may have to say things you should have said at the time. You may have to forgive and release again. Command the negative emotions, where spirits may be attached, to go, in Jesus' name.

Get a constructive image of these things leaving and begin to apply the Blood of Jesus to those broken places. Prophesy scriptures over yourself. Declare who you are in Christ. Use your "I AM" list. Start calling things that be not as though they were and declaring what kind of future you are going to have. It takes just 4 days to change the structure of your brain by renewing your mind. Within twenty-one days of doing this a new nerve pathway will be created. See yourself being made whole.

When you have received healing, you will still have a memory of the event, but the 'sting' it held will be gone. If you have already experienced any kind of healing in your life, you already know this to be true. I can tell you from experience, when the Lord speaks to you, it will instantly heal your emotions and dispel the lie you have believed.

8. The Holy Spirit lives within you. He is your *"Comforter, Counselor, Helper, Intercessor, Advocate, Strengthener and Standby that He may remain with you forever – He is The Spirit of Truth"* - John 14:16,17. So begin to pray for yourself and receive vision of the Holy Spirit channeling through the various chambers of your soul, washing you clean and healing you from the inside out.

Some thoughts were gleaned from *The Experience of Inner Healing* by Ruth Carter Stapleton and *Mending Cracks in the Soul* by Dale Sides.

PRAYER

Father, in the interest of restoring my soul and growing up spiritually, I want to commit myself to not neglect this information. I can see that this is *The Answer* and if I will keep it in front of me, it will continue to make me free and improve my relationships.

I have come to understand that to be carnally or soul minded, operates the law of death in my life. With Your help, Holy Spirit, I choose to be spiritually minded and receive the fruit of life and peace. As I do so, I know I am positioning myself as one the enemy may not devour because I am keeping my hedge of protection up and strong.

Jesus, I am so grateful that healing and deliverance is the children's bread. I am grateful that You came to heal every place I have been broken and shattered in my heart and that You bring recovery of sight to every place that I was blind to Your presence in my life.

I make a conscious decision to come out of agreement with all the destructive imaginations I have had about the people and events in my life.

I ask You, Holy Spirit, to take me to my place of healing and begin to reveal to me where You were. Open the eyes of my understanding to see the events in my life through Your eyes and not mine.

Help me create constructive imaginations, images and considerations concerning these things. Help me to see where my emotions were not being influenced by the truth so they can heal.

As You do these things, I believe I will receive revelation of every evil spirit that has had a place in that part of my life, so that I can effectively drive each one out and close the door of access.

I invite You to flow through every channel of my soul, my mind, my memories, my emotions and my will, overwriting every event with truth and healing me from the inside out. I receive by faith the healing of every wound and trauma. I thank You, Lord, for Your great Love.

A FINAL WORD

I have been teaching this class for many years. I know that each time I have taught it has been a new season with new issues for me, as well as my students. The fruit from going through this material repeatedly has been life changing for us all.

I am confident that the Holy Spirit has revealed many things to you by now. I know from experience, every time you re-read this, you will mature and increase in blessings.

Healing can come in many different ways. Jesus knows exactly how to remove your burdens and destroy your yokes. He knows how to heal you everywhere you hurt. Be open to Him and give Him permission to do it His way. Maybe right now you're not where you need to be, but you can be grateful that you're not where you used to be.

This is a process, we are all on a journey. *The Answer* comes as you begin to change from the inside out, being transformed by the renewing of your mind, maturing in your spirit, soul and body. As you do, the people around you will respond to your changes and your relationships will improve. I encourage you to go through this book often, use it as a study tool and build on the foundation I have laid.

It is my prayer that you will maintain this posture of Kingdom living so you can prosper and be in health even as, in direct proportion and with the same measure, that you will take the time and prosper your soul - III John 2.

Shalom2u,

Donna

Step by step instruction for total soul healing, in all areas of your life.

IDENTIFY YOUR THINKING

- Make a list of the people in your life and write down what you believe about them, include yourself. This will help you to identify deception in your perception.

- Adjust your thinking to see truth through the Father's Eyes.

- Identify and break the power of bitter-root judgments.

- Look for the "roots" of your trouble.

REPENT

- Confess your wrong thinking as sin, and come out of agreement with these thoughts.

- Break the power of all the wrong words you have spoken, using Isaiah 54:17.

- Break the power you have given the kingdom of darkness to destroy you in these places.

- Remember to choose to see everyone and every situation through the "Father's Eyes."

- Renounce any power you gave to occult spirits through your wrong beliefs and loose them from those hiding places.

FORGIVE AND RELEASE

(WHEN YOU STAND PRAYING FORGIVE)

- Forgive yourself and anyone else from every offense and expectation you had.

- Declare before the Lord that they owe you nothing, not even an apology.

- Remember that hurting people hurt people.

BREAK SOUL TIES

- Release people from the mental and emotional places they have had in your soul.

- Call back the broken pieces of you.

- Plead the blood of Jesus over your soul where it was fragmented and declare wholeness.

- Cleanse your gates as necessary.

- Loose any demons that may have been hiding in those places.

BREAK GENERATIONAL CURSES

- Do identificational repentance for the sins in your family line or on your land.

- Declare Isaiah 53:4,5 and Galatians 3:13.

- Bind every evil spirit you see in operation and command them to go.

HEAL TRAUMATIC MEMORIES

- Pray that the eyes of your understanding will be enlightened.

- Ask Jesus to show you where He was.

- Allow yourself to see the truth of the whole picture, as opposed to the partial truth at the time of the event.

- Identify negative emotions, as they may be where demons are hiding.

- Command them to go in Jesus' name.

- Confess Luke 4:18, plead the blood of Jesus, and receive your healing

- Be determined never to see this through a filtered perception again.

Donna is known as a practical Bible teacher. She outlines step-by-step principles with simplicity and warmth as she openly shares from her own personal struggles.

In 2001 she began developing a Bible study called "The Answer" in an effort to find healing for her internal struggles. The Answer identifies soul issues that have caused the problems we experience in life.

The class has evolved over the years and the Lord has used it to mature Donna's character and heal her soul in places she didn't know she needed healing.

She developed a workbook and years later had her class recorded in order to have a corresponding DVD set. This interactive Bible curriculum has been used by churches and home groups around the country. In 2011 Donna released her class in book form and called it "The Answer for Life".

Donna is an ordained minister, wife, mother, grandmother, author, teacher, life coach, conference speaker and mentor. She and her husband Mark live in Rochester, New York where she serves on staff as a teaching pastor at New Testament Christian Church. Her passion is teaching others how to achieve their greatest potential by understanding the authority they have as believers and how to live the blessed life!

The Answer for Life

Video Curriculum and Interactive Workbook

The "must-have" Bible study experience! Discover The Answer for your life and stay on course with it! With this 8-disc DVD Set: It's as if you were actually sitting in Donna's class as she teaches the step-by-step principles found in the Word of God.

Donna talks of her own personal struggles with warmth and humor as she openly shares the x-ray of her soul and her journey to wholeness. You will learn the life-changing truths she has discovered that have matured her character and healed her heart. Each session is closed with a powerful prayer designed to connect your heart to God in a special way for the subject you are learning.

16-Disc CD Set: The average person spends a lot of time driving. Listen again and again in your car or download to your iPod. Every time you hear these life changing truths you get more out of them!

- Discs are in 30 minute segments for small group settings

Blessed Before the Foundation of the World

4 CD set includes:

- Blessed Before the Foundation of the World

- Imagine That!

- The Just Shall Live by Faith

- BE – The Word that Releases "The Blessing!"

Science Proves the Bible

5 CD set includes:

- Quantum Faith
- Thoughts Have a Frequency
- The Anatomy of a Thought
- The Anatomy of Stress
- The Science of Thought and Sound

How to Fight

3 CD set includes:

- Guard Your Mind
- Guard Your Heart
- Our Weapons in Prayer

Honor

2 CD set includes:

- Honor vs. Dishonor
- Conflict Resolutions

www.donnafiorini.com

CPSIA information can be obtained at www.ICGtesting.com
Printed in the USA
BVOW011137261012

303986BV00006B/41/P